Catholicism and Religious Freedom

Catholicism and Religious Freedom

Contemporary Reflections on Vatican II's Declaration on Religious Liberty

Edited by
Kenneth L. Grasso
and Robert P. Hunt

A Sheed & Ward Book
ROWMAN & LITTLEFIELD PUBLISHERS, INC.
Lanham · Boulder · New York · Toronto · Plymouth, UK

ROWMAN & LITTLEFIELD PUBLISHERS, INC.

A Sheed & Ward Book
Published in the United States of America
by Rowman & Littlefield Publishers, Inc.

A wholly owned subsidiary of The Rowman & Littlefield Publishing Group, Inc.
4501 Forbes Boulevard, Suite 200, Lanham, Maryland 20706
www.rowmanlittlefield.com

Estover Road
Plymouth PL6 7PY
United Kingdom

British Library Cataloguing in Publication Information Available

Library of Congress Cataloging-in-Publication Data

Catholicism and religious freedom : contemporary reflections on Vatican II's declaration
on religious liberty / edited by Kenneth L. Grasso and Robert P. Hunt.
    p. cm.
Includes bibliographical references.
ISBN-13: 978-0-7425-5192-3 (cloth : alk. paper)
ISBN-10: 0-7425-5192-X (cloth : alk. paper)
ISBN-13: 978-0-7425-5193-0 (pbk. : alk. paper)
ISBN-10: 0-7425-5193-8 (pbk. : alk. paper)
    1. Vatican Council (2nd : 1962-1965). Declaratio de libertate religiosa. 2. Freedom of
religion. 3. Paul VI, Pope, 1897-1978. I. Grasso, Kenneth L. II. Hunt, Robert P., 1955–
BX8301962.A45 D54 2006
261.7'2—dc22   2006017198

Printed in the United States of America

⊗™ The paper used in this publication meets the minimum requirements of American
National Standard for Information Sciences—Permanence of Paper for Printed Library
Materials, ANSI/NISO Z39.48-1992.

Contents

Acknowledgments

The editors wish to express their heartfelt gratitude to all those, especially our contributors, whose assistance and support made this volume possible. Special thanks should be extended to Kenneth R. Craycraft Jr., who originally conceived of this project and began the process of lining up contributors.

We also wish to thank Jonathan Sisk, Ross Miller, Sarah Johnson, and Katherine Macdonald of Rowman & Littlefield Publishers for their patience, wise advice, and editorial assistance.

We also wish to express our gratitude to our institutions—Texas State University at San Marcos and Kean University—for their ongoing support and encouragement of our scholarship. Most importantly of all, we particularly want to thank our families for their encouragement, support, and understanding.

Introduction

Kenneth L. Grasso and Robert P. Hunt

In his "Message to Rulers" at the conclusion of the Second Vatican Council, Pope Paul VI numbered *Dignitatis Humanae* (*DH*) among the Council's "major" texts.[1] A day earlier during an audience granted to special delegates from various countries and international organizations, he characterized it as "one of the greatest documents" of Vatican II.[2] John Paul II clearly concurred with his predecessor's estimation of *DH*'s importance, frequently invoking it as one of the foundational documents of contemporary Church social teaching. Indeed, insisting that the Church "attaches great importance to all that is stated" in the Declaration,[3] he repeatedly affirmed that the right it proclaimed is the "cornerstone of the structure of human rights"[4] and "the basis" of "all other freedoms."[5]

For all its historic importance, however, as John Courtney Murray reminds us, *DH* is actually "a document of very modest scope."[6] Its subject matter and scope are aptly conveyed by its alternative title: the "Declaration on Religious Freedom: On the Right of the Person and of Communities to Social and Civil Freedom in Matters Religious." "This Vatican Synod," it proclaims,

> declares that the human person has a right to religious freedom. This freedom means that all men are to be immune from coercion on the part of individuals or of social groups and of any human power, in such wise that in matters religious no one is to be forced to act in a manner contrary to his own beliefs. Nor is anyone to be restrained from acting in accordance with his own beliefs, whether privately or publicly, whether alone or in association with others, within due limits.[7]

The limits in question consist of "the just requirements of public order" (*DH*, 3).

This liberty encompasses not merely the freedom "privately" to practice a religion, but also the freedom to "give external expression to . . . internal acts of religion," to "publicly" profess, practice, witness and worship (*DH*, 3). It is important to note that the right proclaimed by the Declaration consists simply of an "immunity from coercion" (*DH*, 4). *DH*, in other words, does not assert the moral right of individuals "whether alone or in association with others" to publicly profess and practice their religious beliefs regardless of their content, but their right not to be "impeded" from doing so by coercive action "provided that the just requirements of public order are observed." This right, it insists, must be recognized as "a civil right" "in the constitutional law whereby society is governed" (*DH*, 2).

In keeping with its modest scope, *DH* is a brief document consisting of two chapters preceded by a brief preface. The preface begins with the contemporary demands for "freedom in human society" (and, in particular, the right to the "free exercise of religion") and the establishment of "constitutional limits" on "the powers of government" as well as the growing sense of "the dignity of the human person" in which these demands are rooted. This Vatican Synod, it declares,

> takes careful note of these desires in the minds of men. It proposes to declare them to be greatly in accord with truth and justice. To this end, it searches into the sacred tradition and doctrine of the church—the treasury out of which the church continually brings forth new things that are in harmony with the things that are old (*DH*, 1).

At the same time, it reiterates the Church's traditional truth claims (affirming both "that God himself has made known to mankind the way in which men are to serve Him, and thus be saved in Christ and come to blessedness" and "that [the] one true religion subsists in the catholic and apostolic Church") and emphasizes that the right with which it is concerned "has to do with" the nature and scope of religious liberty in "civil society," not the Church. It thus "leaves untouched traditional Catholic doctrine on the moral duty of men and societies toward the true religion and toward the one Church of Christ." Finally, it avows its intention "in taking up the matter of religious freedom . . . to develop the doctrine of the recent Popes on the inviolable rights of the human person and on the constitutional order of society" (*DH*, 1).

Beyond affirming the existence of the right to religious freedom, the focus of the first chapter is essentially threefold. First, it outlines the scope of this right, affirming that it extends not merely to individuals but to "religious bodies." Since such bodies "are a requirement of the social nature both of man and of religion itself," it follows that the right to immunity from coercion that belongs to individuals "is also to be recognized as their right when they act in community" (*DH*, 4).

Religious liberty encompasses the right of religious bodies to "govern themselves according to their own norms"; to attempt "to show the special value of their doctrine in what concerns the organization of society and the inspiration of the whole of human activity"; and "to establish educational, cultural, charitable and social organizations, under the impulse of their own religious sense" (*DH*, 4). "Since the family is a society in its own original right," moreover, religious freedom also encompasses the right of parents "to determine, in accordance with their religious beliefs, the kind of religious education that their children are to receive" and thus "to make a genuinely free choice of schools, and of other means of education." This means that "unjust burdens" may not be placed upon parents, "whether directly or indirectly," because of their decision to have their children educated in accord with their religious convictions (*DH*, 5).

Second, the first chapter explores the foundations of religious liberty, arguing that this right "has its foundation in the very dignity of the human person, as this dignity is known through the revealed word of God and by reason itself." "It is in accordance with their dignity as persons," the Declaration proclaims, that "men should be at once impelled by nature and also bound by a moral obligation to seek the truth, especially religious truth" and "once it is known . . . to order their whole lives in accord" with its "demands" (*DH*, 2). Truth, however, must "be sought after in a manner" consistent with our "dignity as persons"—in a manner consistent with our nature "as beings endowed with reason and free will and therefore privileged to bear personal responsibility." Once discovered, it must be adhered to by an act of "personal assent."

Men and women thus "cannot discharge" their "obligations, in a manner in keeping with their own nature, unless they enjoy immunity from external coercion as well as psychological freedom" (*DH*, 2, 3). Truth, moreover, must be sought in a manner consistent with "the social nature of man [which] requires that he should give external expression to his internal acts of religion; that he should participate with others in matters religious; [and] that he should profess his religion in community" (*DH*, 3).

Every man and women, in short, has "the right to seek truth in matters religious" because every human being "has the duty" to seek, and to order his or her life in accordance with, "religious truth" (*DH*, 3). The right to religious freedom thus "has its foundation, not in the subjective disposition of the person" but in our "very nature" and "dignity" as persons (*DH*, 2).

This right, it continues, is also rooted in the limits placed on the jurisdiction of government by virtue of the state's inherently secular character. Since "the religious acts whereby men, in private and in public . . . direct their lives to God transcend by their nature the order of terrestrial and temporal affairs," government "would clearly transcend the limits of its power were it to presume to direct or inhibit" such acts (*DH*, 3).

Third, the first chapter briefly examines the responsibilities this right imposes on government. Since "the function of government is to make provision for the common welfare," it follows that the state must "take account of the religious life of the people and show it favor" (*DH*, 3). Indeed, because "the protection and promotion of the inviolable rights of man" are an integral component of the "common welfare" of society and "ranks among the essential duties of government," it follows that the state has a responsibility

> to help create conditions favorable to the fostering of religious life, in order that the people may be truly enabled to exercise their religious rights and to fulfill their religious duties, and also in order that society itself may profit by the moral qualities of justice and peace which have their origin in men's faithfulness to God and to His holy will.

In fulfilling this function, moreover, government must "see to it that the equality of citizens before the law, which is itself an element of the common welfare, is never violated for religious reasons, whether openly or covertly" (*DH*, 6).

In this context, *DH* explores the limits of religious liberty. Because "it is exercised in human society," the exercise of religious liberty "is subject to certain regulatory norms." These norms arise "out of the need" to protect "the rights of all citizens" and to resolve "conflicts of rights" in a "peaceful" manner, to safeguard "genuine public peace," and to exercise a "proper guardianship of public morality." These norms collectively "constitute" the "public order." The vindication of this "basic component of the common welfare" constitutes "the special duty of government" (*DH*, 7).

The second chapter considers religious liberty in the light of "divine revelation." While admitting that it "does not affirm in so many words the right of man to immunity from external coercion in religious matters," the Declaration nevertheless affirms that the right to religious liberty "has roots in," and is "in accord with," "divine revelation." Revelation discloses "the dignity of the person in its full dimensions" and "gives evidence of the respect Christ showed toward the freedom with which man is to fulfill his duty of belief in the Word of God" (*DH*, 9). Indeed, it attests to the fact that "the act of faith is of its very nature a free act" (*DH*, 10). In proclaiming this right, therefore, "the Church . . . is being faithful to the truth of the gospel, and is following the way of Christ" (*DH*, 12).

"A harmony" exists between the right to religious freedom affirmed by *DH* and "the fundamental principle" governing "the relations between the

church and governments and the whole civil order," namely, "the freedom of
the Church." The Church receives this freedom by a "divine mandate, and to
violate this freedom "is to act against the will of God." The freedom of the
Church encompasses "the independence . . . necessary for the [Church's] fulfillment of her divine mission" and extends to the Church in both "her character as a spiritual authority" charged with the "care" of "the salvation of men"
and as "a society of men" ordering their lives "in accordance with the precepts
of Christian faith." Insofar as the "sincere and practical application" of the
principle of religious liberty affords the Church "the independence" she claims
"in society," the document concludes that there exists "a harmony . . . between
the freedom of the Church and the religious freedom which is . . . the right of
all men and communities" (*DH*, 13).

THE SIGNIFICANCE OF THE DECLARATION

To appreciate its historic importance, it is necessary to set *DH* against the
backdrop of preconciliar Church teaching on the subject of religious liberty,
Catholicism's continuing engagement with what John Paul II describes as
the modern world's "quest for freedom,"[8] and the ongoing debates about the
meaning of religious freedom and the proper role of religion in public life.

   DH marks a dramatic expansion in the Catholic understanding of the
proper scope of religious liberty.[9] At the risk of oversimplifying, it might be
said that, prior to the Second Vatican Council, Catholic thinking on the
whole subject of religious liberty took its bearings from the following premises: that individuals are obligated to embrace religious truth; that Catholicism is the one true religion; that religious liberty is to be understood as an
empowerment, as the moral right of individuals to profess and practice their
beliefs; that total care of the common good—understood as, in Murray's
words, the sum total of "all the social goods, spiritual and moral as well as material, which man pursues here on earth in accord with the demands of his
personal and social nature"[10]—is committed to the state; and that religious
truth is an integral element of this good.

   The implications of these premises for the ordering of human social life
are profound. On the one hand, they imply the legal establishment of
Catholicism as "the religion of the state" with all the privileges that accrue
from such a status. On the other hand, and more important in the present
context, they imply sharp limits on the religious freedom of non-Catholics.
This is not to suggest that non-Catholics may be compelled to profess or
practice a religion in which they do not believe. As Ryan and Millar observe,
inasmuch as "belief depends upon the will" which "is not subject to physical

coercion," non-Catholics may not be "coerced into the Catholic Church." Likewise, they have the right to profess and practice their faith so long as they do so "within the family" or in "an inconspicuous manner."[11] Nevertheless, as Ryan and Millar note, "error has not the same rights as truth."[12]

On this view, religious freedom is a positive concept consisting of the moral right of persons to profess and practice their beliefs. Only the true and the good can be the object of such a right. It follows, as Murray observes, that "the fullness of religious freedom" extends only to the profession and practice of the truth. It also follows that there can be no moral right to do something that is objectively wrong such as disseminating erroneous religious doctrines. As Murray notes, since these doctrines have "no right to external social freedom," the preconciliar view concludes that restrictions on public expressions of non-Catholic religions raise "no issue of religious freedom." Such expressions are a source of "scandal" and "occasion of wrongdoing." They also damage other individuals by violating "their right to be protected from error and to be left undisturbed in the profession of truth," and they damage society as a whole because "the common good [itself] . . . is constituted by what is true and good."[13] In Ryan and Millar's words, since "it is the business of the State to safeguard and promote human welfare in all departments of life,"[14] it follows that government would be remiss if it stood by idly and allowed the public profession and practice of erroneous religious doctrines.

This principle, however, is subject to an important prudential qualification. The foundation of the state's authority to proscribe public expressions of religious error is its responsibility for the common good. This authority, therefore, ought not to be exercised if doing so would prove damaging to that good by endangering values such as public peace and civic amity. In practice, according to Ryan and Millar, this means that such restrictions are appropriate only in "a political community that is either exclusively, or almost exclusively made up of Catholics."[15] In a religiously pluralistic society, a broader tolerance in the interest of public peace is appropriate. Thus, preconciliar Catholic teaching distinguished between the thesis and hypothesis—between, in Murray's words, "the care of religion that constitutional law ought to provide, per se and in principle,"[16] and the care of religion acceptable under less than optimal conditions. It distinguished between the scope of religious freedom that should exist in exclusively or almost exclusively Catholic societies and that which should exist in more religiously diverse communities.

The conclusions about the scope of religious liberty embodied in the preconciliar teaching flow inexorably from the premises that underlie the teaching. While *DH* does not reject these premises wholesale, it nevertheless modifies several of them. While it reiterates the Church's traditional truth claims and insistence that religious truth is an integral element of the common good, it implicitly breaks with the traditional teaching that the total care of the temporal common good is committed to the state. It distinguishes between the common good in toto and that "component" of this good which is entrusted in a "special" manner to the state, thereby affirming that the care of the temporal common good "devolves" not upon the state alone but "upon the people as a whole, upon social groups, upon government, and upon the Church and other religious communities . . . in the manner proper to each" (*DH*, 6). At the same time, it elevates freedom to the status of the preferred method for pursuing the goods that collectively constitute the common good, insisting that "the freedom of man [must] be respected as far as possible, and curtailed only when and in so far as necessary" (*DH*, 7).

At the same time, *DH* makes a distinction that the traditional teaching did not make regarding the nature of religious freedom. It distinguishes between the order of man's relationship to truth and the order of man's relationship to other men and to society as a whole. In the former order, religious liberty is indeed an empowerment; it concerns the moral right of the individual to propagate his religious beliefs. Since no one has a moral right to do something wrong, it follows that there can be no "right" to propagate erroneous religious doctrines. "No one," as Murray observes, "may ever urge 'rights' against the truth."[17] As Francis Canavan points out, however, in the order of intersubjective relations, religious freedom concerns not "a person's moral right to propagate his beliefs" but rather whether he may be "impeded in his propaganda by civil laws and coercive measures."[18] In this order, in other words, religious freedom consists primarily in immunity from coercion by others, including the state. If *DH* insists that it leaves "untouched traditional Catholic doctrine on the moral duty of men and societies toward the one true religion" (*DH*, 1), this is because it is concerned with the order of intersubjective relations. The traditional teaching, on the other hand, is concerned with the order of man's relationship to the truth.

These modifications, combined with several new premises *DH* brings into play (premises about the implications of our dignity as persons to the right ordering of public life, the implications of the subjectivity of the human person for our reception of religious truth, etc.) opened the door to a broader understanding of the proper scope of religious freedom in human society than that embodied in the preconciliar teaching. Rejecting the "thesis/hypothesis" distinction between the scope of religious freedom proper to Catholics and non-Catholics, *DH* understands religious liberty to be a universal right—and thus a right that is enjoyed by all men and women regardless of their religious convictions (or lack thereof), a right enjoyed by Catholics and non-Catholics alike. It is a universal right, as Pietro Pavan notes, because it has its foundation not in the "content" of an individual's religious convictions but "in the very nature of man."[19] It is a right limited, moreover, not by the far-reaching demands of the common good but by the considerably more modest demands of "public order."

DH not only effected a dramatic transformation in the Church's teaching on the subject of religious liberty. It represented a pivotal step in the far-reaching development of Catholic social teaching that George Weigel has aptly called "the Catholic human rights revolution."[20] Indeed, as Walter Kasper has observed, it must be "considered a watershed in the long and controversial history of the relationships between the church and the development of the concept of freedom in the modern era," a milestone in the long-standing conflict between the Church and "the modern idea of freedom."[21]

It is, of course, a commonplace that one of the distinguishing marks of the modern era has been a longing for freedom. "The era we call modern times," as Joseph Ratzinger (now Pope Benedict XVI) has written, "has been determined from the beginning by the theme of freedom." Indeed this "striving for new forms of freedom" is the very hallmark of modernity as a distinct historical epoch.[22] This modern quest for freedom, moreover, found its preeminent political expression in the ideal of "democracy." And it is no secret that the Church initially viewed this quest and the movement for political democracy in which it found expression with deep suspicion, if not outright hostility.

The reasons for this hostility were not mysterious. The intellectual framework through which this quest and the institutions and practices of democratic government were conceptualized in eighteenth- and nineteenth-century Europe were, for the Church, problematic. Carried to their logical conclusion, the philosophical and theological premises that inform what is sometimes called Enlightenment or Continental Liberalism resulted in a naturalism that denied the existence of a supernatural order of revelation and grace and a radical individualism whose effect was to make each individual a law unto himself, subject to no objective order of obligations.

Within this intellectual framework, political society was conceived as created by naturally autonomous individuals, and the "people" were conceived as sovereign in the same manner as the individual citizen. Like the individual, the people as a whole were subject only to laws of their own making. The democratic state, the state embodying the will of the people, was therefore unlimited in its scope, coextensive with society, and officially agnostic in character. The results were an utterly monistic conception of society and—in the name of religious freedom and separation of church and state—the systematic exclusion of the Church from the public life of the community. A secularist ethos was thus imposed on society as a whole.[23]

Under this framework, the Church was restricted to the sacristy, and the whole of human social life was ordered along radically secularist lines. Rejecting not just this ideology but the quest for freedom itself, as well as the political institutions and practices in which it found expression, the Church entered into a fateful alliance with the *ancien regime*, an alliance that was a little more than ironic, given that this regime was the linear descendent of the absolutist state that had emerged from the ruins of the medieval world and that had long been the Church's adversary. Whatever the deficiencies of the *ancien regime*, however, the Church reasoned that it (unlike the polities inspired by Enlightenment Liberalism) was at least an ostensibly Christian order.

In the period running from the pontificate of Leo XIII through the Second Vatican Council, however, Catholic social thought underwent a far-reaching renewal. Two historical experiences played a critically important role in stimulating this renewal. The first was what is perhaps the defining political experience of the twentieth century: the emergence of the totalitarian state. The shattering impact of totalitarianism, whether in Nazi, Fascist, or Marxist-Leninist forms, engendered a newfound consciousness of the value and dignity of the human person and prompted a new exploration of this venerable theme in Christian anthropology.

The second experience was the gradual unfolding of the American experiment in self-government and ordered liberty. As Catholics began to reflect on this experiment, they came to recognize that "democracy" was not a univocal concept and that it neither presupposed the rejection of the Catholic vision of human nature and society nor required the construction of a social order informed by a secularist ethos. The institutions and practices of constitutional democracy need not be conceptualized through the prism of the Enlightenment's vision of human nature and society. In short, it might be possible to embrace constitutional democracy without embracing Enlightenment Liberalism.

These experiences prompted a profound development in Catholic social and political thought. They spurred the recovery of the medieval Catholic commitment to the freedom of the Church, the supremacy of law, constitutionally limited government, and the ruler's responsibility to the community. They also gave rise to an insistence on the dignity of the human person as the fundamental principle informing a rightly ordered society.[24] In Pius XII's classic formulation, man, "far from being the object and, as it were, a merely passive element in the social order, is in fact, and must be its subject, its foundation, and its end." The human person, in short, is "the origin and end of human society."[25]

These intellectual developments found expression in twentieth-century papal thought, which gradually embraced the idea of the juridical (or constitutional) state, a state whose "principal function" is "to safeguard the inviolable rights of the human person, and to facilitate the performance of his duties."[26]

This acceptance of the juridical state was paralleled by a reappraisal of the merits of democratic government. "The democratic form of government," Pius XII noted approvingly, "appears to many a postulate of nature imposed by reason itself."[27]

Thus, as George Weigel points out, in the course of the twentieth century, Catholic social teaching came to recognize that certain "key themes in Catholic social ethics" such as "personalism, the common good, and the principle of subsidiarity" were "not merely congruent" with constitutional democracy "but pointed positively toward the evolution" of this form of governance."[28] These developments culminated in the Catholic human rights revolution, in what Paul Sigmund describes as the embrace by the Church of "the moral superiority of democratic government and guarantees of human rights."[29]

To grasp the significance of this revolution, it is necessary to appreciate that what emerges from within it is not merely a justification of the institutions and practices of democratic government but an alternative model of democracy rooted in the Catholic understanding of human nature and society. Although broadly similar in its institutional framework to the model which emerges under the auspices of Enlightenment Liberalism, this model differs decisively in spirit and substance from the latter.[30] In Jacques Maritain's formulation, over and against the "individualist democracy" that emerged under the aegis of the Enlightenment, contemporary Catholic social teaching has embraced the cause of "personalist democracy."[31]

This embrace, in turn, was accompanied by a newer, more positive and considerably more complicated appraisal of the modern quest for freedom. This reappraisal culminates in this teaching of the Second Vatican Council. As Buttiglione has written, not only does "the fundamental theme of the Council" consist of "the relationship between Catholicism and modernity" but what emerges in its teaching is nothing less than "the reconciliation of the Church with the idea of freedom."[32] At the heart of this reconciliation is the recognition that, like "democracy," "freedom" is not a univocal concept. The problem with the modern world has not been its quest for freedom but rather the understanding of freedom that has informed this quest.

Modernity, *Gaudium et Spes* insists, has "often" understood freedom "improperly."[33] It has generally equated freedom with the sheer capacity for choice—viewing it, Servais Pinckaers writes, as "radical indetermination," as nothing more than "the power to choose between contraries, independently of all causes except freedom."[34] So understood, freedom possesses no intrinsic orientation to an ultimate end or set of ends, no intrinsic orientation toward truth, goodness, and love.

The tragic events of the twentieth century attest to the catastrophic consequences of this flawed understanding. By detaching freedom from "its essential link with the truth,"[35] as John Paul writes, this understanding effectively absolutizes freedom by conferring upon it "the right *to determine what is good and evil*."[36] The severing of the link between freedom and truth ultimately produces a "freedom that negates and destroys itself"[37] by equating liberty with license and reducing politics to the raw contest for power, culminating in nihilism.

To conclude that the modern quest for freedom has been informed by an impoverished understanding of freedom, however, is not to reject the quest as such. "The quest for freedom," John Paul contends, arises inexorably "from a recognition of the inestimable dignity and value of the human person" and from the commensurate desire it arouses "to be given a place in social, political and economic life."[38] In fact, as *Gaudium et Spes* avows, "the people of our time" are "right" to "prize freedom very highly and strive eagerly for it" because "that which is truly freedom is an exceptional sign of the image of God in man."[39]

To understand freedom properly, however, it is necessary to appreciate what John Paul describes as "its essential and constitutive relationship to truth."[40] This relationship is both political and metaphysical. On the political level, freedom has its intellectual foundation in certain fundamental moral and anthropological truths, namely, in the "transcendent dignity of the human person, who, as the visible image of the invisible God, is . . . by his very nature the subject of rights which no one may violate—no individual, group, class, nation or State."[41]

A relativistic view of anthropological and moral truth, by way of contrast, reduces our intrinsic dignity and fundamental rights to the status of mere "social conventions" and deprives us of any "objective criterion of good and evil beyond the will of those in power."[42] "When freedom is detached from objective truth," therefore, "it becomes impossible to establish personal rights on a firm rational basis; and the ground is laid for society to be at the mercy of the unrestrained will of individuals or the oppressive totalitarianism of public authority."[43] Far from being a limitation on freedom, truth is its foundation, its guarantor; freedom simply cannot be sustained absent a shared societal affirmation of certain moral truths about the human person.

At the metaphysical level, the capacity of the mind to discern truth, and the intrinsic orientation of the will toward it, constitutes the very foundation of human freedom. "To be subject to the power of passion and selfish interest whether in oneself or others," as Peter Simpson writes, is to "be determined by something other, by something that merely happens in or to one," and thus "to lose" one's freedom, to "no longer . . . be the true agent of one's own acts." Our capacity to recognize truth, by way of contrast, enables us to recognize "objects of choice . . . as things with a determinate known value that can be compared with other things according to that same known value" and thus to distinguish between greater and lesser goods and between true and false values. By doing so, it "releases" the will "from determination by the object" and thereby "enables the person to be self-determining in his acts."[44] It follows, as Buttiglione observes, that "the light of truth is not extrinsic to the act of freedom, but intrinsically constitutive of it, to the point that an act is not authentically free without it."[45]

This means, in turn, that freedom is not simply the license to do whatever we want. Since freedom is not realized in choices against the truth, such choices do not represent authentic exercises of freedom but its negation. Freedom, in John Paul's formulation, "is ordered to the truth, and is fulfilled in man's quest for truth and in man's living in the truth."[46]

An adequate response to the modern quest for freedom must recognize the legitimate aspirations that have undergirded this quest and seek to assimilate its real achievements. At the same time, however, it must recognize that this quest needs to be, in John Paul's words, "corrected and purified"[47] in the light of Christian truth and the richer metaphysics of freedom this truth affords us. What emerges is a very different posture toward this quest from that adopted by the nineteenth-century Church. This new posture, as Kasper notes, accepts "some essential concerns of the political enlightenment" but seeks to "reconcile the modern understanding of freedom with its Christian origins and [to] bring it again into the comprehensive vision of the . . . Christian tradition."[48]

DH's role in these developments has been so pivotal that Weigel describes it as "the manifesto of the Catholic human rights revolution."[49] For *DH*, he writes, "the right of religious freedom is the juridical expression of the pre-political fact that there is a *sanctum sanctorum* within every person wherein coercive power . . . may not tread." The state therefore "is not omnicompetent," and the effective institutionalization of the "prepolitical human right" proclaimed by *DH* is the "essential" precondition of "a just *polis*" that is "structured in accordance with the inherent dignity of the persons who are its citizens."[50]

This commitment to sharp limitations on the scope of government is reinforced by *DH*'s insistence on the communal dimensions of religious liberty, on the fact that this right belongs not only to individuals but to families and associations. Implicit in this insistence is a "distinction between society and state" and an affirmation of the "ontological priority" of social institutions ". . . over [the] institutions of government."[51] Combined with its celebration of the dignity of the human person, this priority points toward government by consent. The Declaration contains what Murray describes as "a political commitment, however discreet, to constitutional government,"[52] an implicit affirmation that constitutional democracy is, in Paul Sigmund's words, the form of government "most in keeping with the nature of man, and with Christian values."[53]

The Declaration implicitly embraces a more complex posture toward the modern quest for freedom than that which informed preconciliar Church social teaching. It readily acknowledges that the modern world has sometimes misunderstood and misused freedom. "Not a few can be found," it admits, "who seem inclined to use freedom as the pretext for refusing to submit to authority and for making light of the duty of obedience" (*DH*, 8). It insists, however, that this quest cannot simply be rejected because the yearning for freedom it expresses is "in accord with truth and justice" (*DH*, 1). Indeed, the growing appreciation of the dignity of the human person that drives this quest is "due in great measure" to "the leaven of the gospel [which] has long been about its quiet work in the minds of men" (*DH*, 12). It therefore affirms that "the usages of society" must "be the usages of freedom in their full range" and thus that freedom must "be respected as far as possible, and curtailed only when and in so far as necessary" (*DH*, 7).

Rather than rejecting the quest for freedom, *DH* seeks to correct and purify it in the light of Christian truth. Indeed, implicit in its teaching is the richer metaphysics of freedom outlined earlier, a metaphysics that insists on the essential linkage of freedom with truth. On the one hand, religious freedom has its foundation in the truth about man, in our nature and dignity as persons. "True freedom," moreover, realizes itself in striving "after what is true and right," making decisions "in the light of truth," fulfilling the demands of "the moral order," and being obedient "to lawful authority" (*DH*, 8). It involves, in short, both "seeking the truth" and "adhering to it" by ordering our "whole lives in accord" with its demands (*DH*, 2).

The new and distinctive understanding of religious freedom outlined in the Declaration not only marks a milestone in the evolution of Catholic social teaching but makes an important contribution to both the modern world's long-standing debate about the meaning of religious liberty and the ongoing contemporary argument about the proper role of religion in public life. Indeed, even today when the existence of a right to religious liberty is almost universally acknowledged, an intense argument continues to rage about the foundation, nature, and scope of this right.

On the one hand, it is no secret that the dominant modern theories of religious freedom have tended to take their bearings from either the presuppositions of Enlightenment Liberalism or from those of one or another form of Protestantism. Nor is it a secret that the idea of religious liberty has been frequently associated with some type of religious subjectivism, agnosticism, and indifferentism.

At the same time, in recent decades America has witnessed the emergence of a highly influential—and highly controversial—movement demanding what is sometimes called the privatization of religion. On the one hand, the proponents of privatization reject as illegitimate laws, which, in the words of one of the United States Supreme Court's landmark church-state decisions, "aid one religion, aid all religions, or prefer one religion over another."[54] At the same time, they demand the exclusion of religion and religiously grounded moral beliefs from public life and the establishment of what Richard John Neuhaus calls "the naked public square."[55] The proponents of privatization insist that, while individuals should be free to embrace whatever religion they choose, religious beliefs must be checked at the door of the public square, that religion and religiously grounded values must not be allowed to impinge on public life.

The Declaration offers us an understanding of religious freedom rooted not in Enlightenment Liberalism or some form of Protestantism but in the Catholic understanding of the human person, society, and the nature of religious truth. As Canavan observes, the Declaration's approach

> is very much in the rational, natural-law tradition of Catholic thought. . . . [I]t posits a universal human nature, whose natural tendencies and needs are knowable to the human mind. It further assumes the existence of God, who is truth, and the truth about whom answers to the deepest of human needs. By rational analysis of the relationship of God to man it concludes that religious freedom is a natural human right.[56]

DH offers a theory of religious liberty untainted by religious subjectivism, agnosticism, and indifferentism. Its whole understanding of religious liberty takes its bearings from the idea that religious truth is both attainable and of overriding importance. Not only are men and women "at once impelled by nature and . . . bound by a moral obligation to seek . . . religious truth" (*DH*, 2), but there exists "one true religion [which] subsists in the catholic and apostolic Church" (*DH*, 1) which is "by the will of Christ, the teacher of truth" (*DH*, 14). A right to religious liberty exists, moreover, not because religious truth is unattainable or unimportant but because this truth itself—the truth about man's nature, dignity, and destiny as it "is known through the revealed Word of God and by reason itself" (*DH*, 2)—demands the recognition of such a right.

The Declaration offers the broad outlines of a conceptually sophisticated theory of religious liberty that breaks fundamentally with those which have dominated our constitutional law and theory by flatly rejecting the privatization of religion because such privatization is incompatible with authentic religious freedom. Properly understood, *DH* insists, religious liberty requires that government "take account of the religious life of the people and show it favor" (*DH*, 3) and includes the freedom of "religious bodies" to attempt "to show the special value of their doctrine in what concerns the organization of society" (*DH*, 4). The principle of religious freedom demands the establishment not of a naked public square but of a public square open to religion and religiously grounded values. It provides us, in short, with the broad outlines of a new and better approach to the place of religion in public life.

THE UNFINISHED AGENDA

As Murray points out, however, if *DH* constitutes in some sense an "end," it also constitutes a "beginning."[57] It does so because in the process of resolving the question of the Church's teaching about the nature and scope of religious liberty, it raises a host of new questions. By explicitly avowing its intention "to develop" Catholic "doctrine," to "bring forth new things that are in harmony with the things that are old" from "the treasury" of "the sacred tradition and doctrine of the Church" (*DH*, 1), *DH* raises a whole series of complicated questions relating to the development of Church teaching on the subject of religious liberty.

For example, in what sense can the Declaration's teaching on the nature and scope of religious liberty be said to represent a "development" rather than a break with earlier Church teaching? In other words, in what sense can the "new things" affirmed by *DH* be said to be "in harmony with the old?" What has made this evolution in the Catholic conception of the nature and scope of religious freedom possible? Is the movement from the older thesis/hypothesis position to *DH*'s understanding of religious liberty rooted in a change in the Church's understanding of the nature and epistemological status of religious truth? Of the responsibilities and the rights of conscience? Of our nature and dignity as persons? Of the role of the state in the overall economy of human social life? Of the demands of "Christian freedom?" Of several (or all) of the above?

Likewise, the whole question of the relationship between the right affirmed by *DH* and the perennial problem of the proper relationship between Church and state or, more broadly, between religion and government and Church and society is raised. In the language of American constitutional law, for example, *DH* focuses almost entirely on the "free exercise," rather than on the "establishment," of religion. With regard to the latter issue, it limits itself to observing only that "if, in view of peculiar circumstances obtaining among certain peoples, special legal recognition is given in the constitutional order of society to one religious body, it is at the same time imperative that the right of all citizens and religious bodies to religious freedom should be recognized and made effective in practice" (*DH*, 6).

What precisely are these "peculiar circumstances," and how frequently do they obtain? What forms of such "legal recognition" are consistent with the principle of religious freedom? Is there a latent tension between the Declaration's insistence that the state respect the right to religious freedom and its demand that it "take account of the religious life and the people and show it favor" (*DH*, 3)? How can the latter demand be reconciled with its insistence that "the equality of citizens before the law" must "never be violated for religious reasons" (*DH*, 6)? Exactly what forms of recognition and "favor" are consistent with religious liberty and the demands of the equality of citizens before the law?"

Similarly, one must also consider *DH*'s implications for the proper relationship between Church and society or, more broadly, between religion and society. In contrast to certain currents within the Christian tradition that have advocated a posture of radical separation from the world, Catholicism has always understood, as Christopher Dawson notes, that the Church's "essential task" is "the sanctification of humanity as a whole in its corporate as well as in its individual activities."[58] Not surprisingly, therefore, the Declaration reiterates "traditional Catholic doctrine on the moral duty of men *and societies* toward the true religion and toward the one Church of Christ" (*DH*, 1; my emphasis); reminds "the Christian faithful" that "in the formation of their consciences," they are obligated to "carefully . . . attend to the sacred and certain doctrine of the Church"; and affirms the right of "religious bodies" to attempt "to show the special value of their doctrine in what concerns the organization of society and the inspiration of the whole of human activity" (*DH*, 4).[59]

At the same time, however, over and above proclaiming the right to religious freedom, the Declaration implicitly affirms both a distinction between the spiritual order and "the order of temporal and terrestrial affairs" (*DH*, 4) and what *Gaudium et Spes* calls "the rightful autonomy" of temporal matters.[60] Noting how in the contemporary world "men of different . . . religions are being brought into closer relationships" (*DH*, 15), it implicitly acknowledges religious pluralism as an ineradicable fact of contemporary social life.

Against this backdrop, a number of additional questions suggest themselves. What exactly is "the moral duty of . . . societies toward the one true religion and toward the one Church of Christ" of which the Declaration speaks? How can the right of the Church and other religious bodies to seek to organize society in accordance with their doctrines—to seek, in the words of *Gaudium et Spes*, "to impress the divine law of the affairs of the earthly city"—be reconciled with an insistence on the secularity and "rightful autonomy" of the temporal order and the principle of religious freedom? What are the implications of *DH* for our understanding of the action of the Church in the temporal order, for our understanding of the proper role of the Church in the overall economy of human social life and its relationship to the whole range of institutions and communities in which "the social nature of man" (*DH*, 3) finds expression? Is Murray correct that *DH* transforms the traditional problematic of "Church and state" by situating it "at the interior of, and in subordination to, the larger problematic of 'religion and human society'"— religion here being understood "in a historical-pluralist sense"—and if so, what are the implications of this transformation?[61]

This, in turn, raises the whole question of *DH*'s understanding of the nature of the state and its role in the overall economy of human social life. Because *DH* makes a political commitment to constitutional government, it endorses, as Pietro Pavan observes, an understanding of the role and responsibilities of the state that differs from both "the Catholic-confessional" model associated with preconciliar Church teaching and "the laicistic or neutralistic" understanding that emerged under the aegis of Enlightenment Liberalism.[62] What exactly is the understanding of the nature, role, and limits of the state presupposed by *DH*? How does its theory of the state relate to traditional Catholic teaching about the origins and goals of political life? In what sense does it "develop the doctrine of the recent Popes" on the state? How exactly does its theory of the state relate both to the various other political theories that have emerged in the course of Western history and to those which dominate contemporary Western public life?

Finally, there is the whole question of the intellectual foundations of religious freedom. As Richard Regan has shown in his study of the Declaration's drafting, because there was no consensus at the Council about the "rationale for the principle of religious freedom," the argument of the final text represented a compromise that incorporated elements of several different rationales that had been advanced in the course of the conciliar debates (while giving pride of place to the argument moving from the obligation to seek truth).[63] Given the disagreements surrounding it, as Murray observes, the Council did not attempt to articulate a "final and definitive" argument in support of the right it affirmed. Instead, it left "the task" of systematically elaborating such an argument "to the scholars of the Church working in ecumenical spirit with scholars of other religious communities, and in a humanist spirit with scholars of no religious convictions who are concerned with the exigencies of human dignity."[64]

The Declaration, in short, did not attempt to resolve definitively the complicated question of the intellectual foundations of the right it proclaims. Is this right grounded in revelation, reason, or both? Is a philosophical account of this right sufficient, or is a full-fledged theology of religious freedom neces-sary? Are religious liberty's foundations to be found in sacred scripture and the idea of Christian freedom? The rights and duties of conscience? The demands of human dignity? The limited and secular role of government in the overall scheme of human social life? The obligation to pursue truth? Some combina-tion of these? These and other questions remain unanswered.

Taken together, these questions constitute what James Rausch has de-scribed as "the unfinished agenda" of *DH*.[65] The completion of this intellec-tual agenda is essential not only to the proper understanding of the Declara-tion itself but to the successful conclusion of the broader development in Catholic social teaching of which it is a part. One of the pressing tasks con-fronting Catholic social thought today is, as Walter Burghardt has remarked, the deepening of "our understanding of the Declaration's affirmations and the reasons on which they repose."[66]

Unfortunately, little progress has been made toward the completion of this agenda. Indeed, as John Coleman has pointed out, "There has been very little Roman Catholic theological writing or discussion on religious liberty or separation of Church and state since the adoption of *Dignitatis Humanae*."[67] Tragically, the unfinished agenda of *DH* remains not only unfinished but largely ignored.

As surprising as this state of affairs is, what is perhaps even more sur-prising is the widespread neglect of *DH* in contemporary American Catholic thought. After all, if *DH* is among the Council's major texts, it is also the one in which American Catholics and the American Catholic experience played a particularly important role. It was no accident that the Declaration was of-ten referred to during the Council as the "American" schema. The favorable experience of the Church in the United States undoubtedly helped lay the groundwork for *DH*. It demonstrated that religious liberty entailed neither the privatization of religion nor the organization of public life in accordance with a secularist ethos. It also showed that the Church could flourish without enjoying a position of legal privilege, in the context of a political order guar-anteeing a wide-ranging religious freedom and in a social environment char-acterized by far-reaching religious pluralism.

The American experience helped remove a number of obstacles to the Church's embrace of the broader conception of religious liberty that found ex-pression in *DH*. Furthermore, not only were the American bishops among the leading advocates of what became the final schema of *DH* at the Council, but John Courtney Murray, arguably the greatest theologian produced by the American Church, laid the groundwork for the Declaration through his work in the decade prior to Vatican II and also played an important role, as a *peri-tus* at the Council, in its drafting.

Ironically, however, American Catholic scholars have exhibited little interest in addressing the Declaration's unfinished agenda, and *DH* does not assume the sort of central role in American Catholicism's engagement with contemporary American public life that it has played in, say, John Paul II's engagement with the contemporary world. Given that one of the most striking features of post-World War II American public life has been the aforementioned movement toward the privatization of religion, the failure of American Catholics to make the understanding of religious freedom advanced in *DH* a cornerstone of their engagement with contemporary American public life is, to put it mildly, perplexing.

This volume takes shape against this backdrop. Its objectives are essentially twofold. The first is what the Second Vatican Council called *ressourcement*, a return to the sources, in this case to *DH* itself. One of the principal goals of these essays is to explore the teaching of this seminal document—to examine its understanding of the nature and scope of the right to religious freedom; to examine the implications of its teaching for the right ordering of human life in society; to explore its account of the intellectual underpinnings of this right; to investigate what is distinctive about the conception of religious freedom it advances; and to bring that conception into conversation with some of the competing conceptions of religious freedom articulated by other Christian traditions and by secular sources.

The second goal is equally straightforward: to begin the long-overdue task of addressing the questions that collectively constitute *DH*'s unfinished agenda. We say "begin" here because we are under no illusions about the difficulties this will involve. The intellectual project which made the Declaration possible spanned several generations and involved the work of many scholars in a wide array of fields. The successful completion of *DH*'s unfinished agenda will involve a project of similar if not greater magnitude. Our expectations here are thus modest. We hope to do no more than to begin discussing some of the principal questions raised by the Declaration.

A CONSIDERATION OF THE NEW IN LIGHT OF THE THINGS THAT ARE OLD

The Declaration understands itself to be bringing "forth" from "the sacred tradition and doctrine of the Church" a "new" theory of religious liberty that is "in harmony with the things that are old" (*DH*, 1). At the heart of these essays are the questions of the precise nature of these "new things," their relationship to "the sacred tradition and doctrine of the Church," and their harmony with the "old."

In their contribution to the present volume, Robert P. George and William L. Saunders argue that the theory of religious liberty advanced by *DH* represents a salutary development in the Church's understanding of the requirements of a just political order. Employing what has been described as the principles of the "new natural law," they contend that a perfectionist view of natural rights (and of religious liberty) best serves fundamental aspects of human flourishing. Robert P. Hunt argues that a purely negative, antiperfectionist theory of religious liberty as employed, for example, by the U.S. Supreme Court in its church-state jurisprudence—that is, *freedom from* rather than *freedom to*—must depend on a conception of human nature that, in the end, undermines the very religious liberty that it purports to defend. What distinguishes *DH*'s understanding of religious liberty, Hunt argues, is not that it advances a more juridically neutral conception of religious liberty but that it depends for sustenance upon a deeper and richer personal and social ontology than that advanced from within the Enlightenment liberal tradition. Both essays seem to concur that the political theory that undergirds *DH*'s theory of religious liberty should in no way be construed as a concession to the Enlightenment liberal model of man and society.

The theological question of whether *DH* constitutes a reversal of earlier Catholic teaching, a carrying out of the profound intentions (if not the letter) of previous papal teaching, or a genuine development of Church doctrine is explored by Avery Cardinal Dulles. Cardinal Dulles, in a manner reminiscent of John Henry Newman in his magisterial *Essay on the Development of Christian Doctrine*, contends that the Declaration represents true doctrinal progress in the Church's understanding of the nature of religious liberty. Francis Canavan, S.J., focuses more narrowly on the political theory of the Declaration. Father Canavan traces the development of Catholic political theory from the Middle Ages, through its rapprochement with royal absolutism in the seventeenth and eighteenth centuries, to its expression of a preference for the forms and modes of limited, constitutional government in the nineteenth and twentieth centuries. He argues that *DH* represents not a change in the Catholic understanding of religious and moral truth but rather a change in the Catholic understanding of the state.

The essays by Thomas Heilke and David Koyzis analyze the emerging Catholic defense of religious liberty as represented by *DH* from two different Protestant perspectives. Writing from a "radical Protestant" perspective, Heilke discusses what he sees as the Catholic Church's perennial flirtation with political Constantinianism, a flirtation, he contends, that continues in *DH*'s natural law–grounded approach to defending religious liberty. Heilke supports a more biblically oriented defense of religious liberty as a better way of avoiding the pitfalls of Constantinian yearnings. Koyzis discusses what he sees as the rather parallel tracks on which neo-Calvinists and Catholics have been moving regarding the question of religious liberty since the latter part of the nineteenth century. He embraces Abraham Kuyper's notion of "sphere sovereignty"—or what has more recently been called spheres of "differentiated responsibilities"—as a way of defending religious liberty within a limited constitutional order and finds fertile ground for further Catholic/neo-Calvinist dialogue.

The aforementioned "unfinished agenda," and the tensions implicit within it, becomes the focus of the final three essays by John Crosby, Kenneth L. Grasso, and David Crawford. Crosby provides a commentary on John Paul II's personalism and finds such personalism to be an antidote to certain monist conceptions of politics—whether classical or modern—that invariably undermine the possibility of true religious liberty. Grasso contends that further work needs to be done on the Catholic view of the state, especially in light of the Declaration's distinction between the common good and the more limited requirements of public order. He argues that the concept of human dignity supplies a necessary, but not sufficient, foundation for Catholic political theory. This concept must be supplemented by a more comprehensive understanding of the role of the state in the overall economy of social life. Crawford compares and contrasts the arguments of John Courtney Murray and Pope John Paul II on the theological/jural underpinnings of the Catholic defense of religious liberty. He finds Murray's juridical approach to be insufficient and too inclined to collapse into extrincisist concessions to liberal political morality. Like David Schindler and other scholars operating within the Catholic *Communio* movement, he finds John Paul's efforts to develop a more robust theological anthropology to provide a better foundation for *DH*'s defense of religious liberty.[68]

In terms of the work that lies ahead, it is perhaps significant that these essays focus so heavily on the work of two thinkers: John Courtney Murray and Pope John Paul II. The reasons for this are readily apparent. While Murray's influence on its writing was certainly not determinative—he did not, as Higgins notes, have "anything like complete control over . . . the final text"—and he was not entirely satisfied with the final draft of the Declaration,[69] there can be no question that his work at the Council left its imprint on the Declaration.

In the aftermath of the Council, Murray emerged as one of *DH*'s leading interpreters. Suggestive of his role in this regard is that after the Declaration's adoption it was Murray who was asked by the American bishops to explain its contents to the media. In the two years between the promulgation of the Declaration and his untimely death, he wrote upwards of a dozen articles (and delivered countless speeches and lectures) exploring the doctrine of *DH* and its significance.

John Paul's importance to the Declaration, on the other hand, does not stem from his role in its drafting. Although he intervened several times in the conciliar debates on religious liberty, he did not play the type of central role in its drafting that he played in the writing of *Gaudium et Spes*.[70] Rather, his importance stems from the treatment of *DH* in the social teaching of his papacy. Through his encyclicals and addresses he emerged as one of its leading interpreters by insisting on the Declaration's centrality to the Church's social magisterium.

Whether or not a recent writer is correct in suggesting that Murray and John Paul disagree fundamentally about the interpretation of the Declaration, it is undeniable that their glosses on it are characterized by some significant differences in emphasis.[71] Murray's interpretation centers on the natural law argument advanced in the Declaration's first chapter. Indeed, much of the last two years of his life were devoted to trying to address the political dimensions of the Declaration's teaching and, in particular, to elaborate the theory of the state presupposed by *DH*. John Paul, on the other hand, consistently sought to situate the right affirmed by *DH* in the context of a fully elaborated personalist philosophy of human nature, a full-fledged theological anthropology, and a systematically developed theology and philosophy of freedom. If Murray focuses on its juridical and political dimensions, John Paul focuses on its philosophical and theological dimensions; if Murray tries to systematically elaborate *DH*'s theory of the state, John Paul seeks to do the same for the philosophical and theological anthropology that informs it.

DH understands itself as bringing "forth new things that are in harmony with the old" (*DH*, 1). Today, some forty years after its initial promulgation, the precise nature of these "new things" and their relationship to "the old" remain among the most important pieces of unfinished business confronting Catholic social thought. The theological, philosophical, juridical, and political questions that collectively constitute the unfinished agenda of *DH* go to the heart of Catholic teaching not only about the rights and responsibilities of the human person but about the proper ordering of human social life and the development of Catholic social doctrine as well. They also go to the heart of the contemporary debate about the nature, foundation, and scope of religious liberty and the proper role of religion in public life. In the decades since the Second Vatican Council these questions have been largely ignored. The time has come to begin affording them the type of serious and sustained attention they deserve.

NOTES

1. Paul VI, *Closing Speeches: Vatican Council II* (Boston: St. Paul Editions, n.d. [1965]), 25. For purposes of convenience, *Dignitatis Humanae* will be abbreviated as *DH*.

2. AAS 58 (1996): 74; cited in Luigi Misto, "Paul VI and *Dignitatis Humanae*: Theory and Practice" in *Religious Liberty: Paul VI and* Dignitatis Humanae, ed. John T. Ford, C.S.C. (Brescia, Italy: Instituto Paolo VI, 1995), 13.

3. John Paul II, *Redemptor Hominis*, section 12.

4. "World Day of Peace Message," *Origins* 17 (1988): 493.

5. Letter to United Nations Secretary General Waldheim, 2 December 1978; cited in George Weigel, *Freedom and Its Discontents: Catholicism Confronts Modernity* (Washington, DC: Ethics and Public Policy Center, 1991), 19.

6. John Courtney Murray, "The Declaration on Religious Freedom" in *Bridging the Sacred and the Secular: Selected Writings of John Courtney Murray, S.J.,* ed. J. Leon Hooper, S.J. (Washington, DC: Georgetown University Press, 1994), 187.

7. "Declaration on Religious Liberty [*Dignitatis Humanae*]," in *The Documents of Vatican II*, ed. Walter M. Abbott, S.J. (New York: The Crossroad Publishing Co., 1989; reprint, New York: Guild Press, America Press, Association Press, 1966), section 2. This translation is by John Courtney Murray. Further citations of this document will be given parenthetically by section number.

8. Address to the General Assembly of the United Nations," October 5, 1995, in *Make Room for the Mystery of God: Visit of Pope John Paul II to the USA 1995* (Boston: Pauline Books & Media, 1995), 19.

9. For good statements of the preconciliar teaching, see John A. Ryan and Moorhouse F. X. Millar, S.J., *The State and the Church* (New York: Macmillan, 1922), 26–61, and John Courtney Murray, "The Problem of Religious Freedom," in *Religious Liberty: Catholic Struggles with Pluralism,* ed. J. Leon Hooper (Louisville, KY: Westminster/John Knox Press, 1995), 128–97. *The Problem of Religious Liberty* is a short volume written by Murray during the Council comparing and contrasting the preconciliar teaching on religious liberty with the newer approach that eventually found expression in *DH*.

10. Murray, *The Problem of Religious Liberty*, 145.

11. Ryan and Millar, 35.

12. Ibid., 36.

13. Murray, *The Problem of Religious Freedom*, 130–33.

14. Ryan and Millar, 37.

15. Ibid.

16. Murray, *The Problem of Religious Liberty*, 132.

17. Murray, "The Declaration on Religious Freedom: A Moment in Its Legislative History," in *Religious Liberty: An End and a Beginning*, ed. John Courtney Murray, S.J. (New York: Macmillan, 1968), 24.

18. Francis Canavan, "Church, State and Council," in *Ecumenism and Vatican II*, ed. Charles O'Neill, S.J. (Milwaukee: The Bruce Publishing Co., 1964), 53.

19. Pietro Pavan, "Declaration on Religious Liberty," in *Commentary on the Documents of Vatican II*, vol. IV, ed. Herbert Vorgrimler (New York: Herder & Herder, 1969), 65.

20. Weigel, *Freedom and Its Discontents*, 25.

21. Walter Kasper, *The Christian Understanding of Freedom and the History of Freedom in the Modern Era* (Milwaukee: Marquette University, 1988), 2, 4.

22. Joseph Ratzinger, *Truth and Tolerance*, trans. Henry Taylor (San Francisco: Ignatius Press, 2004), 236.

23. For an in-depth discussion of this ideology and the model of democracy it inspired, see John Courtney Murray, "The Church and Totalitarian Democracy," *Theological Studies* 13 (December 1953): 525–63; and "Leo XIII: Separation of Church and State," *Theological Studies* 14 (June 1952): 145–214.

24. On this tradition, see R. W. Carlyle and A. J. Carlyle, *A History of Medieval Political Theory in the West*, 6 vols. (Edinburgh: William Blackwood and Sons, 1936).

25. Pius XII, "1944 Christmas Message" (Washington, DC: National Catholic Welfare Conference, n.d.), 3.

26. Pius XII, radio message, 1 June 1941, in *Acta Apostolicae Sedis* 33 (1941): 200.

27. "1944 Christmas Message," 4.

28. Weigel, *Freedom and Its Discontents*, 25.

29. Paul Sigmund, "The Catholic Tradition and Modern Democracy," in *Religion and Politics in the American Milieu*, ed. Leslie Green (Notre Dame, IN: *The Review of Politics* and Office of Policy Studies, n.d.), 20.

30. For an account of the model of democracy that emerges in contemporary Catholic social teaching that stresses its distinctive character and the gulf that separates it from models that have emerged under the auspices of what we have here called "Enlightenment Liberalism," see Kenneth L. Grasso, "Beyond Liberalism: Human Dignity, the Free Society, and the Second Vatican Council," in *Catholicism, Liberalism and Communitarianism: The Catholic Intellectual Tradition and the Moral Foundations of Democracy*, ed. Kenneth L. Grasso, Gerard V. Bradley, and Robert P. Hunt (Lanham, MD: Rowman & Littlefield, 1995), 29–58.

31. See Jacques Maritain, *Scholasticism and Politics* (New York: Macmillan, 1940), 70–88.

32. Rocco Buttiglione, *Karol Wojtyla: The Thought of the Man Who Became Pope John Paul II* (Grand Rapids, MI: William B. Eerdmans Publishing Co., 1997), 365, 371.

33. *Gaudium et Spes*, section 17. We are employing the translation that appears in *Vatican II: The Conciliar and Post-Conciliar Documents*, ed. Austin Flannery, O.P. (Collegeville, MN: The Liturgical Press, 1975).

34. Servais Pinckaers, *The Sources of Christian Ethics*, trans. Mary Thomas Noble, O.P. (Washington, DC: Catholic University of America Press, 1995), 242.

35. *Evangelium Vitae*, section 19.

36. *Veritatis Splendor*, section 35.

37. *Evangelium Vitae*, section 19.

38. "Address to the General Assembly of the United Nations," 21–22.

39. *Gaudium et Spes*, section 17.

40. *Veritatis Splendor*, section 4.

41. *Centesimus Annus*, section 44.

42. Ibid., section 45.

43. *Evangelium Vitae*, section 16.

44. Peter Simpson, *On Karol Wojtyla* (Belmont, CA: Wadsworth, 2001), 28, 84.

45. Buttiglione, 372.

46. "Address to the General Assembly of the United Nations," 30–31.

47. *Veritatis Splendor*, 31. "The heightened sense of the dignity of the human person and . . . of the respect due to the journey of conscience," he writes, "certainly rep-

resents one of the positive achievements of modern culture. This perception, authentic as it is, has been expressed in a number of more or less adequate ways, some of which however diverge from the truth about man . . . and thus need to be corrected and purified in the light of faith." Ibid.

48. Kasper, 2, 18.

49. Weigel, *Catholicism and the Renewal of American Democracy* (Mahwah, NJ: Paulist Press, 1989), 83.

50. *Freedom and Its Discontents*, 11, 39–40.

51. Ibid., 40.

52. "The Issue of Church and State at Vatican Council II," in *Religious Liberty: Catholic Struggles with Pluralism/John Courtney Murray*, 218.

53. Sigmund, 13.

54. *Everson v. Board of Education*, 330 U.S. 1, 15–16 (1947).

55. See Richard John Neuhaus, *The Naked Public Square: Religion and Democracy in America* (Grand Rapids, MI: William B. Eerdmans Publishing Co., 1984).

56. Francis Canavan, "The Catholic Concept of Religious Freedom as a Human Right," in *Religious Liberty: An End and a Beginning*, 71.

57. Murray, "Preface," in *Religious Liberty: An End and a Beginning*, 7.

58. Dawson, *Beyond Politics* (London: Sheed & Ward, 1939), 134.

59. On the latter point, it should be noted that the Council forcefully affirms both the responsibility of laity "to impress the divine law on the affairs of the earthly city" and the right and responsibility of the Church "to proclaim its teaching about society . . . and to pass moral judgments even in matters related to politics, whenever the fundamental rights of man or the salvation of souls requires it." *Gaudium et Spes*, sections 43 and 76.

60. *Gaudium et Spes*, section 36. It should be noted that the Council distinguishes this "rightful autonomy" from a "false autonomy" that refuses to acknowledge God and the order established by Him. See *Gaudium et Spes*, sections 36 and 41.

61. "The Issue of Church and State at Vatican Council II," in *Religious Liberty: Catholic Struggles with Pluralism/John Courtney Murray*, 215.

62. Pietro Pavan, "Declaration on Religious Freedom," 64.

63. Richard J. Regan, *Conflict and Consensus: Religious Freedom and the Second Vatican Council* (New York: The Macmillan Co., 1967), 170, 174.

64. This observation is found in the notes Murray attached to his translation of *DH*. See Abbot, 680, n. 7.

65. See James S. Rausch, "*Dignitatis Humanae*: The Unfinished Agenda," in *Religious Freedom: 1965 and 1975*, ed. Walter J. Burghardt, S.J. (Mahwah, NJ: Paulist Press, 1977).

66. Walter J. Burghardt, "Critical Reflections," in *Religious Liberty: 1965 and 1975*, 72.

67. John A. Coleman, *An American Strategic Theology* (Mahwah, NJ: Paulist Press, 1982), 211.

68. For an introduction to Schindler's thought, see his *Heart of the World, Center of the Church*: Communio *Ecclesiology, Liberalism, and Liberation* (Grand Rapids, MI: William B. Eerdmans Publishing Co., 1996).

69. Ibid., 3.

70. On John Paul's role in the Conciliar debates on what became the Declaration, see Regan, 82, 151; Buttiglione, 187–93; and George Weigel, *Witness to Hope: The Biography of Pope John Paul II* (New York: HarperCollins, 1999), 163–72.

71. See Hermínio Rico, S.J., *John Paul II and the Legacy of Dignitatis Humanae* (Washington, DC: Georgetown University Press, 2002).

Dignitatis Humanae: The Freedom of the Church and the Responsibility of the State

Robert P. George[1] and William L. Saunders Jr.[2]

$\mathcal{O}$n January 24, 2002, more than two hundred religious leaders representing creeds and peoples from around the world gathered in Assisi, Italy, the home of St. Francis, at the invitation of Pope John Paul II to participate in the second Day of Prayer for Peace for the World. (The first was held on October 27, 1986.) Catholics and Jews, Orthodox and Protestants, Confucians, Buddhists, and Muslims all came together to pray for that peace that had been so brutally repudiated with the attacks of September 11.

While crediting the late pope's good intentions, some Catholics—and other Christians—nonetheless disapproved of the Assisi gathering. These critical voices alleged that John Paul II's appearance with the others compromised the claims of Christianity to be divinely revealed truth. These critics believe that, by appearing with these other religious leaders and despite his statement that there were no moments of common prayer during the Day, John Paul II continued and deepened a fundamental mistake made at the Second Vatican Council.

In this essay, we will examine whether the critics' charges are justified. Assuming John Paul II was, as he always claimed to be, a faithful interpreter and implementer of Vatican II, did Vatican II teach in a way so as to undermine Christian truth claims? More specifically, did Vatican II's teachings on the subject of religious freedom break with Catholic tradition? Did Vatican II put the Catholic Church on a path that fosters religious indifferentism?

In *Dignitatis Humanae*, the Council Fathers set forth principles of religious freedom. Taking note of the "spiritual aspirations" of contemporary man, particularly his yearning for freedom, the Council's "Declaration on Religious Freedom" called for protection of the right of each person to religious liberty within the constitutional order. The Declaration found this "civil right" to be rooted in the personal dignity and social nature of the human being. Thus, subject (only) to the just demands of public order, all forms of "coercion" aimed at forcing a person to act contrary to his conscience in matters of religion were declared to be unjust.

It is commonly acknowledged that the thinking of John Courtney Murray, S.J., shaped the development of this teaching, and we will spend some time on that point below. However, it is also true that the Council saw itself as "develop[ing] the doctrine of recent popes on the inviolable rights of the human person and on the constitutional order of society" (*DH*, 1). It is, however, on precisely this point—conformity to the teaching of prior popes—that *Dignitatis Humanae* is frequently challenged. Although a thorough analysis requires systematic treatment by historians and theologians, we would like to note a few points.

First, critics often allude to the teaching of one prior pope in particular to illustrate what they claim are discontinuities between the larger tradition and the teaching of *Dignitatis Humanae*—Pius X. Leaving aside the point that, from the perspective of Catholic faith, the teaching authority of an ecumenical council such as Vatican II is superior to the non–ex cathedra teaching of an individual pope —something that would resolve the matter if there *were* a contradiction—we might consider whether there *is* a contradiction between the teaching of Pius X and that of *Dignitatis Humanae*.

Perhaps the heart of Pius X's teaching is contained in his encyclical letter "On the Doctrine of the Modernists" and the companion "Syllabus Condemning the Errors of the Modernists," both issued in 1907. In these documents, he grapples with the problems posed by Catholics adhering tenaciously to heretical doctrines as if by right. As a result, he condemns the view that "[i]n proscribing errors, the Church cannot demand any internal assent from the faithful by which the judgments she issues are to be embraced."[3] In other words, according to Pius X, the Church may demand the internal assent of its members. Vatican II asserts that man "is not to be forced to act in a manner contrary to his conscience" (*DH*, 3).[4] Is this a contradiction?

While Pius X speaks to the *Church's* right, *Dignitatis Humanae* speaks of the *individual's* right. These rights do not contradict each other. The Church presents the truth undiminished and may demand that its members adhere to its tenets. But individuals are to be free in the civil order to heed the Church or not. Indeed, people are to be free in the civil order to leave the Church, if that is what they wish to do. *Dignitatis Humanae* expressly "leave[s] untouched traditional Catholic doctrine on the moral duty of men and societies toward the true religion and toward the one Church of Christ" (*DH*, 1)[5]—precisely the moral duty that Pius X was at pains to assert[6]—but *supplements* that teaching with new (but not contradictory) teaching on how the individual is to find that truth.[7]

The teaching of *Dignitatis Humanae* that (subject to the demands of public order) neither the state nor anyone else may exercise coercion on the individual in matters of religion appears to be a development of the teaching of a successor of Pius X, namely, Pius XII. According to John Courtney Murray's account,[8] in a discourse to Italian journalists in 1953, Pius XII approached the issue by referring to the parable of the tares (Matthew 13). Therein Jesus tells the story of the master whose enemy sows weeds among his wheat. When his workers ask if they should remove the weeds, the master says

> Let them grow side by side until harvest time, and at harvest time I shall direct the reapers to collect the weeds first, bundle them up and burn them, but to bring the grain into my barn.

Pius XII drew the lesson that to facilitate civil peace and the common good in the face of modern pluralism:

> The duty of repressing religious and moral error cannot . . . be an ultimate norm of action. It must be subordinated to higher and more general norms which in some circumstances permit, and even perhaps make it appear the better course of action, that error should not be impeded to promote a greater good.[9]

Pius's insight is developed in the writings of Murray, particularly those gathered together as a book entitled *We Hold These Truths*. As Murray wrote, "[t]he First Amendment [to the Constitution of the United States] is simply the legal enunciation of the papal statement."[10] In Murray's view, American democracy provides precisely those "circumstances" to which the pope refers, circumstances in which there is neither a duty nor a right of the state to stamp out error. America, given its diversity of Protestant sects alone, was pluralistic in religion from the beginning, unlike European societies "decayed" into this condition from an original unity. In such circumstances, to achieve the civil peace and the common good, the only course was for the state to respect the religious beliefs of each citizen, secured by the provisions of the First Amendment that Murray famously described as "articles of peace," not "articles of faith."[11]

At Vatican II, Pius XII's teaching (and, indirectly, Murray's reflection) was developed further.[12] Instead of limiting the right to religious freedom to "certain circumstances," such as those obtaining in the United States, *Dignitatis Humanae* teaches that, in *every* circumstance, the "right of the human person to religious freedom is to be recognized in the constitutional order whereby society is governed. Thus it is to become a civil right" (*DH*, 2). In so teaching, the Council Fathers rely, *inter alia*, upon the parable of the tares (*DH*, 11). Further, they appeal, in part, to notions of the common good and a just civil peace to justify their teaching, as did Pius XII (and Murray).

The second point we would like to make is that in considering *Dignitatis Humanae* we must recall the situation then facing the Church. That situation contained both promise and contradiction.

The promise was the widespread acceptance, in both international and national law, of the principle of religious freedom.[13] Given this "happy sign of the times," the Vatican Council was not announcing the principle of religious freedom in the absence of an international consensus in its favor. The right of the individual, even to join with others in community, was widely acknowledged. Nonetheless, this acknowledgment often ignored the necessary corollary, without which these "rights" lacked coherence. In examining this ignored corollary, we must first consider what Murray, echoing Romano Guardini, called "the interior disloyalty of modern times." That requires a brief look at history.

In 494 AD, in a letter to Byzantine Emperor Anastasius I, Pope Gelasius I asserted that "two there are . . . by which this world is ruled on title of original and sovereign right—the consecrated authority of the priesthood and the royal power."[14] Thus was announced the principle that would shape the West—"the freedom of the church." The freedom of the Church meant both the freedom of the Church as a corporate body to teach, to evangelize, to organize its life, etc., *and* the freedom of the individual to receive that teaching, to conform his life to it, etc. These principles had, in turn, important sociopolitical consequences. First, the Church limited the secular power of government. Second, "the church . . . mobiliz[ed] the moral consensus of the people and br[ought it] to bear upon the [secular governmental] power, thus . . . insur[ing] that the king, in the phrase of John of Salisbury, would 'fight for justice and for the freedom of the people.'"[15]

This system of "dual" sovereignties—state *and* church—formed the basis of societal organization for centuries. However, once the balance between the two sovereigns was destroyed by the rise of national "absolute" monarchies, men found themselves trampled under the unchecked power of the monarch. In rebelling, they posited a new way to check the sovereign—free political institutions. These, not the separate corporate reality and power of the Church, would mediate between the state and society and hold the former accountable to the latter. This, in effect, reduced the original "dualism" to a "monism," "a oneness of society, law, and authority."[16] In the modern monist system, everything was staked on the proposition that the individual conscience was, and should be, the sole interpreter of the moral order. Whatever moral imperatives the free individual conscience acknowledged would then be transmitted as binding norms on the secular governmental power through free political institutions.

An early manifestation of this idea was Jacobinism, or what Murray calls "sectarian Liberalism," in France. Its "cardinal thesis" was the primacy of the political—"everything within the state; nothing above the state." Thus, the Church was "under" the state and controlled by it. It was this system—not the tenets later prescribed in *Dignitatis Humanae*—that the Church fought when it denounced "separation of church and state" and "religious liberty."

The modern idea came to a kind of logical conclusion in the Communist systems, where everything was (theoretically) subject to the "masses" under the direction of "the Party." But it continues, in a subtler form, in a certain conception of secular liberalism as well. In this conception, liberal ideology will, in the name of "tolerance" and "neutrality," exercise political hegemony; religion will be effectively "privatized"; and the Church will be rendered politically irrelevant.[17]

This attitude of rejection of the need for a moral teacher on the part of the well-taught student is what Guardini and Murray meant by "the interior disloyalty of modern times." It is also the problem that, we believe, *Dignitatis Humanae* was chiefly designed to address.

In effect, Vatican II acknowledged that modernism had recognized an important truth, which, when removed from its context, becomes a potentially treacherous half-truth. Modernism rightly emphasized the dignity of individual conscience, for the entire Christian message likewise turns on this; but the modernists were wrong to neglect the importance of sound formation of conscience to the moral life. And their error abetted the "privatization" of religion and the marginalization of the Church, whose role, as bearer of truth, is to challenge and exhort individuals and communities to just and upright living.

Modernism was correct to recognize that the political common good and public authority had centrally to do with the dignity of the individual, his reason, and free will, but it failed to recognize that freedom could not be exercised responsibly by an ill-formed or unformed conscience. A primary aim of *Dignitatis Humanae* was, then, to defend and, indeed, to restore the principle of "the freedom of the Church," as a corporate, visible body, with the right to *evangelize*, to speak to the consciences of citizens and rulers. The Declaration teaches that

> Among the things which concern . . . the welfare of society here on earth
> . . . , this certainly is preeminent, namely, that the Church should enjoy
> that full measure of freedom which her care for the salvation of men requires. . . . The freedom of the Church is the fundamental principle in

what concerns the relations between the Church and governments and the whole civil order. . . .

[W]here the principle of religious freedom . . . is given sincere and practical application, there the Church succeeds in achieving a stable situation of right as well as of fact and the independence which is necessary for the fulfillment of her divine mission. . . . Therefore, a harmony exists between the freedom of the Church and the religious freedom which is to be recognized as the right of all men and communities and sanctioned by constitutional law (*DH*, 13).

When the freedom of the Church is recognized, the monism of modernism is replaced by a new form of "dual sovereignties." Where once there was emperor and Church, now there will be "the constitutional democratic state" and the Church, with the Church, through its teaching and evangelization, mobilizing consciences to (among other things) guide and check the state. (Here one might usefully consider the highly effective public witness of religious leaders and communities, Protestant and Jewish as well as Catholic, against state-sponsored racial segregation and other forms of injustice.) Restoring the freedom of the Church replaces modernism's half-truth with full truth. It acknowledges the "corollary" to religious freedom (which modernism ignored) by restoring the balance between the individual conscience in search of truth and the wise teacher of truth.

Of course, one thing *Dignitatis Humanae* does not insist upon is that there be only one teacher, the Catholic Church. As noted above, it is clear that the teaching of Pius XII had been developed so as to permit other teachers, those with partial truths and even those who peddle untruths, to teach as well. The remaining question is whether this is wise and philosophically sound.[18]

Some persons argue for religious freedom on the basis of the controversial religious view that all religions are (equally) true or untrue, or the equally controversial religious view that religious truth is a purely subjective matter, or the pragmatic political ground that religious freedom is a necessary means of maintaining social peace in the face of religious diversity, or the political-moral view that religious liberty is part of the right of personal autonomy, or the religious-political view that "religion," if a value at all, is a value with which government lacks the jurisdiction or competence to deal. Each of these arguments inclines toward some form of public and governmental agnosticism —what might be described as political antiperfectionism—on the question of the goods that make for human flourishing.

A wise and philosophically sound defense of religious freedom—one consistent with the patrimony of Church teaching—cannot appeal implicitly to some form of religious skepticism, subjectivism, or relativism. Nor can it be inconsistent with a belief in objective religious truth or imply that religion is a purely private matter. Serious Roman Catholics would be right in rejecting any defense grounded in such questionable premises. A pluralistic perfectionist theory of religious liberty, we would argue, supplies a better foundation for that liberty than some variant of liberal antiperfectionism.

The right to religious freedom is grounded precisely in the value of religion, considered as a basic human good or fundamental aspect of human flourishing. Since religion is an intrinsic value, government need not, and should not, be indifferent to the value of religion. The nature of that value is such, however, that it simply cannot be realized or well served by coercive imposition. Any attempt by government to coerce religious faith and practice, even *true* religious faith and practice, will be futile, at best, and is likely to impair people's participation in the good of religion. While religious liberty is not absolute, government has compelling reasons to respect and protect religious freedom.

Even though people come to different conclusions about religious matters, no one can reasonably ignore the religious question of whether there is anything greater than ourselves, that is to say, an ultimate, or at least more nearly ultimate, source of meaning and value that we must take into account and with whom we can enter into friendship and communion. One's answer to the question, even if atheistic or agnostic, profoundly affects one's life. One is bound, therefore, to explore the religious question and act on the basis of one's best judgment.

Moreover, no one can search for religious truth, hold religious beliefs, or act on them authentically, for someone else. Searching, believing, and striving for religious truth are interior acts of individual human beings. As interior acts, they cannot be compelled. If they are not freely done, they are simply not done at all. Compelled prayers or religious professions, or other apparently religious acts performed under compulsion, may bear the external marks of religious faith, but they are not, in any meaningful sense, "religious." If religion is a value, the value of religion is simply not realized in such acts.

On this view, for a Roman Catholic, communion with God is like communion with other human beings in its *reflexivity*; it is not communion unless it represents a free self-giving, unless it is the fruit of a *choice* to enter into a friendship, mutuality, and reciprocity. Such a relationship simply cannot, in the nature of the thing, be established by coercion. Coercion can only damage the possibility of an authentic religious faith, a true realization of a fundamental aspect of human flourishing. Coercion deflects people from really choosing the good of religion, for it seeks to dominate their deliberations with the prospect of a quite different good—of freedom from imminent pain, loss, or other harms or of some other nonreligious advantage.

For the sake of religion considered as an intrinsic aspect of the integral good of all human beings, government may never legitimately coerce religious belief, nor may it require religious observance or practice, nor may it forbid them for religious reasons. Government, for the sake of the good of religion, should protect individuals and religious communities from others who would try to coerce them in religious matters on the basis of theological objections to their beliefs and practices.

The argument for religious liberty we have advanced here is described at times as an integral element of "new" natural law theory, particularly as that theory has been advanced by Germain Grisez, John Finnis, and Joseph Boyle.[19] As such, it postdates the explicit arguments for religious liberty found in *Dignitatis Humanae*. Yet it would be fair to say that the authors of the conciliar document make a similar case for noncoercion in religious matters.

While explicitly reaffirming its decidedly nonrelativist teaching that "the one true religion subsists in the catholic and apostolic Church, to which the Lord Jesus committed the duty of spreading it abroad among all men" (*DH*, 1), *Dignitatis Humanae* teaches that religious coercion is contrary to true religion and sound political morality even when it is exercised on behalf of the Church in which the fullness of religious truth subsists.

> It is in accordance with their dignity as persons—that is, beings endowed with reason and free will and therefore privileged to bear personal responsibility—that all men should be at once impelled by nature and also bound by a moral obligation to seek the truth, especially religious truth. They are also bound to adhere to the truth once it is known, and to order their whole lives in accord with the demands of truth.
>
> However, men cannot discharge these obligations in a manner keeping with their own nature unless they enjoy immunity from external coercion as well as psychological freedom. Therefore, the right to religious freedom has its foundation, not in the subjective disposition of the person, but in his very nature. In consequence, the right to this immunity continues to exist even in those who do not live up to their obligations of seeking the truth and adhering to it. Nor is the exercise of this right to be impeded, provided that the just requirements of public order are observed (*DH*, 2).

The Declaration teaches that the right to religious liberty is grounded precisely in the value of religion itself: coercion, even on behalf of religious truth, harms people by impeding, even as it misguidedly seeks to advance, people's genuine appropriation of religious truth and participation in the good of religion:

> For, of its very nature, the exercise of religion consists before all else in those internal, voluntary, and free acts whereby man sets the course of his life directly toward God. No merely human power can either command or prohibit acts of this kind (*DH*, 3).

Does this teaching that religious faith consists "above all else" in the "internal, voluntary, and free acts" of individual human beings imply a radically individualistic view of religion? Certainly not, for as the Declaration immediately observes:

> [T]he social nature of man itself requires that he should give external expression to his internal acts of religion: that he should participate with others in matters religious; that he should profess his religion in community. (*DH*, 3)

Only an instant later the Declaration unambiguously affirms the status of religion as a reason for (noncoercive) political action:

> The religious acts whereby men, in private and public and out of a sense of personal conviction, direct their lives to God transcend by their very nature the order of terrestrial and temporal affairs. Government, therefore, ought indeed to take account of the religious life of the people and show it favor, since the function of government is to make provision for the common welfare. (*DH*, 3)

Those who support what they describe as the "strict separation" of church and state will be troubled by the Declaration's statement that government must "show [religion] favor." The Declaration's position, however, is entirely consistent with a strict regard for religious freedom and is, in fact, preferable to "strict separationism" because it does not relegate religious belief to the realm of interior dispositions and purely private acts. The intrinsic value of religion provides a compelling reason for government not only to respect religious freedom but to encourage and support religious reflection, faith, and practice. While that norm of political morality that requires respect and protection for religious liberty limits the means whereby government may legitimately act for the sake of religion, it does not require governmental agnosticism about the good of religion as a fundamental aspect of human flourishing.

Perhaps some light can be shed on the matter by considering the issue of pornography and how its treatment compares with Vatican II's teachings about religious freedom. As with truths about religion, human beings, if they are to flourish, must understand and integrate into their lives the truth about sexuality. Pornography, however, presents an untruth about sexuality, just as false religion (precisely to the extent of its falsehood) presents untruths about God and man. Now the production and dissemination of pornography are often prohibited by society, and the Church approves of this. A central reason (though not the only one) is that such material may influence the mind of the consumer in ways destructive of the common good (perhaps leading, for example, to spousal or child abuse). However, false religious teachings can also influence the mind of a consumer in ways destructive of the common good (leading, for example, to the Jonestown massacres in Guyana), yet *Dignitatis Humanae* seems to require that such teachings be legally tolerated. Is this inconsistent?

Before we can answer that question, we must refine our analysis. Not all sexually explicit material is "pornography." Rather, so far as it is prohibited (and we are speaking here of American law), such material is prohibited only when it is "obscene," meaning it is without redeeming value and appeals to the prurient interest in sex. Otherwise, American society leaves it to individual adults to decide whether to read or view nonobscene sexually explicit material (though the consumption of this material is subject to certain restrictions).[20] In other words, our society leaves it to the conscience of the individual to decide.

This is parallel to the position in *Dignitatis Humanae* regarding abuses of religious liberty. The religious liberty it advocates is not a rogue elephant, free to wreak what destruction it will. Rather, "society has the right to defend itself against possible abuses committed on pretext of freedom of religion" (*DH*, 7). Thus, even religious freedom may be restricted where the failure to do so imperils the common good ("public order"). For instance, if neo-Aztecs were to reintroduce the practice of human sacrifice, civil authorities could prohibit it (as obscenity is prohibited) without violating the principles of *Dignitatis Humanae*. Likewise, public authority might restrict other harmful acts, even where those acts are thought by some to be religiously required and even where the restriction implied or entails that the religious proposition that gives rise to the harmful act is false.[21] This power of public authorities to regulate in order to protect public health, safety, and morals (the traditional "police power") and to promote the general welfare is consistent with the principles of the Declaration.

In sum, just as the state prohibits the distribution of some, but not all, sexually explicit material (that which is obscene), it may effectively inhibit the dissemination of some but not all false religious teaching (e.g., Aztec religion of human sacrifice). In each case, the common good is protected by the civil authorities (that which is most damaging is prohibited), but individual citizens (adults) are left free to make choices about less damaging but still false religious propositions. This is in accord with both democratic theory and the Catholic understanding of the human person.

Of course, it may be asserted that this marks a fundamental shift in Catholic thinking and teaching away from the responsibility of the state to promote all aspects of the common good. But such an objection misses the point. The state, if it is doing as *Dignitatis Humanae* requires, *is* promoting the common good; it is creating the conditions in which human flourishing is possible.

But we may ask: where the common good is not placed in jeopardy, must people be left entirely free to choose from a bewildering potpourri of religious options? The answer given by *Dignitatis Humanae* is "yes." Still, the Declaration emphasizes the obligation of society to assist its members in the responsible exercise of their freedom. Above all, society—and "especially those who are charged with the task of educating others"—must be concerned with the proper formation of consciences (*DH*, 8). Thus, if the state educates children, it must, while respecting the rights of parents, ensure that its education is at least compatible with the truth about man, including his creation by, and orientation to, God. The state may not, in the name of neutrality among religions, teach agnosticism or atheism; rather it should present a theocentric worldview to the students or, at least, refrain from teaching incompatibly with such a worldview. For this reason, it would be permissible (though not mandatory) for the Catholic Church (or another religious body) to be in charge of education within a political entity (as the Church was, until recently, in Quebec) so long as it (1) respected the religious freedom of students and their families to dissent from Catholic (or other) teachings and (2) maintained an atmosphere in which students felt free to search for God (and, should they so judge, believe and even defend atheism) as their consciences dictated. (Under the principles of *Dignitatis Humanae*, minority religious positions must be respected, and psychological coercion is prohibited [*DH*, 2 and 6].) Again this is parallel to what we demand of the state regarding education about sexuality: if state schools are to teach sex education, they must do so in ways that do not, in the guise of neutrality, present an antireligious worldview or deny fundamental truths about human sexuality. Thus, Planned Parenthood, for example, should certainly not be placed in charge of sex education in the schools.

However, the Declaration goes further—it places *demands* on *public authority*. Not only must the state protect religious freedom through legislation, it must "help to create conditions favorable to the fostering of religious life" (*DH*, 6). Here we believe is the heart of the Declaration. *Dignitatis Humanae* is, we believe, commonly misunderstood. While it clearly rejected the old assumption that the state was to coercively stamp out religious falsehood, it did not, as is sometimes believed, endorse state neutrality and individual libertarianism.

There is a third model, which is the model of *Dignitatis Humanae*. Under this model, the state, recognizing the value of religion as an intrinsic aspect of human well-being, and the importance of religion for the common good, actively works to promote religion and religious practice. It does this in part and, perhaps above all, by respecting and protecting religious freedom, including the full and generous recognition of the freedom of the Church. Moreover, it may foster and promote religion by providing for the accommodation of its free exercise.

Thus, for the sake of the good of religion, governments may (and, perhaps, ought) legitimately concern themselves with the health and well-being of various communities of faith within their jurisdiction, just as they legitimately concern themselves with the health and well-being of families and other valuable institutions of civil society. No norm of political morality requires that governments always and everywhere refrain from working with churches and religious organizations to combat social evils or solve social problems. The common good is often served by government, however, when it respectfully refrains from taking over social welfare functions that are better served by religious institutions, interdenominational and nondenominational charities, families, and other nongovernmental providers.

Several examples here might help clarify how this principle could be applied in practice. Government may, for example, provide tax deductibility for contributions to religious institutions, tax relief for religious communities, aid to religious schools, etc. It may also provide for the regular spiritual care of people in military, educational, and other public institutions (in accordance, to the greatest extent practicable, with people's own religious beliefs and commitments). It could even prepare "public service announcements" encouraging citizens to attend the church or synagogue of their choice.

May the state proclaim a day of "Sabbath rest"? Yes, though the state in certain religiously pluralistic societies would not have available to it the luxury of selecting a day that is the common Sabbath of all faiths. Of course, under *Dignitatis Humanae*, the state must avoid acting "in arbitrary fashion or in an unfair spirit of partisanship" (*DH*, 7). However, since the state is to promote religious practice, it would not be "unfair" if it chose the Sabbath day of the majority religion, particularly if it also provided legal recognition and protection of the right of other believers to observe their own Sabbath (and, perhaps, to work on the officially recognized Sabbath day as well).

It should be remembered that the norm of political morality enjoining government to "show favor" in political ways to the spiritual lives of the people is not especially stringent. Prudential considerations (for example, a concern that governmental intervention might compromise the integrity of the religious institutions that government wishes to assist) will often militate against particular proposals for governmental support for religion.

The norm of political morality endorsed by the Declaration requiring governmental respect and protection of the right to religious liberty is much more stringent. Government should permit religious practice unless there is a compelling reason not to permit it; it should never attempt to coerce religious belief and practice, and in most circumstances, it should discourage and even prevent purely private religious coercion.

In short, we believe the philosophical underpinnings of *Dignitatis Humanae* are sound. It advocates an approach to religion quite similar to that which hard-earned experience has taught us to take with respect to other important aspects of human life, such as sexuality. It does not naively exalt human freedom but respects it, placing freedom in the service of truth. Further, it requires the state to take an active role in promoting the good of religion, thereby avoiding that "neutrality" that is such in name only.

In defending principles such as religious freedom, political equality, constitutional democracy, the rule of law, and limited government, Vatican II might be said to be adopting an "old-fashioned" liberal approach to the nature of man and society. This "old-fashioned" liberalism—the liberalism of the American founding and of the Constitution of the United States—stands in marked contrast to much of "contemporary" liberalism and its purported agnosticism toward the goods that make for human flourishing.

But even today certain Catholic conservatives remain suspicious of the type of "old-fashioned" liberalism represented by Vatican II's Declaration on Religious Liberty and of "rights talk" in general.[22] They tend to understand the idea of religious freedom only as it was manifested in French Revolutionary ideology and Continental Liberalism, with their anticlericalism, demands for liberation from traditional moral constraints, and belief in the subordination of the Church to the state. These "old-fashioned" conservative Catholics argue that *Dignitatis Humanae* contradicts authoritative, and even unchangeable, teachings of nineteenth-century popes. They deny that that the new teaching commands the religious assent of faithful Catholics.

Pope John Paul II, who as a young bishop was instrumental in shaping and winning approval for that document, was no friend of these "old-fashioned" conservatives. He consistently, and even emphatically, reaffirmed the Council's teaching. If there was ever a doubt about its authoritative status and the obligation of Catholics to give it their wholehearted assent, his pontificate erased that doubt. On the question of religious freedom, to be a good Catholic one must be a kind of "old-fashioned" liberal. To deny the moral right to freedom from coercion in religious matters is to place oneself in opposition to an important principle of Catholic faith.

The principles of *Dignitatis Humanae*—that document's "old-fashioned" liberalism, as it were—recognize the validity of the modern insight concerning the importance of individual freedom in matters of religion.[23] Internal assent cannot be compelled, and external religious acts without internal assent are worthless. Man must *freely* search for the truth, and he can hardly search for it if he cannot advocate what he judges to be true, even if his conscientious judgment is imperfect or erroneous. Vatican II insists, however, on respect for the freedom of the Church to confront man with that truth.

In the end, it is the judgment of Vatican II and, thus, of the Catholic Church that everything turns on the individual's judgment and decision, on a conscience free to seek God.[24] That is also the truth taught by our Master while he was on earth.[25] This truth need not bring discouragement about the future of the Church. It may, in fact, be the mustard seed of a new era of evangelization. In a valuable book, *The Rise of Christianity*, the eminent sociologist of religion, Rodney Stark, tells us that Christianity did not triumph in the Roman Empire because it was *established* by Constantine. Rather, it had grown so widespread by the time Constantine came to power that it was prudent for him to embrace it. The curious thing is the mechanism by which it became widespread. It was not, as is commonly thought, by way of forced mass conversion.[26] Rather, the sociological evidence shows that Christianity won the Roman Empire through the conversion of individual consciences, one person at a time. Many people came to Christian faith because of the good example of the faithful Christians whose conduct they observed. In endorsing precisely this approach to evangelization, *Dignitatis Humanae* prepares the way for the Church, once again, to win a "pagan empire" to Christ, one conscience at a time.

NOTES

1. Robert P. George is McCormick Professor of Jurisprudence and Director of the James Madison Program in American Ideals and Institutions at Princeton University.

2. William L. Saunders, Jr., is Senior Fellow and Human Rights Counsel at the Family Research Council in Washington, DC. He is a member of the board of the Fellowship of Catholic Scholars.

3. Syllabus, no. 7.

4. "On his part, man perceives and acknowledges the imperatives of the divine law through the mediation of conscience. In all his activity a man is bound to follow his conscience faithfully, in order that he may come to God, for whom he was created. It follows that he is not be forced to act in a manner contrary to his conscience" (*DH*, 3).

5. Against the objection of Archbishop Marcel Lefebvre and others that, in *Dignitatis Humanae*, Vatican II abandoned traditional Catholic teaching on this point, Murray had the following to say:

> It is worth noting that the Declaration does not base the right to the free exercise of religion on "freedom of conscience." Nowhere does this phrase occur. And the Declaration nowhere lends its authority to the theory for which the phrase frequently stands, namely,

that I have the right to do what my conscience tells me to do, simply because my conscience tells me to do it. This is perilous theory. Its particular peril is subjectivism—the notion that, in the end, it is my conscience, not the objective truth, which determines what is right or wrong, true or false.

The Documents of Vatican II, ed. Walter M. Abbott, S.J. (New York: America Press, 1966), note 5 at p. 679.

6. The Declaration teaches both that

(1) "All men are bound to seek the truth, especially in what concerns God and His Church, and to embrace the truth they come to know, and to hold fast to it" (*DH*, 1); and

(2) "[I]n the formation of their consciences, the Christian faithful ought carefully to attend to the sacred and certain doctrine of the Church. The Church is, by the will of Christ, the teacher of the truth" (*DH*, 14).

7. "[E]very man has the duty, and therefore the right, to seek the truth in matters religious, in order that he may with prudence form for himself right and true judgments of conscience, with the use of all suitable means.

"Truth, however, is to be sought after in a manner proper to the dignity of the human person and his social nature. The inquiry is to be free, carried on with the aid of teaching or instruction, communication, and dialogue" (*DH*, 3).

8. See *We Hold These Truths: Catholic Reflections on the American Proposition* (Sheed and Ward, 1960) (hereinafter, *We Hold These Truths*), 61–63.

9. Ibid., 62.

10. Ibid. Murray noted that Roger Williams, the man usually considered the leading champion of religious freedom in American history, learned the same lesson from the parable as did Pius XII.

11. "[I]n regarding the religion clauses . . . as articles of peace and in placing the case for them on the primary grounds of their social necessity, one is not taking low ground. . . . In the science of law and the art of jurisprudence the appeal to social peace is an appeal to high moral value. . . . This is the classic and Christian tradition." *We Hold These Truths*, 60. For a critique of Murray's position, see Gerard V. Bradley, "Beyond Murray's Articles of Peace and Faith," in *John Courtney Murray and the American Civil Conversation*, ed. Robert P. Hunt and Kenneth L. Grasso (Grand Rapids, MI: William B. Eerdmans Publishing Co., 1992), 181–204.

12. As John Paul II said in *Tertio Millennio Adveniente*:

"The Second Vatican Council . . . drew much from the experiences and reflections of the immediate past, especially the intellectual legacy left by Pius XII" (no. 18). The teaching of Pius XII is cited, for example, as support for the key proposition that "in forming their consciences the faithful must pay careful attention to the sacred and certain teaching of the Church" (*DH*, 14).

13. "Indeed it is a fact that religious freedom has already been declared a civil right in most constitutions and has been given solemn recognition in international documents" (*DH*, 15). For instance, the Universal Declaration of Human Rights adopted by the United Nations General Assembly on December 10, 1948, declared:

Everyone has the right to freedom of thought, conscience and religion; this right includes freedom to change his religion or belief, and freedom, either alone or in community with others and in public and private, to manifest his religion or belief in teaching, practice, worship and observance [Article 18].

14. For Murray's discussion of "the freedom of the church," see *We Hold These Truths*, chapter 9.

15. *We Hold These Truths*, 205.

16. Ibid., 208.

17. See Gerard V. Bradley, *Dogmatomachy—the "Privatization" Theory of the Religion Clause Cases*, 30 ST. LOUIS U LAW J 275–330 (1986).

18. Much of what is found in the next several paragraphs is taken from Robert P. George, *Making Men Moral: Civil Liberties and Public Morality* (New York: Oxford University Press, 1993), 219–26.

19. See, for example, Joseph M. Boyle, Jr., Germain Grisez, and Olaf Tollafsen, *Free Choice: A Self-Referential Argument* (Notre Dame, IN: University of Notre Dame Press, 1976); John Finnis, *Natural Law and Natural Rights* (Oxford: Clarendon Press, 1980); Germain Grisez, "A Contemporary Natural-Law Ethics," in *Moral Philosophy: Historical and Contemporary Essays*, ed. William C. Starr and Richard C. Taylor (Milwaukee: Marquette University Press, 1989), 125–43.

20. See Robert P. George, *Making Children Moral: Pornography, Parents, and the Public Interest*, 29 ARIZONA STATE LAW JOURNAL 569–80 (1997). Our personal view is that American constitutional law sweeps too widely in protecting much sexually explicit material that is truly pornographic (though not legally obscene) and damaging to the consumer and to society, e.g., such material could, and, we think, should, justly be prohibited or severely restricted for the sake of public morality.

21. For instance, if a particular brand of false religion encouraged children to commit suicide as a "quick ticket" to heaven, its advocacy in media available to children could legitimately be restricted in certain ways. Other brands of religion, however, which do not suffer such extensive and fundamental defects but still fall short of full truth may not be legitimately subject to such restrictions. As John Paul II reminded us, the Catholic Church recognizes "seeds of truth" in non-Christian religions, and "the Catholic Church does not reject anything in these religions that is holy and true." *The National Catholic Register*, September 20, 1998, quoting from his weekly audience on September 9.

22. For further elaboration of this distinction between old-fashioned conservative Catholics and old-fashioned liberal Catholics, see Robert P. George and William L. Saunders, Jr., "Religious Values and Politics," chapter 12 of *The Clash of Orthodoxies: Law, Religion, and Morality in Crisis* (Wilmington, DE: ISI Books, 2001), 231–58.

23. As John Paul II said during his greeting in the Cathedral in Baltimore on October 8, 1995:

> Religious tolerance is based on the conviction that God wishes to be adored by people who are free: a conviction which requires us to respect and honor the inner sanctuary of conscience in which each person meets God.

24. "It is one of the major tenets of Catholic doctrine that man's response to God in faith must be free. Therefore no one is to be forced to embrace the Christian faith

against his own will. This doctrine is contained in the word of God and it was constantly proclaimed by the Fathers of the Church. The act of faith is of its very nature a free act" (*DH*, 10).

25. "He bore witness to the truth, but He refused to use force to impose the truth by force on those who spoke against it" (*DH*, 11).

26. The forced mass conversion under a ruler who officially embraced Christianity for his people became the practice after Constantine in many parts of Europe. Starks believes this was bad for the faith:

> You look at the spread of Christianity beyond the empire, and you see that it was almost entirely by treaty and by baptizing kings. I think one reason medieval church attendance was so bad in Scandinavia and Germany was because these people weren't really Christians. If it hadn't been for establishment, they might have been.

Interviewed in *Our Sunday Visitor*, April 19, 1998, 10–11.

Two Concepts of Religious Liberty: *Dignitatis Humanae v.* the U.S. Supreme Court

Robert P. Hunt

Ideas do matter. Especially in law, ideas are of dominant import. As Johnson told Boswell, law is a cultural study. It is as wide as human life and always rests on a philosophy of life. Therefore I think it useful, especially at this time, to recall an enduring idea of the basis of law and the intellectual defense of human rights— an idea that has come to us from our immemorial past, but in our day has been questioned and denied to the peril of what we are and of all we possess.[1]

—Edward S. Dore
Former Associate Justice
New York Supreme Court

I

One of the most influential lectures of the past fifty years, as George Weigel has noted recently, is Isaiah Berlin's "Two Concepts of Liberty," in which Berlin compellingly laid out what might be described as an intellectual foundation for the liberal anti-Communist consensus of the post–World War II period. Searching for a means whereby Western democracies might avoid the dangers of monistic totalitarianisms of the Right and Left and thereby secure the blessings of constitutionally limited government and a "robust pluralism," Berlin distinguished between negative liberty and positive liberty.[2]

Berlin's concept of negative liberty, according to Weigel, was freedom *from* the coercive power of the state, and it implied the legal (but not necessarily moral) right of persons to live their lives largely as they saw fit, provided they did not interfere with other persons' liberty. Positive liberty, on the other hand, was defined by Berlin as a freedom *to*: a freedom to pursue some greater good that is itself acknowledged to be a *good* by the state. Under the dispensation of a juridical order committed to negative liberty, the blessings of constitutionally limited government can be secured in a world of "inevitably conflicting interests, diverse concepts of the good, and competing projects." By contrast, when the state affirms a more positive concept of liberty and becomes determined "to use political power to liberate human beings, whether they [like] it or not, for the realization of some higher historical end," the most likely result, according to Berlin, will be the loss of political freedom. Totalitarian regimes of the Right and of the Left do not necessarily reject the idea of freedom. Rather, they trade upon a positive notion of freedom that corrodes the very possibility of constitutionally limited government.[3]

Berlin's form of (liberal) consensus building might be described as a mid-twentieth-century variant of antiperfectionist political/ juridical theory. Berlin does not go so far as to claim overtly that competing conceptions of the good are provably equally valid *at the moral level*. To make such a claim would, for Berlin, require that the state explicitly *affirm* the good of moral subjectivism and thereby, paradoxically, place the state in the service of a (subjectivist) concept of positive liberty. Rather, the success of Berlin's dichotomy depends upon a conscious effort on the part of the legal/juridical order to prescind from any question of what constitutes the good for human beings.

For Berlin, a type of official state agnosticism regarding the nature of the good provides the context within which varying conceptions of the good can be more effectively realized. One might describe Berlin's theoretical efforts by using intellectual categories once employed by the Reverend John Courtney Murray, S.J., in a slightly different context: Berlin seeks to defend juridical articles of peace for religiously and morally divided societies. Politico/juridical articles of peace grounded in the concept of negative liberty supply a better foundation for limited constitutional government than do the metaethical and comprehensive conceptions of the good (and positive liberty) that lie at the twisted heart of the totalitarian regimes of the twentieth century.

Weigel acknowledges the virtues of Berlin's efforts to construct an intellectual foundation for this liberal anti-Communist consensus. "[H]is insistence that politics is not therapy, his resolute refusal to deny the reality of conflicts among social goods, and his insistence that utopian politics inevitably become coercive politics (and, in the modern world, extraordinarily brutal coercive politics) were all important ideas to defend, in Europe and America, against the coercive utopians of the twentieth century."[4]

Berlin's defense of "negative liberty"—and, more comprehensively, his effort to disengage the language of law and rights from architectonic conceptions of the good—trades, however, upon a more comprehensive notion of the foundation of freedom that is by no means neutral on the question of what constitutes the good for man. John Hallowell once remarked that "underlying every system of government there is some predominant conception of the nature of man and the meaning of human existence. More often than not, this idea of man is implicit rather than explicit. But if not always explicit, it is always fundamental."[5] Former Justice Edward Dore of the New York Supreme Court applied the same argument in matters juridical when he claimed that "law is a cultural study. It is as wide as human life and always rests on a philosophy of life."[6]

Try as he might, Berlin cannot avoid placing his argument for freedom *from* the power of the state within a larger philosophy of life and the meaning of human existence. Moreover, the very invocation of the categories of negative and positive liberty *and how he defines their respective contours* are themselves a product of a mind shaped and influenced by the nominalism and voluntarism of the Enlightenment.

As Weigel notes, Berlin himself conceded that "conceptions of freedom directly derive from what constitutes a self, a person, a man."[7] And, according to Weigel, Berlin's conception of freedom is Ockhamite in both substance and form:

> When Berlin writes that "I am normally said to be free to the degree to which no man or body of men interferes with my activity," such that "political liberty is simply the area within which a man can act unobstructed by others," he is taking an Ockhamite tack from the outset. Berlin openly admits that his "positive liberty" begins in "an act of will." In fact, however, his formulation of "negative liberty" also assumes that freedom is essentially a matter of the will. "Negative liberty" is simply that which allows me to avoid too many collisions with the wills of others.[8]

For Berlin, when the state sets itself up as the arbiter of what constitutes the good and *promotes* that conception of the good through the exercise of coercive power, it is doing little more than imposing its will on the will of the individuals who comprise the state. When the state refrains from making such judgments and sets a framework of law in which individuals pursue their own ends (consistent with a respect for the chosen ends of others), it is deferring to the will of those individuals. Citing Servais Pinckaers's magisterial *The Sources of Christian Ethics*, Weigel describes Berlin's account of both positive and negative liberty as grounded in a notion of *freedom of indifference*. Under this dispensation, "freedom is simply a neutral faculty of choice and choice is everything, for choice is a matter of self-assertion, of power."[9] The *terminus ad quem* of Berlin's voluntarist conception of liberty (both positive and negative), once it has evacuated from within itself any notion of the Divine Will, is "autonomous man," who has the right to attach his will to any object.[10]

Weigel draws a sharp contrast between the notion of the freedom of indifference (upon which Berlin's intellectual dichotomy between positive and negative liberty draws) and Pinckaers's notion of freedom for excellence, which consists of "the capacity to choose wisely and to act well as a matter of habit . . . Freedom is the means by which, exercising our reason and our will, we act on the natural longing for truth, for goodness and for happiness that is built into us as human beings."[11] Berlin's voluntarist notion of freedom cannot tell us much about how we ought to resolve the conflicts of wills among members of society other than by resorting to sheer coercion. Moreover, "Berlin's 'negative liberty' cannot provide an account of why that freedom has any moral worth beyond its being an expression of my will."[12] By replacing freedom for excellence with the freedom of indifference, Berlin has unintentionally undermined his own efforts to provide a coherent account of the foundations of liberal constitutional democracy.

Berlin makes a conscious effort to suppress his own conception of the good in the name of a larger, seemingly neutral juridical framework of laws. His argument for such a framework depends, however, upon a nominalist, voluntarist, and, ultimately, subjectivist, anthropology that, whether Berlin likes it or not, will, if accepted by most members of society, have a profound effect on the way in which they conceive of the manner in which freedom should (or should not) be exercised. Berlin openly acknowledges that "political theory is a branch of moral philosophy," and his own political theory in no way brackets, or prescinds from, his own skepticism about the ultimate incommensurability of individual and social goods. Michael Sandel has noted that Berlin's argument

> . . . comes perilously close to foundering on the relativist predicament. If one's convictions are only relatively valid, why stand for them unflinchingly? In a tragically configured moral universe, such as Berlin assumes, is the ideal of freedom any *less* subject than competing ideals to the ultimate incommensurability of values? If so, in what can its privileged status consist? And if freedom has no morally privileged status, if it is but one value among many, then what can be said about liberalism?[13]

One might well draw from Weigel's and Sandel's criticism of Berlin two important conclusions, both of which impact significantly on the effort to develop a theory of freedom (and, most important, of religious freedom) that meets the needs of a true *ordo iuris*. First, a purely negative conception of liberty is an impossibility. Once one has argued that persons must have freedom *from* the state, one must perforce explain *why* it is important, or right, or good for them to be free. One might invoke the idea of the autonomous self (a la David Richards), or the notion of "equal concern and respect" (a la Ronald Dworkin and other supporters of political Rawlsianism), or one might claim more modestly (a la Berlin) that the practical fact of incommensurable values requires such freedom. Or one might, to play it safe, formulate a hodgepodge of these three (and other) justifications at the same time. But the mere fact that one feels compelled to answer the question *why* tells us that even the most adamant opponent of teleological conceptions of human nature has his own (disguised) *telos*.[14] *Freedom from* necessarily becomes *freedom to*, even if that freedom entails little more than adherence to Polonius's maxim: "To thine own self be true." And the advocate of this freedom of indifference is often quite willing to employ the power of the state to impress this notion of freedom on others.

Second, since every theory of political and juridical freedom must be grounded, as Hallowell argued, in some conception of human nature and the goods attendant to that conception, the true test of the validity of that theory cannot be whether it conforms more closely to Berlin's concept of negative liberty. All theories of religious and political liberty—even those that claim to be merely negative by reining in the power of the state, or those that pretend to be supportive of "articles of peace" for morally fractured societies—cannot fully suppress their underlying philosophical commitments. They must be judged, therefore, on the basis of whether the society entailed by these commitments (and the regimen of law based on those commitments) makes possible the goods of human flourishing.

Since "a purely procedural republic is logically impossible," as Ralph McInerny has noted,[15] the fundamental choice confronting the citizens of a constitutional democracy is not between political orthodoxy on the one hand and some purported alternative to orthodoxy (which pretends to be advancing a purely *negative* conception of liberty) on the other. The choice is between at least two rival philosophical anthropologies of freedom, between Pinckaers's (and Thomas Aquinas's) freedom for excellence, "an anthropology that," according to Weigel, "contains thick moral convictions about the inalienable dignity and value of every human life" and of the positive role that religious liberty plays in promoting the true goods of human flourishing, and Ockham's freedom of indifference, an anthropology that inclines toward a defense of the sovereign self of contemporary liberalism.[16]

These two anthropological conceptions of liberty (and not Berlin's distinction between positive and negative liberty) can be brought to bear on the effort to clarify the development of Roman Catholic social teaching on the subject of religious freedom inspired by *Dignitatis Humanae*. They demonstrate how that teaching differs from the predominant model of church-state relations inspired particularly by the U.S. Supreme Court's religion clause jurisprudence since the mid-1940s.[17]

II

One of the central questions confronting scholars who work from within the Catholic intellectual tradition is the relationship between Catholicism and liberalism. For those persons who, like the late Reverend John Courtney Murray, S.J., describe the "liberal tradition of politics" as a tradition committed to "constitutionalism, the rule of law, the notion of sovereignty as purely political and therefore limited by law, [and] the concept of government as an empire of laws and not of men," the relationship is not a particularly problematic one.[18]

When the word "liberal" is used in a narrower sense—to designate a particular and highly individualistic model of man and society (even modeled perhaps on the distinctions made by Isaiah Berlin)—the relationship becomes more problematic, especially given the Roman Catholic emphasis on man's intrinsically social nature.

There are many scholars who argue, however, that the developments in Roman Catholic social teaching inspired by the Second Vatican Council make rapprochement between Catholicism and liberal individualism possible. Since the Second Vatican Council, so the argument goes, Roman Catholics have come fully to embrace human rights and religious freedom, not merely as prudential accommodations to the empirical fact of religious diversity but as exigencies of the moral order that reflect an ever-deepening Catholic commitment to personal dignity. In fact, because Catholics have largely abandoned the thesis/hypothesis distinctions of an older "confessionalist" perspective, rapprochement with the liberal tradition of politics becomes more than the establishing of a modus vivendi between two somewhat incompatible worldviews. It becomes a sine qua non of a principled Catholic commitment to constitutional government, a dynamic "working out" of the principles embedded—but for so long latent—within the Catholic tradition itself.

These integrationist assumptions are overly sanguine about possible overlap between the Catholic and liberal traditions. Even in the area of "religious freedom," where there seems at first glance to be principled agreement regarding the need to rein in the coercive power of the state—to secure what Berlin describes as "negative liberty"—the underlying philosophical anthropologies that direct each tradition toward a defense of "religious freedom" virtually guarantee that each tradition will conceive of this freedom in a manner vastly different from the other. And what follows, therefore, are differing *reasons* why state power must be curtailed in matters "religious" and, ultimately, differing arguments regarding the role of the state in promoting what *Dignitatis*᷅Humanae᷅describes as "the just requirements of public order."[19] In short, any effort to effect a "deep" rapprochement between *Dignitatis Humanae*'s notion of "freedom for excellence" and the liberal notion of "freedom of indifference" (as embodied most notably in the U.S. Supreme Court's religion clause jurisprudence) is both morally and politically problematic.

III

The most memorable words of *Everson v. Board of Education of Ewing Township, New Jersey* (1947) are not those in which a bare majority of five justices *upheld* the constitutionality of a New Jersey program of reimbursing the parents of parochial (primarily Catholic) schoolchildren for the cost of bus transportation to and from school. The most memorable, and constitutionally significant, words are those in which Justice Hugo Black (with none of his confreres writing to the contrary) lays out what he believes to be the foundational principles upon which the First Amendment's nonestablishment component rests: "Neither a state nor the Federal Government can set up a church. Neither can pass laws which aid one religion, aid all religions, or prefer one religion over another. . . . In the words of Jefferson, the clause against establishment of religion by law was intended to erect 'a wall of separation between church and state.'"[20]

The four dissenting justices in *Everson* take issue not with Black's invocation of Jefferson's metaphor but rather with Black's inability to apply what they believe to be the juridical principles embodied within the metaphor to the case at hand, as Justice Robert Jackson rather sardonically points out, quoting Lord Byron's Julia, who "whispering 'I will ne'er consent,' consented."[21] Dissenting Justice Wiley Rutledge argues for a more consistent application of the separationist principle, arguing that the purpose of the First Amendment's nonestablishment component "was to create a complete and permanent separation of the spheres of religious activity and civil authority by comprehensively forbidding every form of public aid and support for religion."[22]

Rutledge and the other dissenters attempt to make short shrift of Black's claim that the statute at hand is a facially neutral statute that neither advances nor hinders religion. Reading the nonestablishment component as the virtual equivalent of the proposed (but unratified) nineteenth-century Blaine Amendment, Rutledge would foreclose any form of direct or indirect aid to religion in general on the part of federal and state levels of government. To employ terminology later used by Berlin, the type of *freedom from* governmental coercion embodied in the First Amendment's religion clauses requires that government not act in such a manner as to "support religion." (How one goes about squaring this argument with the protection of the "free exercise" of religion will be touched on momentarily.)

Justice Black's argument *in support of the law* is significant because it sets the parameters within which the Court will be forced to operate at the level of juridical principle in future religion-clause cases, *even when it chooses to uphold the constitutionality of some ostensible general welfare statute*. The First Amendment, Black argues, "requires the state to be neutral in its relations with groups of religious believers and non-believers, it does not require the state to be their adversary. State power is no more to be used to handicap religions, than it is to favor them."[23]

There is much in Justice Black's practical effort to resolve the case that would not, at first glance, contradict what *Dignitatis Humanae* argues almost two decades later about the proper juridical foundation for religious freedom, particularly as the conciliar document is interpreted by John Courtney Murray. First and foremost, Black attempts to set limits to the constitutional powers of federal and—more controversial for those who refuse to accept incorporationist arguments—state authority. Moreover, he attempts to do so in a way that seems to reflect Murray's later comment that the juridical principle at the heart of *Dignitatis Humanae* pronounces no "moral or theological judgments of value on the activity [of religious freedom] itself."[24] Second, in affirming constitutional limits on the powers of government in religious matters, Black maintains that such limits should in no way be construed as displaying hostility to religion. Finally, and assuming for present purposes that Black's argument for incorporating the nonestablishment component of the First Amendment through the due process clause of the Fourteenth Amendment is correct, state public welfare statutes that incidentally treat religionists as eligible for the same benefits as the general population can in no way be said to violate the nonestablishment prohibition.

Why then did Murray, who took an active part in supporting the statute, soberly claim after the Court's *Everson* decision that "we have won on busing, but lost on the First Amendment?"[25]

Most anti-*Everson* constitutional and/or legal scholars contend that Black's rationale (and, more obviously, the dissenters' conclusions *and* rationales) centers, mistakenly, around the use of Jefferson's "wall of separation" metaphor and a selective reliance upon the Virginia debates on religious freedom in the mid-1780s in general and James Madison's *Memorial and Remonstrance* in particular. These scholars would agree that the debates conducted in the First Congress over the scope and nature of the religion clauses are more determinative of the framers' intent than was Madison's more grandiose and controversial argument several years earlier, in a decidedly different political context.

Philip Hamburger's recent study of the historical development of the term "separation of church and state" points to an even larger problem with Black's rationale than its historical inaccuracy. Hamburger contends that the "wall of separation" metaphor, and the uses to which it has been put, is particularly unfortunate not merely because it does injury to what the Framers believed about the manner in which the First Amendment secured *freedom from* government in matters religious but, ultimately, because it undermines the effort to secure *freedom for* religious believers.[26]

Black's effort to develop a juridical principle that limits the powers of government in matters religious breaks out from within its supposedly juridical limits, and it cannot help but do so precisely because it depends upon a larger (and by no means neutral or negative) view of the role of religion in public life. Black's (and the dissenters') "separationism," to the extent upon which it relies upon Jefferson's and Madison's views on the proper role for religion within a liberal society, is rooted in what Stephen Monsma has accurately described as an "Enlightenment worldview that is itself anything but neutral and universal. If the great world religions such as Catholicism and Judaism are 'sectarian'—as the Supreme Court's opinions have often referred to them—the worldview in which Everson is rooted is no less sectarian. As John Courtney Murray wrote two years after the decision, it was rooted in an 'irredeemable piece of sectarian dogmatism.'" Monsma goes on to explain that "in an effort to prove that 'no establishment of religion' means 'no aid to religion' the Supreme Court proceeds to establish a religion—James Madison's."[27]

Black is not forced to reach the conclusion that "non-establishment" of religion means "no aid" to religion because some putative preoccupation with the placement of limits on the powers of government requires him to do so. Arguing for *limits* on the power of government in matters of religion in no way requires that government *do nothing* to benefit religion generally. Nor is Black forced to do so because he is maintaining fidelity to some (impossible) Archimedian standard of "negative liberty"—read as a constitutional *freedom from* religious establishments—that makes no judgments of value about the good of religion.

Black is forced to reach the conclusion about the meaning of nonestablishment precisely because his effort to define the contours of this negative liberty (or *freedom from* religious establishments) depends on a notion of freedom that is itself a child of the Enlightenment. Black is forced by virtue of this larger anthropological notion of freedom to define the "general welfare" in such a way as to exclude, in principle, any governmental support for religion whatsoever. In short, Black's reading of "non-establishment" as legal shorthand for Jefferson's or Madison's larger philosophical agenda turns the religion clauses into precisely what John Courtney Murray believes the clauses were intended to avoid. They are hardened into a secularist "article of faith."

Monsma chastises the Court for this "wrong road taken," and the implication one might draw from his rejection of the reading of Enlightenment dogma into the First Amendment is that Monsma would prefer an interpretation of the amendment that adheres more closely to Murray's "articles of peace" reading. In other words, by reading the religion clauses in a more purely juridical manner (and not filling them with the baggage of a dogma that would have the practical effect of privatizing all matters of religious belief and practice), states would retain a greater flexibility to assist both religionists and nonreligionists in matters of education, for example, in a truly even-handed manner. The right juridical road would comport with a pluralistic, religion-friendly social and cultural environment. For Monsma, a chastened and "neutralized" *Everson* shorn of its radical separationist underpinnings might lay a proper juridical foundation for American church-state relations.

Clearly, the "no aid to religion" thrust of Black's (and the dissenters') opinion has the practical effect of undermining *Dignitatis Humanae*'s later claims "that the right of all citizens and religious bodies to religious freedom should be recognized and made effective in practice" and that one way in which the state can make such religious freedom effective in practice is to "show religion favor" as an aspect of its concern for the common welfare.[28] An article of Enlightenment dogma that would wall off matters of state from "sectarian" influences is manifestly inconsistent with the right of religious bodies to make their faith "effective in practice," unless the religious bodies themselves accept as true the same piece of Enlightenment dogma and seek to keep private all matters of belief and practice.

The question, however, is whether the solution to the problem of a juridical orthodoxy that eschews support for religion in general is a supposed juridical alternative to orthodoxy that claims to be "neutral" between religion and nonreligion and is thereby purportedly more open to plural forms of religiosity in the public square.

Monsma's effort to embrace juridical neutrality while rejecting "no aid" separationism is reflected in the plurality opinion of Justice Clarence Thomas in *Mitchell v. Helms* (2000), an opinion that clearly displays a greater openness to general welfare statutes that treat religionists and nonreligionists in a more even-handed manner. In *Mitchell*, the Court upheld, against an establishment clause challenge, the constitutionality of the Education Consolidation and Improvement Act of 1981 and the ability of state and local agencies of government, with the support of federal funds, to lend educational equipment and materials (including library and media materials and computer software) to public and private (including religious) elementary and secondary schools. Justice Thomas attempts to prove that, if a state's purpose is secular (i.e., has neither the purpose of advancing nor inhibiting religion), the lending of such materials meets constitutional muster even if those materials could later be diverted to advance the religious mission of some of the schools in question. Says Thomas:

> In distinguishing between indoctrination that is attributable to the State and indoctrination that is not, we have consistently turned to the principle of neutrality, upholding aid that is offered to a broad range of groups or persons without regard to their religion. If the religious, irreligious, and areligious are all alike eligible for governmental aid, no one would conclude that any indoctrination that any recipient conducts has been done at the behest of the government.[29]

For Thomas and a Court plurality, juridical neutrality between religion and irreligion—Black's phrase—should not be construed as hostility toward religious institutions, and the "secular purpose" test should not be construed as constitutional shorthand for liberal political morality. Thomas thus advances what purports to be a juridical alternative to separationist orthodoxy, an alternative that is "neutral" between the claims of religionists and nonreligionists.

One could argue—and I certainly would so argue—that Thomas's reading of the nonestablishment component of the religion clause is less dependent on secularist foundational principles than is Black's separationist rhetoric in *Everson*, but it is most certainly not more juridically neutral. In fact, the irony of the three major judicial opinions in *Mitchell v. Helms*—Thomas's for a Court plurality, Justice Sandra Day O'Connor's in concurrence, and Justice David Souter's in dissent—is that they engage in a rather comical interchange over whose reading of what does and does not constitute an establishment of religion is more neutral in matters religious. O'Connor, for example, does not "quarrel with the plurality's recognition that neutrality is an important reason for upholding government-aid programs against Establishment Clause challenges" but wonders whether such a need for neutrality would have been met if funds had been truly diverted for religious purposes, even indirectly.[30] Souter contends that in "endorsing the principle of no aid to a school's religious mission . . . government can in fact operate with neutrality in its relation to religion."[31]

Just as Isaiah Berlin's defense of "negative liberty" (i.e., *freedom from* governmental coercion) must explain *why* it is important that individuals be accorded liberty and can do so only in light of a larger and by no means neutral conception of human personhood, so Thomas's, O'Connor's, and Souter's defenses of "juridical neutrality" in matters religious must ultimately depend upon a larger and by no means neutral conception of the role of religion in public life and *why* the U.S. Constitution places limits on the powers of government in advancing that role. Their arguments must be judged, therefore, not on the basis of whose juridical theory is more "neutral"—a chimerical goal, to say the least—but on whose juridical theory is grounded in a fuller and more coherent account of the purposes for which religious freedom exists. A richer and more adequate conception of the relationship between human personhood and religious freedom will provide us with a better sense of *why freedom from* governmental coercion in matters religious ought to be secured and also *at what point* government can intervene legitimately to maintain "the just requirements of public order." Absent this conception of purpose as both limit on and (under certain circumstances) justification for governmental intervention, the comical effort to judge whose juridical orthodoxy is less of an orthodoxy, and therefore more neutral, will continue.

The larger problem with what might be described as "no-aid separationism" is not that it fails to be "neutral"—Thomas's defense of facially neutral general welfare statutes is no more neutral than Souter's opposition to them—but that it must ultimately affirm a conception of human freedom that drives a stake through the heart of religious freedom, especially as that freedom is understood by the authors of *Dignitatis Humanae*. If the Vatican Document on Religious Freedom represents a defense of *freedom for excellence*, the predominant strain of the U.S. Supreme Court's First Amendment jurisprudence represents a defense of *freedom of indifference*.

A brief analysis of the trajectory of American church-state relations since *Everson* bears witness to the onset of this *freedom of indifference*, even among jurists who would undoubtedly abjure the title of moral philosopher. For example, Hugo Black's own idiosyncratic constitutional literalism and desire to avoid becoming a self-ordained moral philosopher/jurist probably assisted him in avoiding the logic of his own position: a desire to privatize *all* fractious religious and moral issues. Yet, when Black was forced to explain, for example, why the optional daily recitation of prayer in public elementary schools is unconstitutional, he advanced a view of religion itself that would constitutionally privilege a liberal Protestant brand of religiosity: "the Establishment Clause . . . stands as an expression of principle on the part of the Founders of our Constitution that religion is too personal, too sacred, too holy, to permit its 'unhallowed perversion' by a civil magistrate."[32] A constitutional opinion that presents itself at first glance as guaranteeing "articles of peace" for children in a public school setting *justifies* itself of necessity by reference to a more comprehensive liberal individualist "article of faith."

This article of faith runs the danger, once permitted to follow its natural trajectory, of eviscerating any "thick" notion of the common good and of subordinating the free exercise component of the religion clause, and thus of religious freedom itself, to the demands of the nonestablishment component. The supposed "tension" that jurists such as Warren Burger see in the commands of "non-establishment" and "free exercise" is dissolved in the name of a larger *moral* right: the right to freedom of conscience, conceived in liberal individualist terms.

Several conscientious objector cases from the 1960s provide examples of this movement on the Court's part toward a purely formal, individualistic interpretation of what the "free exercise" component protects. In *U.S. v. Seeger* (1965), for example, the Supreme Court ruled in favor of an individual who had been denied conscientious objector status because he did not believe in a "Supreme Being." The Selective Service Act in question had clearly specified that a religious claim to objector status must be grounded in an acknowledgment of "duties superior to those arising from any human relation." Seeger by contrast had claimed a religious faith in a "purely ethical creed." The U.S. Supreme Court, writing a gloss on the statute that had the practical effect of rewriting the statute, argued that any set of beliefs in ultimate reality, whether grounded in religion or a purely ethical creed, might serve as grounds for exemption from facially valid federal Selective Service laws. "A sincere and meaningful belief which occupies in the life of its possessor a place parallel to that fulfilled by the God of those admittedly qualifying for [conscientious objector status] comes within the statutory definition."[33] Justice Black, in *Welsh v. U.S.* (1970), extended the logic of *Seeger*, claiming that "beliefs that are purely ethical in source and content," if held strongly, are sufficient to justify exemption from military service.[34]

The logic of the Court's argument is certainly consistent. The overarching demand of the nonestablishment component requires that the state not *prefer* religion to irreligion or nonreligion. The state therefore can make no judgments about the veracity, the utility, or even the religiosity of a person's innermost convictions. To decide the case on the latter grounds in particular is to violate the demand for nonestablishment. If the free exercise component protects anything then, it protects not religious exercise *per se* but rather individual beliefs, whether religious or not.

The development of the Court's interpretation of the "free exercise" component makes it quite clear that the type of "negative liberty" being secured through the asserted "fundamental right" of free exercise (and the concomitant assertion that government, at both federal and state levels, must have a "compelling state interest" justifying incursions upon such a right) is grounded in a larger *freedom to* live according to one's beliefs. This larger trajectory of the Court's religion clause jurisprudence precedes even *Everson;* in fact, *Everson's* ostensible "neutrality" between religion and nonreligion is anticipated by *West Virginia Board of Education v. Barnette* (1943), a case that, ironically, is often depicted as a victory for religious freedom.[35]

In *Barnette*, the Court struck down as unconstitutional a mandatory Pledge of Allegiance in public elementary schools as violative of the First Amendment as absorbed through the due process clause of the Fourteenth Amendment. At first glance, *Barnette* seems to be a victory for the cause of religious freedom since the persons whose rights were being vindicated were members of the Jehovah's Witnesses. But in his opinion for the Court, Justice Robert Jackson (a supporter of a more radical separationist position, it must be remembered, in *Everson*) grounds the Court's opposition to the mandatory Pledge not so much in the fact that religionists' (*qua* religionists) religious liberties were being violated but rather in the fact that individuals (who happened to be religionists but need not have been) were being forced to affirm publicly a set of beliefs to which they did not adhere. In short, the case was more about the freedom not to speak than it was about religious liberty. And, given the logic of what would later become the separationist position, it *needed* to be primarily about something other than religion if government was to maintain a position of neutrality in matters of religion.

How do we accommodate religious practices (or the refusal of religionists, in the case of Barnette, to affirm that which they conscientiously oppose) without acknowledging, per *Everson's* supposed "neutrality" principle, that *religious* belief is a *good* thing that, to paraphrase *Dignitatis Humanae*, must be shown favor and respect? By accommodating them, as Gerard V. Bradley points out, not as religious practices *per se* but as activities that flow from deeply held beliefs. And we turn again to Justices O'Connor and Souter for confirmation of this foundational understanding of (religious) liberty. Justice O'Connor, in *Board of Education of Kiryas Joel v. Grumet* (1994), maintains that "[w]hat makes accommodation permissible, even praiseworthy, is not that government is making life easier for some religious group as such. Rather, it is that government is accommodating a deeply held belief."[36] Justice Souter, in *Employment Division v. Smith* (1990), argues that "in freeing the Native American Church from federal laws forbidding peyote use . . . the government conveys no endorsement of peyote rituals, the church, or religion as such; it simply respects the centrality of peyote to the lives of certain Americans."[37]

Thus, the Court's ostensible neutrality between religion and nonreligion (and its effort to square this neutrality with *freedom from* the coercive power of the state in matters religious) becomes a defense of liberal individualism, of what Pinckaers and Weigel describe as *freedom of indifference*. In questions of free exercise, as Bradley states, "the coherent rationale for a 'superneutral' religious liberty is this: it's about liberty, not religion."[38]

The practical effect of this "retheoretizing" of the religion clauses of the First Amendment is that the clauses are transformed from political/juridical principles that *limit* the powers of government out of a respect *for the good of religious freedom* into something quite different: a potentially exhaustive philosophical defense of something quite similar to the *conscientia exlex* of nineteenth-century laicism—a position against which the church fathers addressed their arguments for religious freedom in *Dignitatis Humanae*. Francis Canavan captures the paradoxical nature of this brand of statist individualism:

> Recent constitutional law in the United States has limited government by insisting more and more upon individual rights. Still more recently, so has civil rights legislation enacted by Congress or by the several state legislatures. This undoubtedly limits what government may do to individuals, but by the same token, and necessarily, it increases what government may do for individuals and institutions.
>
> Consequently, government is obligated to be, at one and the same time, individualistic and statist. It is individualistic when it serves an expanding array of rights. But insofar as it uses the power of the state to impose those rights upon institutions, government is statist, and the fingers of the bureaucracy reach more and more into all of the institutions of society.[39]

The liberal understanding of religious freedom is problematic not because it fails to offer a defense of negative liberty. Like Berlin, the U.S. Supreme Court's jurisprudential perspective is shaped by the notion that a constitutionally legitimate form of government must provide its citizenry with a *freedom from* the type of state-sponsored coercion that is the hallmark of totalitarian regimes. In securing this negative liberty, the Court must protect those fundamental aspects of human autonomy that suffer under a regime that advances too comprehensive a view of positive liberty.

Nor is that understanding problematic because it fails to place limits on the powers of government. As Canavan notes, the recent history of American constitutional law is the history of an increasingly broadened category of "rights" that require the Courts' protection against anything other than what constitutes a "compelling state interest." This "compelling state interest" is synonymous with the securing of individuals' rights to live according to their deeply held beliefs.

The Court's church-state jurisprudence (as well as its jurisprudence in other areas related to civil rights and liberties) is grounded in a voluntarist conception of human freedom that finds it impossible to explain *why* freedom of any sort, religious or otherwise, is an essential aspect of human flourishing. Absent this understanding of *freedom for excellence*, and of an *ordo iuris* that sustains this freedom, our constitutional system is placed in the untenable position of embracing in turn some variant of individualism, statism, or a combination of the two. John Courtney Murray has pointed out the inadequacy of the liberal model of freedom:

> We see that the modern concept of freedom itself was dangerously inadequate because it neglected the corporate dimension of freedom. We see too that modernity was wrong in isolating the problem of freedom from its polar terms—responsibility, justice, order, law. . . . We know that the myopic individualism of modernity led it into other errors, even into a false conception of the problem of the state in terms of the unreal dichotomy, individualism vs. collectivism.[40]

IV

Dignitatis Humanae is acknowledged to be the centerpiece of the Second Vatican Council's reflections on the political-juridical order, the nature of constitutional government, and the proper foundations for religious freedom in the modern world. While the document itself, as Kenneth L. Grasso points out, is not a systematic treatise of political theory, its content has become fodder for both Catholic integrationists and neoconfessionalists.[41] Integrationists such as David Hollenbach and Michael Novak embrace the document for what they see as its support for liberal political institutions; neoconfessionalists such as Robert Kraynak criticize it for what they see as its insufficiently Catholic view of human society and overly cribbed view of the common good.[42]

However strongly their substantive views of the proper role for the Church in society may differ, integrationists and neoconfessionalists seem to agree on one point: by embracing human rights and religious freedom, the Second Vatican Council embraced some variant of liberalism.

John Courtney Murray's commentary on the document, as embodied in his essay entitled "The Declaration on Religious Freedom: A Moment in Its Legislative History," seems to confirm such an interpretation precisely because Murray, like Berlin, focuses on the concept of negative liberty, which he sees as an integral part of the conciliar argument.

A study of the nature of the juridical order, Murray argues, reveals it to be "the order of rights, [having] to do with intersubjective relations among men." Within this juridical order—a deliberately limited order—man faces "'the others,' who also have their own duties and rights. No one may ever urge 'rights' against the truth; the very notion is non-sensical. Rights are urged against the others."[43] Conceived in juridical terms alone, religious freedom is a freedom from coercion by "the others," especially from those who, by giving the concept of religious freedom positive juridical content (that is, by adopting a comprehensive political "article of faith"), are quite willing to advance a comprehensively statist notion of the common good or public order.

A juridical approach to the problem of human freedom, according to Murray, makes no exhaustive claim for the rights of conscience. It tries "to set outside limits to a sphere of human activity, and to guarantee this sphere against forcible intrusion from without, but not to penetrate into the interior of this sphere and to pronounce moral or theological judgments of value on the activity itself."[44] The sphere in question is that of religion, and the political-juridical theory appropriate to this sphere, according to Murray's reading of the conciliar argument, is one that places limits on the coercive power of government, not on the compulsory power of the truth itself.

Murray's analysis of the conciliar argument for religious freedom is reminiscent of his analysis of the original purposes of the First Amendment. In the case of the conciliar argument, as just noted, Murray insists that a proper juridical notion of religious freedom make no "moral or theological judgment of value" on religious activity itself. By refusing to do so, one avoids endorsing an overly comprehensive (e.g., confessionalist) view of the common good. In the case of the First Amendment, Murray contends that its Framers gave a distinctively Catholic answer to the problem of religious liberty. They displayed a "prejudice in favor of the method of freedom in society and therefore the prejudice in favor of a government of limited powers, whose limitations are determined by the consent of the people."[45] The Framers saw the First Amendment's religion clauses as "articles of peace" for a dogmatically divided nation. These clauses say nothing about the nature of religion itself; they are not "articles of faith" with a particular religious (i.e., liberal Protestant) content. The genius of the American constitutional system (and, one might infer, of the conciliar argument as well) was that civic rulers were "constitutionally inhibited from passing judgment in matters of religious faith."

Murray's practical "articles of faith/articles of peace" distinction (and the reflections of that distinction found in his analysis of the conciliar argument) is ill used when it is hardened into a principled dichotomy. What might have been an effective rhetorical device when directed against a particular statist substantive orthodoxy (e.g., liberal Protestantism, confessionalism, or secularism) might easily become, in the hands of an able Hobbesian or historicist interpreter of Murray, a pronouncement against all orthodoxies and a preoccupation with toleration as the only enforceable norm in a liberal regime. In other words, Murray's reading of the conciliar argument, and of the intentions of the Framers of the U.S. Constitution, is easily convertible, at the practical level, into Berlin's defense of "negative liberty."[46]

Murray's argument seems to assume, however, that this negative juridical notion of religious liberty provides a positive foundation upon which society will display respect for the affirmation of persons' (and faith communities') religious sensibilities. Murray contends that

> by reason of its negative [juridical] content [religious freedom] serves to make possible and easy the practice of religious freedom for men and society. It serves to assure full scope for the manifold manifestations of freedom in religious matters. . . . It is to create and sustain a constitutional situation, and to that extent to favor and foster a social climate, within which the citizen and the religious community may pursue the higher ends of human existence without let or hindrance by other citizens, by society, or by government itself.[47]

But clearly, as has already been noted, a purely juridical theory that prescinds from any judgment about the value of religion is just as much a historical impossibility as is a purely "negative" conception of liberty in general or a theory of the First Amendment that prescribes "neutrality" between religion and irreligion. Murray's reading of the conciliar argument can be distinguished from liberal orthodoxy not in its purported effort to eschew judgments about *why* religion is valuable but, rather, in its dependence on a theory of human personhood, and the type of public order that flows therefrom, that *assumes* religiosity to be a fundamental aspect of human flourishing. In short, Murray's theory of negative juridical liberty works precisely because it depends on what Weigel describes as *freedom for excellence.* Murray implicitly acknowledges this dependence by his juridical theory on something larger than itself:

> First, [the notion of] public order . . . was explicitly related to the common good; in consequence, the notion was given not only a juridical, but also a moral, content. Second, and more important, the third schema [of the conciliar document] included, for the first time, a statement of the principle of the free society: "The freedom of man is to be respected as far as possible, and it is not to be restricted except in so far as necessary." This principle is rooted in the dignity of the human person. When it is recognized effectively, abuses of governmental power in the order of religion, as in other orders of social life, are likewise effectively barred.[48]

The state, while limited to pursuing the requirements of a moral public order, cannot adopt a truncated, Hobbesianized view of civic life if it is to create those conditions under which "the higher ends of human existence" can develop. The concept of "public order" must be set against a backdrop of a more comprehensive conception of the temporal common good if true public order and religious freedom are to be actualized. In short, the success of Murray's political "articles of peace" depends upon a societal "article of faith" that is open to religion as an aspect of human flourishing.

In fact, the conciliar document seems to be clearer on this point than is Murray's analysis of it. *Dignitatis Humanae* advances a distinctly Christian differentiation on political things by moving in the direction of a principled defense of limited constitutional government and religious freedom that differs markedly from the liberal model and its dependence on the freedom of indifference. Unlike the liberal model of man and society, it recognizes "the social nature of man." Rather than endorsing a privatized religiosity in the name of civil peace, it acknowledges that man "should give external expression to his internal acts of religion; that he should participate with others in matters religious; that he should profess his religion in community."[49] Rather than attempting to be neutral between religion and irreligion, it argues that "government . . . ought indeed to take account of the religious life of the people and show it favor, since the function of government is to make provision for the common welfare."[50]

This favoritism is displayed, according to the conciliar argument, not through the state's establishment of a particular confessional perspective but by its maintaining a morally grounded public order within which religious freedom (construed by the public as a positive good) and those institutions that support such freedom can flourish. In fact, the confessional state is to be discouraged in principle not because religion is a private matter, nor because the state must respect choice *qua* choice, but because religious freedom in particular is an intrinsic human good that the state advances indirectly through its juridical commitment to constitutional limits and forms. Robert P. George captures the truly Christian dimension of *Dignitatis Humanae*'s argument for religious freedom when he contends that "[c]oercion can only damage that possibility of an authentic religious faith, a true realization of the human good of religion. Coercion deflects people from really choosing that human good, for it seeks to dominate their deliberations with the prospect of a quite different good—of freedom from imminent pain, loss, or other harms, or of some other non-religious advantage."[51]

If *Dignitatis Humanae* represents a change in the political theory of the Catholic intellectual tradition—that is, a salutary movement away from the understanding of church-state relations that marks confessionalism—it remains unchanged in its ultimate commitment to Pinckaers's notion of freedom for excellence, however much it may express itself in the contemporary grammar of negative liberty. For as Francis Canavan notes in a commentary on *Dignitatis Humanae,* the success of limited constitutional government depends on more than a commitment to juridical norms and procedures. It depends on a people's commitment to a higher order of morality and law that is not of its own choosing. Canavan argues that "under a constitutional form of government (which the declaration [on religious freedom] seems to consider normal), the moral order and the public order derived from it will be effective restraints on government insofar as they are accepted by the collective conscience of the larger and sounder part of society and are upheld by constitutional organs, such as the courts of law."[52]

V

Robert P. George's and Francis Canavan's apt words capture the essence of the teaching of *Dignitatis Humanae*—a teaching that stands in sharp relief against the metaethical principle of human autonomy that lies at the heart of the U.S. Supreme Court's effort to develop a "neutral" juridical theory of church-state relations. For the authors of *Dignitatis Humanae,* religious freedom is an intrinsic human good and the Church's developing commitment to its juridical protection reflects its larger commitment to a personalist rather than individualist notion of human dignity. *Dignitatis Humanae*'s politico-juridical notion of religious freedom as *freedom from* coercion has an anthropological dimension that distinguishes it from the type of negative liberty supported by Berlin. While the state needs to be reminded constantly of its own intrinsic limitations in matters religious, the attainment of larger human ends and purposes is possible only when a society commits itself to preserving not only constitutional forms and structures but also the moral law upon which these forms and structures depend for sustenance.

Angela C. Carmella has observed that "religious liberty, not separation or parity, is the goal of the religion clauses" of the First Amendment of the U.S. Constitution.[53] To the extent that the antiperfectionist vision of *freedom of indifference* has provided philosophical underpinnings for the Supreme Court's jurisprudence, it has been difficult to provide a coherent account of the nature of *religious* liberty and of the *ordo iuris* under which it can be sustained. *Everson* and its progeny have had the effect of reifying the sovereign self. In so doing, *Everson* has, whatever its intentions, articulated a thoroughly "retheoretized" (to use Murray's term) view of church-state relations that is, in many respects hostile to the arguments advanced by the church fathers in *Dignitatis Humanae.* Stephen Monsma's argument for a chastened (and less secularist) reading of what governmental neutrality in matters religious means opens the public square to persons of religious sensibilities, but it must be supplemented at the philosophical and social level by a theory of man and society that grounds a defense of religious freedom (and of the state's limited juridical role) in something other than the voluntarism of *freedom of indifference*.

George Weigel's critique of Isaiah Berlin's "Two Concepts of Liberty" ends with a post-September 11 warning that "a society without 'oughts' tethered to truths cannot defend itself against aggressors motivated by distorted 'oughts'. . . . The answer to a distorted concept of the good cannot be a radical relativism about the good. It must be a nobler concept of the good."[54] *Dignitatis Humanae* supplies us with this "nobler concept of the good" and a more viable conception of the politico-juridical order. John Courtney Murray's interpretation of the trajectory of the Second Vatican Council's efforts properly emphasizes the limited juridical nature of the state in religious matters. Those who wish to develop further the Church's teaching in these matters must demonstrate convincingly that this commitment to juridical limits should in no way be construed as an endorsement of a regime of antiperfectionist "negative liberty."

NOTES

1. Edward S. Dore, *Human Rights and the Law*, 15 FORDHAM LAW REVIEW 1, 5 (1946).
2. George Weigel, "A Better Concept of Freedom," *First Things* 121 (March 2002): 14–20. Berlin's original essay is contained in Berlin's *Four Essays on Liberty* (New York: Oxford University Press, 1969).
3. Weigel, 14.
4. Ibid., 15.
5. John Hallowell, *The Moral Foundation of Democracy* (Chicago: University of Chicago Press, Midway reprint, 1973), 89.
6. Dore, op. cit.
7. Berlin, cited in Weigel, 15.
8. Weigel, 17.
9. Weigel, 16. For a full account of Pinckaers's distinction between freedom of indifference and freedom for excellence, see *The Sources of Christian Ethics*, translated from the third edition by Sr. Mary Thomas Noble O.P. (Washington, DC: Catholic University of America Press, 1995), 327–78.
10. Weigel, 17.
11. Ibid., 15.
12. Ibid., 17.
13. Michael Sandel, "Introduction" to *Liberalism and Its Critics* (New York: New York University Press, 1984), 8.

14. For another extended treatment of this theme, see Charles Taylor, "What's Wrong with Negative Liberty," in *The Idea of Freedom*, ed. Alan Ryan (New York: Oxford University Press, 1979), 175–93. Reprinted in Charles Taylor, *Philosophy and the Human Sciences: Philosophical Papers 2* (Cambridge: Cambridge University Press, 1985), 211–29.

15. Ralph McInerny, "Those Mothers on the Mall," *Crisis* (December 1989), 3.

16. Weigel, 17.

17. The remaining sections of this essay extend upon themes I addressed in "Catholicism, Liberalism, and Religious Liberty," in *A Moral Enterprise: Politics, Reason, and the Human Good: Essays in Honor of Francis Canavan*, ed. Kenneth L. Grasso and Robert P. Hunt (Wilmington, NC: ISI Books), 2002, 143–63.

18. John Courtney Murray, *We Hold These Truths: Catholic Reflections on the American Proposition* (New York: Sheed and Ward, 1960), 32.

19. *Dignitatis Humanae*, sections 3 and 4. All further references to this document will be taken from the translation supplied by John Courtney Murray in *Religious Liberty: An End and a Beginning* (New York: Macmillan, 1966), 162–89.

20. *Everson v. Board of Education of Ewing Township, N.J.*, 330 U.S. 1, at 15–16.

21. Ibid., at 19.

22. Ibid., at 31–32.

23. Black, cited in David M. O'Brien, *Constitutional Law and Politics*, vol. 2, *Civil Rights and Liberties*, 3rd ed. (New York: W. W. Norton & Company, 1997), 86.

24. John Courtney Murray, "The Declaration on Religious Freedom: A Moment in Its Legislative History," in *Religious Liberty: An End and a Beginning*, 29.

25. Murray cited in Jo Renee Formicola, "Catholic Jurisprudence on Education," in *Everson Revisited: Religion, Education, and Law at the Crossroads*, ed. Jo Renee Formicola and Hubert Morken (Lanham, MD: Rowman & Littlefield, 1997), 86.

26. Philip Hamburger, *Separation of Church and State* (Cambridge, MA: Harvard University Press, 2004).

27. Stephen Monsma, "The Wrong Road Taken," in *Everson Revisited*, 127–28.

28. *Dignitatis Humanae*, section 6.

29. *Mitchell v. Helms*, 120 S. Ct. 2530, at 2541.

30. Ibid., at 2557.

31. Ibid., at 2597.

32. Black, *Engel v. Vitale*, 370 U.S. 421 (1962), cited in *The Supreme Court on Church and State*, ed. Robert S. Alley (New York: Oxford University Press, 1988), 199.

33. *U.S. v. Seeger*, 380 U.S. 163, at 184. For further discussion of the ramifications of *Seeger*, see James Hitchcock, *The Supreme Court and Religion in Public Life*, vol. 1, *The Odyssey of the Religion Clauses* (Princeton, NJ: Princeton University Press, 2004), at 63–67.

34. *Welsh v. U.S.*, 398 U.S. 333, at 341–43.

35. *West Virginia Board of Education v. Barnette*, 319 U.S. 624 (1943), at 630–42.

36. *Board of Education of Kiryas Joel v. Grumet*, 512 U.S. 687 (1994), cited in Gerard V. Bradley, "Déjà Vu, All Over Again: The Supreme Court Revisits Religious Liberty," *Crisis* 13, no. 4 (April 1995), 41.

37. *Employment Division v. Smith*, 110 S. Ct. 1595 (1990), cited in Bradley, "Déjà Vu," 41.

38. Bradley, "Déjà Vu,"42.

39. Francis P. Canavan, *The Pluralist Game: Pluralism, Liberalism, and the Moral Conscience* (Lanham, MD: Rowman & Littlefield, 1995), 139.

40. Murray, *We Hold These Truths*, 200.

41. Kenneth L. Grasso, "Beyond Liberalism: Human Dignity, the Free Society, and the Second Vatican Council," in *Catholicism, Liberalism, and Communitarianism: The Catholic Intellectual Tradition and the Moral Foundations of Democracy*, ed. Kenneth L. Grasso, Gerard V. Bradley, and Robert P. Hunt (Lanham, MD: Rowman & Littlefield, 1995), 39ff.

42. For the respective positions of Hollenbach and Kraynak, see David Hollenbach, "A Communitarian Reconstruction of Human Rights: Contributions from the Catholic Tradition," in *Catholicism and Liberalism: Contributions to American Public Philosophy*, ed. R. Bruce Douglass and David Hollenbach (New York: Cambridge University Press, 1994), 133, and Robert Kraynak, *Christian Faith and Modern Democracy: God and Politics in the Fallen World* (Notre Dame, IN: University of Notre Dame Press, 2001).

43. Murray, "The Declaration on Religious Freedom," 24.

44. Ibid., 29.

45. Murray, *We Hold These Truths*, 47.

46. For a further discussion of this theme, see my own "The Quest for the Historical Murray," in *Catholicism, Liberalism, and Communitarianism*, 197 ff.

47. Murray, "The Declaration on Religious Freedom," 29.

48. Ibid., 36.

49. *Dignitatis Humanae*, section 3.

50. Ibid.

51. Robert P. George, *Making Men Moral: Civil Liberties and Public Morality* (New York: Oxford University Press, 1993), 221–22.

52. Francis Canavan, "The Catholic Concept of Religious Freedom as a Human Right," in *Religious Liberty: An End and a Beginning*, 76.

53. Angela C. Carmella, "Everson and Its Progeny: Separation and Nondiscrimination in Tension," in *Everson Revisited*, 117.

54. Weigel, 19.

Dignitatis Humanae and the Development of Catholic Doctrine

Avery Cardinal Dulles, S.J.

Dignitatis Humanae (*DH*) is, I believe, the only document of Vatican II that explicitly claims to be a development of doctrine. The Fathers express their intention "to develop the teaching of the more recent popes on the inviolable rights of the human person and on the constitutional order of society."[1] The debates on the Council floor revolved not so much about the concept of religious freedom itself as about the process of doctrinal development. John Courtney Murray in his commentary on *DH* calls it

> the most controversial document of the whole Council, largely because it raised with sharp emphasis the issue that lay continually below the surface of all the conciliar debates—the issue of the development of doctrine. The notion of development, not the notion of religious freedom, was the real sticking point for many of those who opposed the Declaration even to the end.[2]

Elsewhere Murray writes that the chief theoretical interest of *DH* lies in the problems of development it presents.[3]

The problem of religious freedom, as understood today, has emerged only since the Enlightenment. In the Middle Ages, no doubt, the Church tolerated or authorized practices that strike us today as inconsistent with due respect for religious freedom, but it is difficult to find doctrinal statements that address the jurisprudential question as we know it today. The formal teaching of the Church on the theme is generally understood as beginning in the early nineteenth century, when Rome condemned the ideas of the Abbé Félicité de Lamennais. Since that time the Roman magisterium has produced a wealth of documents dealing with the freedom of religion and of conscience. Is there a homogeneous line of development or a reversal? Can the facts be squared with the theory of doctrinal development as it has been understood since John Henry Newman's classic work, *An Essay on the Development of Christian Doctrine*?[4]

Although commentators generally agree that *DH* marks a shift in doctrine, they differ in their ways of understanding the nature of the change. At the outset, we may distinguish three basic positions, which will be examined more thoroughly as our investigation proceeds.

One school contends that Vatican II reversed earlier Catholic teaching. There are two expressions of this position. Archbishop Marcel Lefebvre and the Catholic traditionalists argue that the previous teaching was correct and that Vatican II erred. Catholic revisionists, on the contrary, treat *DH* as a clear example of the correction of erroneous noninfallible magisterial teaching.

Commentators of a second group hold that the Declaration, while it departs from the letter of previous papal teaching, respects and carries out the profound intention of the earlier magisterium. These authors distinguish between what was meant from what was said. Vatican II, they say, may contradict the conceptuality and language of earlier popes, but it adhered to their doctrine, in the sense that it upheld what these popes meant.

Third, there are some who see the development in *DH* as leaving intact the explicit teaching of the magisterium in the previous century. The development, for this school, consists in clarifying what was previously ambiguous and in finding new implications and applications of the Church's teaching in view of new situations.

In order to decide which, if any, of these positions is correct, I shall examine the teaching of *DH* in two principal areas. First, what does it say about the right or duty of the state to uphold some given religion, more particularly Catholic Christianity, as true or worthy of support? Second, what does the Declaration say about the rights of persons and groups of persons who in good conscience fail to accept the true religion?

DH asserts that the Council "searches into the sacred tradition and doctrine of the Church—the treasury out of which the Church continually brings forth new things that are in harmony with the things that are old" (*DH*, 1). With reference to each of our two problem areas, then, three questions may be put. First, in what respects does the Declaration bring forth something genuinely new, as it must in order to be reckoned as a development? Second, in what way are the new elements drawn from the treasure of sacred tradition and doctrine? Third, are the new elements in harmony or in conflict with what was previously taught? In the following pages we shall consider successively *DH*'s novelty, its roots in Scripture and tradition, and its compatibility with earlier teaching. Before directly comparing *DH* with earlier papal teaching, we shall briefly review the developments of papal teaching in the twentieth century prior to Vatican II.

NOVELTY

The relativities of history, as many theologians have pointed out, play a role in the development of ideas, especially those related to the political and social order.[5] Popes and bishops quite properly address the religious questions of their own day, and they do so with the tools offered by the scientific, cultural, and philosophical world in which they live. It is not surprising, therefore, that Church teaching on civil and religious freedom has varied somewhat over the centuries.

Early Stages

The Christianity of Catholic Europe inherited from the Middle Ages an organic vision of society in which the spiritual and temporal authorities (the *sacerdotium* and the *imperium*) collaborated in governing the *civitas christiana*. The religious authority, exercising a kind of spiritual paternity over the faithful, admonished kings and princes to respect the mission and liberties of the Church, which was charged with the task of leading souls to eternal salvation. The temporal ruler, likewise playing a paternal role, was regarded as having direct responsibility for the temporal realm and as taking indirect responsibility for the spiritual by working in harmony with the Church.

In early modern times, with the advent of absolutist monarchies, total authority—both spiritual and temporal—was frequently transferred to the secular ruler. Kings assumed the headship of the Church in their respective domains, treating the clergy almost as their chaplains. The Peace of Augsburg in 1555 canonized the pernicious principle *cuius regio eius religio*.

With the advent of the Enlightenment, however, both the medieval and early modern settlements were challenged by religious individualism, in which each person was seen as autonomous and as responsible for professing or not professing a particular faith. This development was often accompanied by an anticlerical spirit. The French Jacobin tradition went to an extreme in excluding the Church from public life and in denying the right of secular rulers to defend Christian orthodoxy. Inspired by similar principles, the Piedmontese government under Count Camillo di Cavour pursued a ruthless policy of laicization, exiling members of religious orders and congregations, imprisoning priests, closing Catholic schools, and encouraging anti-Catholic propaganda.[6]

The Holy See in the nineteenth century reacted strongly against the privatization of religion in this "laicist" liberalism. To give public status to the faith, the popes sought to shore up the remnants of the medieval model, in which the ruler of the state, as a father of the people, was accorded some limited responsibility for protecting their spiritual as well as their temporal welfare.

Popes of the Twentieth Century

In the first half of the twentieth century, a new series of threats arose with the Mexican Revolution, Italian Fascism, German National Socialism, and Soviet Communism. In these systems the secular state or the political party constituted itself as the rival of the Church, demanding quasireligious loyalty. Reacting against this totalitarianism, the Church saw itself called to the defense of human dignity and freedom. Emphasizing the limited competence of the state, the popes increasingly spoke out in favor of constitutional forms of government in which the rights and freedom of the citizens were guaranteed by law. The dignity of the human person emerges with ever greater clarity and emphasis in the writings of Pius XI, Pius XII, and John XXIII.

Pius XI in a series of powerful encyclicals reacted strongly against the idolatry of the state or regime. Speaking principally as shepherd of the Catholic faithful, he upheld their right to worship God according to the dictates of their consciences and warned them against falling prey to the seductions of Fascism, National Socialism, and Communism in its various forms. He admonished secular rulers that the Church's freedom to carry out her mission is sacred and inviolable.

As the popes directed their gaze beyond the confines of European Catholicism and witnessed the destructive impact of totalitarianism across the face of the globe, they spoke in more universalistic terms. They taught more explicitly that in view of the diversity of religions in many commonwealths, there is no strict necessity for Catholic Christianity to be established by law. A variety of religious beliefs could and should be tolerated. Thus Pius XII, in his allocution *Ci Riesce* (1953), predicted that in the international community then coming into being, positive law would provide for diversity:

> Within its own territory and for its own citizens, each State will regulate religious and moral affairs by its own laws: nevertheless, throughout the whole territory of the international community of States, the citizens of every member-State will be allowed their own beliefs and ethical and religious practices, in so far as these do not contravene the penal laws of the State in which they are residing.[7]

The pope understands the penal laws as embodying the exigencies of public order. In later sections of his talk, he implies that the Church does not need to have a privileged legal status in the international community. Concordats can guarantee to the Church her full independence in the fulfillment of her divine mission.[8]

John XXIII, in *Pacem in Terris* (1963), called attention to the "signs of the times" and noted that "the men of our time have become increasingly conscious of their dignity as human persons."[9] Advancing beyond his predecessors and even beyond what he himself had taught in *Mater et Magistra* (1961), John XXIII here recognizes freedom as a "fourth pillar" of society alongside of truth, justice, and love. The social order, he writes, is grounded in *truth*; it must function according to the norms of *justice*; it should be inspired and perfected by mutual *love*, and it should be brought to completion and refinement in full *freedom*.[10] He reckoned among the inviolable rights of every human person the right to worship God "according to the correct norms of their conscience."[11]

The gains in Catholic social teaching during the decades preceding Vatican II may be summarized in four points:

1. The human person is seen not as an object to be shaped passively by government but as the "subject, foundation, and goal" of social and political life.[12] This affirmation of Pius XII, in the context of the world of 1944, was a clear protest against dictatorial totalitarianism.

2. Among the chief purposes of government is that of protecting and fostering the dignity of the human person. In the words of Pius XII, "The purpose of all social life remains always the same, always sacred and obligatory, namely, the development of the personal values of man as the image of God."[13]

3. The dignity of the person includes religious freedom, in the sense that all citizens have the moral duty, and consequently the right, to seek religious truth, to adhere to it when found, and to profess their faith, "within the limits laid down by the moral order and the common good."[14]

4. The state has only limited competence. Its distinctive role is to assure temporal peace and prosperity, not to decide questions of truth with reference to revealed religion. In *Ci Riesce*, as we have seen, Pius XII holds that members of the larger civil society should be allowed to maintain their own ethical and religious beliefs and practices insofar as these do not contravene the penal laws of the state.

DH

DH takes up where Pius XII and John XXIII had left off. In its opening sentences, it declares that the Council is taking careful note of the way in which the sense of the dignity of the human person has been imposing itself more and more on the contemporary consciousness (*DH*, 1). Among the auspicious signs of our times, the Council joyfully recognizes the increasing recognition of religious freedom as a civil right (*DH*, 15). *DH* thus situates itself within the dynamic development of the Church's consciousness to which the Council adverted in its Pastoral Constitution on the Church in the Modern World (*Gaudium et Spes*).[15]

The first two sentences of *DH*, in words virtually quoted from *Pacem in Terris*, focus on the dignity of the human person and responsible freedom.[16] Religious freedom, says the Council, has its foundation in the very dignity of the human person, as this dignity is known through the revealed word of God and by reason itself (*DH*, 2). The right to immunity from coercion, says the Council, continues to exist even in those who do not live up to their obligation of seeking the truth and adhering to it (*DH*, 2). Every human being, therefore, has the right and the duty to seek religious truth and to profess it, when found (*DH*, 3). In promoting the common welfare, governments ought to take account of the religious life of the people and show it favor (*DH*, 3). Since the social nature of religion requires the external and public expression of faith, religious bodies have a right not to be hindered in their witness to the faith, unless in so doing they abuse their own rights and violate the rights of others (*DH*, 4). Governments are required to help to create conditions favorable to the fostering of religious life (*DH*, 6). The usages of society require that freedom be respected as far as possible and curtailed only when and insofar as necessary (*DH*, 7). It is a major tenet of the Christian religion that the response to God in faith must be free (*DH*, 9). The Catholic Church claims for herself not only the freedom common to all human associations but the sacred freedom to carry out the saving mission entrusted to her by the Son of God (*DH*, 13–14).

As if to ratify the whole process of development, Paul VI, in a message to political rulers given at the close of the Council (December 9, 1965), summarized the new relationship between the Church and the political powers:

> And what is it that this Church asks of you, after nearly two thousand years of all sorts of vicissitudes in her relations with you, the powers of the earth? What does the Church ask of you today? In one of the major texts of the Council she has told you: she asks of you nothing but freedom—the freedom to believe and to preach her faith, the freedom to love God and serve him, the freedom to live and to bring to men her message of life.[17]

BASIS IN SCRIPTURE AND TRADITION

The problem of doctrinal development arises not simply with regard to *DH* but with regard to the four preconciliar advances already noted. According to John Henry Newman, whose *Essay on the Development of Christian Doctrine* remains a classic reference point, authentic developments may be tested by criteria such as continuity of principles, logical sequence from what precedes, anticipation of what was to come, and conservative action on past teaching.[18] It can be argued persuasively, I believe, that the four principles of twentieth-century Catholic social teaching listed above pass these tests. These principles, although they are less prominent in the teaching of earlier centuries, are anticipated in that teaching and logically implied in it, so that it is in its turn confirmed by them.

1. Catholic social teaching had traditionally viewed the human person as prior to the state, which exists in order to help the members of society to attain their own perfection. Leo XIII in *Immortale Dei* insisted that "government should moreover be administered for the well-being of the citizens, because they who govern others possess authority solely for the welfare of the State."[19] In *Rerum Novarum* Leo XIII insists that man is not a chattel but a creature having inviolable dignity.[20]

2. The dignity of the human person has been a major theme of Christian literature since patristic times. It was celebrated in the Italian Renaissance by Giannozzo Manetti and Giovanni Pico della Mirandola. That dignity, in the perspectives of theology, depends on the biblical teaching that we have been created in God's own image and likeness, redeemed by the blood of the Incarnate Son, and called to eternal life as adopted children of God. All these points are recalled by Leo XIII in *Rerum Novarum*.[21]

3. Throughout the centuries Catholic teaching has strongly insisted on the importance of human freedom in opposition to Manichaeanism, Jansenism, and other errors. In opposition to some Protestants, the Council of Trent anathematized the teachings that free will was lost by the Fall of Adam and that human beings are merely passive in accepting the grace of justification.[22] The First Vatican Council taught under anathema that the assent of faith is a free, voluntary response to grace and cannot be coerced.[23] Leo XIII in *Libertas Praestantissimum* defended true liberty and called it the protector of personal dignity.[24] Heed must be taken, he said, "that no one shall be forced to embrace the Catholic faith against his will."[25] Human freedom, Leo declared, far from being hindered by grace, is enhanced by the interior workings of God in the mind and will.[26] Leo also taught that just as God tolerates the abuse of freedom in human sin, the state may tolerate evil for the sake of the common good.[27] In line with the dominant theological tradition, furthermore, Francisco Suárez in

the sixteenth century denounced forced conversions on the ground that they lead to hypocrisy and sacrilege and arouse scandal and blasphemy against the Christian religion.[28]

4. In opposition to Erastianism on the one hand and theocracy on the other, the Church has maintained the biblical distinction between the things that are Caesar's and those that are God's (Mt 22:21). Since Gelasius II this distinction has frequently been seen as requiring a "dyarchy"—a differentiation between the secular and spiritual powers, each having its own sphere of competence. Suárez, for example, insisted that the State has merely human authority and is ordered to a natural end, consisting chiefly in the preservation of peace, the maintenance of natural justice, and the fostering of the moral probity conducive to such an end. It has no mandate to punish for sins of infidelity.[29]

The distinction between the ecclesiastical and civil powers lay at the heart of Leo XIII's encyclical *Immortale Dei*. Here and in *Libertas Praestantissimum* he taught that the proximate and proper end of the state is the welfare of the governed in the present life. By working toward this end, the state can enhance the capacity of the citizens to attain the supreme good of everlasting happiness, which is the distinctive concern of the Church.[30] Since the members of both societies are frequently the same persons, the two powers must work in harmony and avoid giving contrary commands.[31]

The freedom of the Church to pursue her divinely given mission, which we have seen eloquently stated by Pius XI and Paul VI, is likewise well-grounded in the tradition. Since the Gregorian Reform in the eleventh century, and especially when religious freedom was suppressed under Soviet Communism and German National Socialism, the Church has insisted on her God-given mandate to propagate her faith and to conduct services of worship in private and in public. Leo XIII speaks for the tradition when he proclaims in *Immortale Dei* that the authority of the Church, deriving from her divine mission, cannot be restricted by any human power.[32]

NONCONTRADICTION OF PREVIOUS TEACHING

Notwithstanding the continuities already noted, problems have arisen about whether *DH* reversed earlier Catholic teaching. When one compares the statements of nineteenth-century popes with *DH*, neglecting the intermediate development, the contrast appears so sharp that the casual reader spontaneously suspects that the earlier teachings have been reversed.

Conscious of these objections, a whole series of speakers at Vatican II addressed the issue of continuity. Bishop Émile De Smedt, in his first *relatio* on behalf of the Secretariat for Promoting Christian Unity (November 18, 1963), took up this problem at length.[33] Several other speakers such as Archbishop Pedro Cantero Cuadrado of Saragossa,[34] Cardinal Gabriel-Marie Garrone of Toulouse,[35] and Cardinal Lawrence Shehan of Baltimore[36] argued that *DH* was in continuity with earlier papal teaching.[37] During and since the Council, many distinguished theologians and historians have likewise made the case for homogeneous development.[38]

In a preliminary version of *DH* distributed to the fathers on November 17, 1964, a section of four paragraphs dealing with the historical question was inserted.[39] But the treatment was too concise to do justice to the complexity of the matter and was for that reason suppressed in subsequent drafts.[40] At the very end of the Council, just before the final vote, Bishop De Smedt declared: "Some Fathers affirm that the Declaration does not sufficiently show how our doctrine is not opposed to the Church documents up to the time of the sovereign pontiff, Leo XIII. As we have already said in the last *relatio*, this matter will have to be fully clarified in future theological and historical studies."[41]

Theologians and historians, however, express no consensus. From a Traditionalist perspective, Michael Davies agrees with Archbishop Lefebvre that *DH* improperly contradicts the teaching of Gregory XVI and Pius IX.[42] From an opposite perspective, Juan Luis Segundo, objecting to the censure of certain aspects of liberation theology by the Holy See, argues that *DH* properly overturned the teaching of Pius IX in the *Syllabus of Errors*.[43] In the United States, opponents of *Humanae Vitae* frequently use *DH* as evidence that the ordinary teaching of the popes is subject to later correction. Daniel C. Maguire, in a collection of essays in support of Charles E. Curran, writes: "Gregory XVI and Pius IX both condemned notions of religious liberty and freedom of conscience later to be blessed in Vatican II."[44] In general, Catholic doctrinal revisionists seize on *DH* as a showcase example of doctrinal reversal.[45]

J. Robert Dionne in *The Papacy and the Church* devotes some seventy-five pages to the exposition and defense of his thesis that the teaching of the ordinary papal magisterium since Gregory XVI had been reversed by Vatican II in *DH*. He takes *DH* as a salient instance of the correction of noninfallible teaching thanks to feedback coming from the People of God.

The discussion has centered particularly on two themes in the teaching of Pius IX and Leo XIII. Did these popes teach as a matter of divine law that Roman Catholicism should be established as the religion of the state? Did they reject the religious freedom of non-Catholics, individually and corporately, to practice their religion publicly and to propagate their beliefs?

Duties of the State toward the True Religion

In the teaching of Pius IX, the encyclical *Quanta Cura* (1864) and the *Syllabus of Errors* accompanying it have been cited to prove that he maintained that the State must publicly accept and protect the Catholic faith—a doctrine allegedly renounced by *DH*. In *Quanta Cura* the pope opposes naturalism, which he defines, in the words of Gregory XVI, as the system according to which "the best constitution of public society, and (also) civil progress, altogether require that human society be conducted and governed without regard being had to religion any more than if it did not exist; or, at least, without any distinction being made between true religion and false ones."[46] The *Syllabus* condemns the proposition that "the Church must be separated from the state, and the state from the Church" (Prop. 55) and denies that "in our age it is no longer suitable for the Catholic religion to be considered the sole religion of the state, excluding all other religions" (Prop. 77).[47]

Leo XIII quotes with approval the statements of Pius IX and the *Syllabus* on the separation of church and state. In *Immortale Dei* he proclaims that "it is not lawful for the State, any more than for the individual, either to disregard all religious duties or to hold in equal favor different kinds of religion." He denies that the state should favor the unrestrained freedom of citizens to express whatever they think as though this were an inherent personal right.[48] It is unlawful, he says, "to place various forms of divine worship on the same footing as the true religion."[49]

These statements of the two popes at first sight seem inconsistent with the teaching of *DH* that, although "the civil government, whose proper purpose it is to provide for the temporal common good, should certainly recognize and promote the religious life of its citizens, . . . it must be said to transgress the limits of its authority if were it to presume to direct or inhibit religious activity" (*DH*, 3). Provided that the demands of public order are respected, says *DH*, religious bodies must be free to govern themselves, to worship, and to bear witness to their faith publicly in speech and writing (*DH*, 4). The civil government, according to *DH*, is to create conditions in which all the citizens are able to exercise their religious rights (*DH*, 6). "If, in view of peculiar circumstances obtaining among certain peoples, special legal recognition is given in the juridical order to one religious body, it is at the same time imperative that the right of all citizens and religious bodies to religious freedom should be recognized and upheld in practice" (*DH*, 6). These statements seem to renounce the view that the state must give special recognition and support to the Catholic faith.

Any attempt at a reconciliation must begin from a correct understanding of the *Syllabus*. The propositions, as they stand, are not composed by Pius IX.

They are summaries or digests from earlier papal documents, all of which are explicitly referred to.[50] From careful study of these documents, it becomes clear that some of the propositions are not, strictly speaking, condemned as errors. Many must be understood as warnings against applying certain defensible principles in too sweeping a way, without recognition for the need of caution in particular situations. Each proposition, moreover, has to be interpreted in its context in the document from which it is drawn.

Proposition 55, on the separation of church and state, for instance, is drawn from the allocution *Acerbissimum* given to cardinals in 1852. It referred to the persecution of the Church in New Granada (modern Colombia), where the state had taken possession of all seminaries, reduced marriage to a merely civil contract, and claimed the right to appoint all bishops and pastors. Likewise, proposition 77, referring to the establishment of the Catholic religion, is taken from an allocution of 1855 in which the pope was expressing his wonderment at the breach of the Concordat on the part of the Spanish government. In the light of the context, it may be seen that, as Roger Aubert points out, "The error of proposition 77 consisted in affirming that there was no longer any situation, in the mid-nineteenth century, in which the maintenance of Catholicism as the religion of the state was still justified."[51]

In many of his documents Pius IX was writing about situations arising in areas such as Mexico and rural Italy, in which poorly educated classes were being unfairly subjected to the aggressive propaganda of a secularism that ruthlessly attacked the Church. Under the circumstances the pope quite properly refused to condemn arrangements in which Catholic kings and princes felt a paternal responsibility to protect their people from being robbed of the precious gift of faith. Nothing in the teaching of Pius IX would preclude a judgment in the latter part of the twentieth century that the establishment of the Roman Catholic religion would be undesirable in most parts of the world.

In *Quanta Cura* Pius IX rejected the view "that is the best condition of human society, in which no duty is recognized, as attached to the civil power, of restraining by enacted penalties, offenders against the Catholic religion, except so far as public peace may require."[52] Questions have been raised about the compatibility of this condemnation with the teaching of Vatican II that citizens enjoy the right to be free from external coercion provided that the just requirements of public order are observed (*DH*, 2). While it is undeniable that a development has occurred, the two documents do not contradict each other. *Quanta Cura* does not call for the universal establishment of Catholicism as the state religion, nor does *DH* claim that the civil authority should have no duties at all to the Catholic faith except to maintain public peace. "Public order" as described by *DH* is a larger concept than "public peace." It has three components: safeguarding the rights of all citizens, public peace, and public morality (*DH*, 7). The "rights of all citizens" and "public morality," while here left somewhat vague, may be understood as including respect for the rights of the Church and for "the objective moral order," which the Church interprets with authority (*DH*, 7, 14).[53]

The case of Leo XIII is more complex. In *Immortale Dei*, for example, he reaffirms many of the condemnations of Gregory XVI in *Mirari Vos* and of Pius IX in the *Syllabus of Errors*. But while reiterating the teaching of his predecessors about naturalistic rationalism and state secularism, he speaks in more measured terms, making it clear, as they had not, that the Church is not opposed to true progress, civil liberties, and participatory forms of government. Unlike Gregory XVI and Pius IX, Leo does not content himself with condemnations. In place of the rejected theories, he sets forth the principles of a Catholic social and political theory, grounded in the philosophy of Aristotle and Thomas Aquinas.

John Courtney Murray, on the basis of an exhaustive study of the Leonine corpus, concludes that there is a certain tension in Leo's thinking between his desire to uphold the secular character of the state and his approval of the confessional state, in which the prince had a paternal relationship to the people. According to the first model, which may be called "constitutional," the state would have no competence (even indirect or instrumental) in the religious area, but according to the second, political sovereigns would have a responsibility for the common good in all its aspects, including the moral, the spiritual, and the religious.[54]

If Leo had taught that the confessional state is a universal and exceptionless norm, his teaching could be difficult to reconcile with *DH*, which treats the confessional state as a special case and refers to it only in a hypothetical clause (*DH*, 6). But this aspect of Leo's teaching was in Murray's view conditioned by the situation of his day in countries where the faithful, because of low educational standards, were ill prepared to meet the onslaughts of secular liberalism as it sought to secure the apostasy of the masses and establish a naturalist, atheistic order. The pope, writing as a pastor concerned for his flock, took a position that Murray regards as "reasonable and prudent, in view of the circumstances."[55]

According to Murray, then, the paternalist conception of secular government may be considered an emergency measure, adopted to meet a crisis.[56] The center of gravity of Leo's thought lay elsewhere—in striving to awaken the consciousness of the world to the true dignity of human persons. If this be true, *DH* may be judged faithful to the profound intentions of Leo XIII, even if not to all his verbal formulations.

Brian W. Harrison, like Murray, holds that there is no contradiction, but he adopts a different rationale.[57] He holds that Leo XIII's position on the obligation for the state to profess the true faith expresses the constant position of the Church, taught by all the popes since Pius IX and reaffirmed, though in muted terms, by *DH*. Leo XIII, he holds, was not speaking simply in the context of certain Catholic countries. He was familiar with the American system of separation of church and state and appreciated its practical benefits for the Church but found it unsatisfactory from the standpoint of revelation.[58] Harrison quotes from Leo's encyclical *Immortale Dei* to the effect that society as such, and the government through which it acts, has a duty to recognize the truth of Catholicism. Objectively, the obligation is to worship God "in that way in which he has shown to be his will."[59] This doctrine, already taught by Pius IX in the *Syllabus*, was to be reaffirmed by Pius XI in his encyclical on Christ the King, *Quas Primas*.[60] Establishment of the Catholic Church is therefore the norm. In principle the claim of the Catholic Church to be the one true religion is binding on the state.

Murray himself, according to Harrison, disliked arrangements that gave a juridically privileged position to any religious group, even the Catholic Church. In the draft of 1964, corresponding to Murray's views, the Declaration asserted that the state was incompetent to make judgments about truth in religious matters, but this statement was dropped in all subsequent drafts.[61] In like manner the final version eliminated the ambiguous statement in the draft presented at the beginning of the 1965 session that the civil authority should "restrict itself to the things of this world" and should not "involve itself in those things which concern man's orientation to God." Instead the final text asserted that religious acts "transcend by their very nature the order of terrestrial and temporal order" (*DH*, 3).

DH's assertion concerning the incompetence of the state "to direct or inhibit religious activity" (*DH*, 3) is a rejection of the state's authority to usurp the magisterial role of the pope and the bishops. It does not deny that the holders of political office are obliged to discern the truth of Catholicism and to reflect the results of that discernment in appropriate ways.[62]

The general principle for interpreting these texts must be the affirmation in the opening paragraphs of *DH* that the Council "leaves untouched traditional Catholic doctrine on the moral duty of men and societies toward . . . the one Church of Christ" (*DH*, 1).[63] Even this text leaves a possible ambiguity, since it could be understood as placing an obligation on society but not on the government. But in response to questions that had been raised, Bishop De Smedt in his final *relatio* cleared up the ambiguity. He explained that the text, as revised, did not overlook but clearly recalled Leo XIII's teaching on "the duties of the public authority (*potestatis publicae*)" toward the true religion.[64] De Smedt's *relatio*, as Harrison explains, is the only official commentary on the text of *DH*.[65]

Vatican II, however, does not simply reaffirm the teaching of popes prior to Pius XII. It makes a real advance by treating the dignity and freedom of the person as the common concern of civil and religious society. Church and state do not confront each other as two powers over a passive mass of humanity. Each of them is at the service of human persons, who play an active role in bringing about harmony. Without being the legally established religion, Catholicism can exert an influence through members of the government, who may be expected to act according to their faith and to engage in private and public acts of worship. The people, likewise, express their religious commitments by voting for certain candidates for public office and by proposing, approving, and applying particular laws. Juridical establishment is only one of many ways—and perhaps one of the less effective—by which the Church can have a social impact.[66]

Religious Freedom

Although the duty of the state toward the true religion is closely connected with the religious freedom of citizens, the two issues should be distinguished, because in any given arrangement between Church and state, various degrees and forms of religious freedom are possible.

In *Quanta Cura* Pius IX approves the judgment of his predecessor Gregory XVI to the effect that it is "insanity" (*deliramentum*) to assert with Lamennais "that liberty of conscience and worship is each man's personal right, which ought to be legally proclaimed and asserted in every rightly ordered society; and that a right resides in the citizens to an absolute liberty, which should be restrained by no authority, whether ecclesiastical or civil, whereby they may be able openly and publicly to manifest and declare any of their ideas whatever, by word of mouth, by the press, and in any other way."[67] Following up on this principle, the *Syllabus of Errors* denies that "each individual is free to embrace and profess the religion that he judges true by the light of reason" (Prop. 15; DS 2915).

Read outside their historical context, these condemnations might seem to contradict the assertions of *DH* that all human persons have a right to religious freedom and are not to be coerced by any human power to act in a manner contrary to their own beliefs (*DH*, 2). But the statements can be reconciled. In denying the citizen's freedom to embrace any religion, Proposition 15 of the *Syllabus* need not be interpreted as favoring religious coercion. The statement may be understood as rejecting only the moral right to profess error. The reference to the "light of reason" in the same proposition should presumably be read in the context of Proposition 3: "Human reason, without any relation at all to God, is the sole judge of true and false, good and evil, is a law unto itself, and is sufficient by its natural powers to procure the welfare of men and peoples." According to Catholic teaching, the articles of faith are not demonstrated by autonomous human reason but believed on the authority of God the revealer.[68] Faith requires a free and willing submission of our judgment to the Word of God, to which our minds are drawn by the interior movement of grace.

What is being consistently opposed in *Quanta Cura* and the source documents of the *Syllabus* is a rationalistic naturalism that makes autonomous human reason the supreme judge of truth and goodness, allowing no place for a free submission to divine revelation. *DH*, on the contrary, was insisting on the freedom of individual persons and groups of persons to accept and live up to the truth disclosed to them through the biddings of their conscience and the solicitations of grace. When Pius IX rejected freedom of conscience and of worship, therefore, he was not opposing what Vatican II would later approve.[69]

Leo XIII in *Libertas Praestantissimum* elaborated on the doctrine of Pius IX. True liberty, he maintained, is a mark of human dignity. It consists not only in a natural or psychological freedom, whereby we are responsible for our acts, but in a moral freedom—the capacity to do what we ought. The so-called modern freedoms of worship, speech, teaching, and conscience are unacceptable if freedom is too loosely defined. Liberty of worship cannot mean an entitlement to choose any religion or none according to one's pleasure.[70] Liberty of speech and academic freedom should not extend to unfounded and deceptive statements.[71] Liberty of conscience is desirable if it means the right to follow the dictates of God as made known through natural religion and revelation, but it turns into license if it means the right to do whatever one pleases.[72]

Because of his high esteem for human dignity and freedom, Leo XIII set the Church on the course that would be followed, with progressively deeper penetration, by Pius XI, Pius XII, and John XXIII. Murray therefore feels entitled to render the judgment: "The legitimate conclusion is that between Leo XIII and the Second Vatican Council there was an authentic development of doctrine in the sense of Vincent of Lerins, 'an authentic progress, not a change of the faith.'"[73]

As we have seen, the progress was gradual. New distinctions were introduced only as new situations emerged. Leo XIII saw the necessity to distinguish between the different meanings that could be attached to terms such as "freedom of conscience" and "freedom of religion." A further stage was reached when Pius XI distinguished between "freedom of conscience" (i.e., the independence of conscience with regard to God), which he condemned, and "freedom of consciences" (i.e., willing submission to the sense of duty), which the Church defended in opposition to the totalitarian state.[74] Still another major breakthrough was achieved by Pius XII in his address to jurists, *Ci Riesce*, in which he teaches that the state may sometimes be obliged to tolerate immorality or error for the sake of a more general good, even though it has the physical power to repress these evils.[75]

John XXIII, in *Pacem in Terris*, came closest to *DH* by building the principle of freedom into his theory of society. The dignity of the human person, he points out, requires that all citizens be permitted to act responsibly, according to their intelligence and free will. The process from Gregory XVI to Vatican II, therefore, is not a passage from negation to affirmation but a gradual perception of the theological implications of human dignity as taught in the immemorial tradition of the Church.

The case against continuity has been strongly argued by J. Robert Dionne in the book mentioned above. He holds that all the popes up to, and perhaps including, John XXIII denied, at least implicitly, that non-Catholic Christians or non-Christians could have a strict right to worship according to their beliefs. But *DH*, he believes, reversed their teaching on this point. To make the difference clear, he asks: "Does a human being in the present economy of salvation have the *objective* right to worship God in the manner in which a responsible use of intellect indicates he or she should?"[76] Dionne does not contend that either the popes or Vatican II directly answered this question, but he finds indications of a negative answer in the papal teaching prior to Vatican II, whereas "the inner logic of *Dignitatis Humanae* suggests an affirmative answer" to the question.[77] Had Dionne's question been put to them, the popes and the Council would have admitted, I believe, that the responsible use of the intellect creates an "objective right" to perform objectively good acts of worship, but these popes would have denied that it creates a right to perform objectively disordered acts, such as human sacrifice or temple prostitution.

As Murray notes in his commentary, *DH* does not base its right to the free exercise of religion on "freedom of conscience."[78] The Council avoided teaching that anyone can have an objective right to do something that is objectively wrong. Religious freedom, strictly speaking, is not a right to *do* anything. In technical terms, it is not a *ius agendi* but a kind of *ius exigendi*—a right to make a demand on the state. Negatively, it is a right not to be coerced in one's religious life unless one is jeopardizing public order. Positively, it is a right to be supported in one's quest to know religious truth and live accordingly.[79] This twofold right, rooted in the dignity of the person, is not a merely "civil" right—one that could be conferred or abrogated by the state—but a natural right that may and should be protected by civil law. The right, moreover, does not depend upon the individual's living up to the obligation incumbent upon all to seek the truth and adhere to it (*DH*, 2). The recognition of this distinctive *ius exigendi* is, I believe, one of the most significant advances of Vatican II. It is a true development that harmonizes with the traditional theology concerning human freedom and dignity, and also with the traditional teaching, reaffirmed by Bishop De Smedt in his final *relatio* on *DH*, that there can be no right to hold or disseminate error.[80]

The *Catechism of the Catholic Church* supports the interpretation of Bishop De Smedt. Citing both Leo XIII and *DH*, it declares:

> The right to religious liberty is neither a moral license to adhere to error, nor a supposed right to error, but rather a natural right of the human person to civil liberty, i.e., immunity, within just limits, from external constraint in religious matters by political authorities. This natural right is to be acknowledged in the juridical order of society in such a way that it constitutes a civil right. (CCC §2108)

DH should be read in the context of Vatican II as a whole and with the realization that it, like the Declaration on the Jews, was at one point chapters of the Decree on Ecumenism. The Council's teaching on religious freedom, therefore, is intrinsically connected with its teaching on ecumenism and interreligious relations. Whereas earlier popes and councils often seem to have assumed that the teaching and worship of these bodies are objectively evil, Vatican II gives a more favorable appraisal. Non-Catholic churches and communities can be centers of genuine faith, dispense certain valid sacraments, and foster authentic holiness. The Holy Spirit has not refrained from using them as means of salvation.[81] Judaism, as the root from which Christianity arose, has a precious heritage of revealed truth.[82] Religions such as Hinduism and Buddhism, though they do not profess biblical monotheism, contain elements of truth and holiness, greatly esteemed by the Catholic Church.[83] Statements such as these suggest that the teachings and practices of non-Catholic Christian and non-Christian religious groups are often good. When evil is present, it may be tolerated according to the principles of Leo XIII and Pius XII, which the Council did not abrogate.[84]

WHAT KIND OF DEVELOPMENT?

At the opening of this essay a distinction was made among three ways of understanding the development achieved by *DH*. The three positions may now be evaluated.

Representing the first position in its first form, Lefebvre and the traditionalists, including Michael Davis, contend that there is a conflict and that

Vatican II was unfaithful to the Catholic tradition. Dionne, representing the other form of the first position, argues that Vatican II corrected the earlier teaching of the ordinary papal magisterium. It reversed two key teachings, he believes: that Catholicism ought to be established as the religion of the state and that the state should not tolerate non-Catholic religious groups except as necessary for the sake of the common good.

The findings of the present study do not support this first position in either of its forms. Regarding the official adoption of Catholicism as the religion of the state, the preconciliar magisterium never taught that Catholicism must be established; it condemned only the view that it may never be established. Vatican II, for its part, provided for circumstances in which Catholicism could be granted special legal recognition (*DH*, 6). As for religious freedom, *DH* never affirmed that individuals or groups were entitled to follow and propagate erroneous views—a position that would indeed have overturned the tradition. *DH* recognized the right of such individuals and groups to be free from coercion and to enjoy the protection of the laws unless they violated the demands of public order. It left intact the teaching of the popes on religious toleration.

The second position, that a reversal was made on the level of conceptual formulation but not on the level of deep intention, has been impressively argued by John Courtney Murray. He appeals to the transcendental philosophy of Bernard Lonergan to justify his view that certain magisterial statements of the nineteenth-century popes were historically conditioned and need not be literally accepted in our day. Confronted by Leo XIII's "paternalist" support of the confessional state, Murray denounces the "classicist" view that "what matters is what he [Leo XIII] said—the propositions that he put down on paper."[85]

Murray's distinction is not between principles and applications but between the "profound intention" of the popes and their historically conditioned formulations. "The progress," he writes:

> cannot be explained by the facile categories of "principles" and "applications." The principles of faith—and even more, those of reason—are not in the genus of Platonic ideas, eternally immutable, given all at once in perfect understanding, awaiting only occasions for their application in history. On the contrary, the Church matures in her understanding of the principles themselves. And a principle newly understood is new as a principle. Besides, the new growth of this understanding is normally achieved under the tutelage of experience, both religious and secular.[86]

Murray's transcendental argument raises difficult questions, far beyond the scope of the present essay. For example, does the magisterium have the authority to proclaim any specific moral and dogmatic norms as permanently and universally binding? Without going into these difficult matters, one may question Murray's contention that Pius IX and Leo XIII, in the statements that he rejects, were not intending to formulate Catholic doctrine. Brian Harrison, in his reply, shows that the popes from Gregory XVI through Pius XII consistently taught that the political community has an obligation from divine law to acknowledge and support the Catholic faith. To reject this position can only be dissent.[87]

The most satisfactory position, I believe, is the third: that there has been true progress without reversal, even on the plane of propositional declarations. The teaching has developed in important ways but has not undergone contradictory change. In describing the development we may suitably follow Harrison, who takes note of three features.[88]

First of all, *DH* registered a change of emphasis, corresponding to a changed context. Following in the footsteps of Pius XII and John XXIII, the Council saw fit to speak in the perspectives of a world-consciousness rather than within the relatively narrow confines of Catholic Christendom. In addition, Vatican II presupposed a more optimistic assessment of non-Catholic Christianity and of non-Christian religions than had been current before the middle of the twentieth century. And finally, *DH* preferred to speak in the context of what was de facto most common, whereas previous papal teaching had concentrated on what was de jure most perfect. This threefold change of emphasis was in harmony with the missionary, ecumenical, and phenomenological orientations of Vatican II as a whole.

In a second respect, *DH* marks a development insofar as it spells out fresh implications of traditional doctrines such as the dignity of the human person, the freedom of the act of faith, and the limited role of the secular state. In this context *DH* is more consistent than some doctors of the Church, such as Thomas Aquinas, who taught that heretics and apostates should be subject to physical compulsion in living up to their baptismal commitment.[89]

In the third place, *DH* makes an advance by clearing up certain ambiguities in previous magisterial teaching. Although the popes had recognized that the state could and even should sometimes tolerate false worship, they had not answered the question whether groups in error had a right to worship and proclaim their faith. *DH* affirmed that they did have a true moral right (not a merely civil right) to exist and act without external coercion in ways that favor religious life. Although the particular actions of these groups are not always objectively right, they may be immune from coercion by the civil authority.

DH is often dismissed as a belated affirmation by the Catholic Church of a principle that had long been recognized in constitutional democracies and in other religious traditions. But as the preceding analysis shows, Vatican

II did not take over a ready-made doctrine from any non-Catholic source, least of all from individualistic liberalism. It forged a new position in line with the "traditional Catholic doctrine on the moral duty of men and societies toward the true religion and the one Church of Christ" (*DH*, 1). The Council proceeded on the understanding that all human persons are made for the truth and that the state itself has obligations toward the true faith.

POSTCONCILIAR DEVELOPMENTS

The developments in *DH* have proved themselves by their broad acceptance and by their fruitfulness in the pontificates of Paul VI[90] and John Paul II,[91] both of whom had supported the Declaration at the Second Vatican Council and enlarged upon it after the Council. Since Vatican II, the doctrine has continued to develop along the three lines already indicated.

In terms of emphasis, the first facet of development, the concept of religious freedom, has to be proposed today in ways that challenge the pervasive relativist agnosticism. John Paul II ceaselessly proclaimed that human freedom does not mean that everything is permitted. Freedom exists for the sake of orienting human beings toward the truth, which is fully given in Christ. The truth revealed in Christ does not enslave but on the contrary makes one free (Jn 8:32). Giving a Christological focus to the concept of religious freedom, John Paul II insists that a new culture of freedom, finding its basis in the unique dignity of the children of God, "includes the right to discover and freely to accept Jesus Christ, who is man's true good."[92]

The second aspect of development consists in the discovery of new implications. An example from the pontificate of John Paul II would be the Church's need to conduct a collective examination of conscience concerning the intolerance and violence that have at times been practiced in the service of truth. Such violence, according to John Paul II, runs contrary to *DH*'s affirmation that "the truth cannot impose itself except by virtue of its own truth, as it makes its entrance into the mind at once gently and with power" (*DH*, 1).[93]

In the third place, the ambiguities that have occasioned conflicting interpretations of *DH* are being addressed. As we have seen, some have understood the Declaration as disapproving of the special recognition of Catholicism as the state religion. Some have thought that it endorsed a strict separation, barring the state from any responsibility toward the true religion. Some, finally, have imagined that *DH* taught that people have a conscientious right to disseminate their erroneous views concerning religious matters. The present essay is submitted with the hope of dissipating these and other misunderstandings, thereby contributing to the postconciliar phase of the development.

No development within history may be seen as terminal. As Newman said long ago, true developments prove themselves by their capacity of expansion. "A living idea becomes many, yet remains one."[94] The tradition of religious freedom continually gives rise to new insights as it encounters new cultural situations.

NOTES

1. *Dignitatis Humanae*, section 1, in *The Documents of Vatican II*, ed. Walter M. Abbott and Joseph Gallagher (New York: America Press, 1966). Further citations of this document will be given parenthetically in the text with *Dignitatis Humanae* abbreviated as *DH*. The author has at some points modified the translation in the Abbott-Gallagher edition.

2. John Courtney Murray, "Introduction to *Dignitatis Humanae*," in *The Documents of Vatican II*, 673.

3. John Courtney Murray, "Vers une intelligence du développement de la doctrine de l'Eglise sur la liberté religieuse," in *La Liberté Religieuse: Déclaration "Dignitatis humanae personae,"* ed. J. Hamer and Yves Congar (Paris: Ed. du Cerf, 1967), 111.

4. John Henry Newman, *An Essay on the Development of Christian Doctrine* (Notre Dame, IN: University of Notre Dame Press, 1989).

5. Murray, "Vers une intelligence," 114–15. Roger Aubert has made the same point in various places. See, for example, "L'enseignement du Magistère ecclésiastique au XIXe siècle sur le libéralisme," in *Tolérance et communauté humaine* (Tournai: Casterman, 1952), 75–103.

6. Roger Aubert, "La liberté religieuse du Syllabus de 1864 à nos jours," in *Essais sur la liberté religieuse* (Paris: A. Fayard, 1965), 13–25, at 17–18.

7. Pius XII, Allocution *Ci Riesce*, AAS 45 (1953): 797; trans. "Religion in the Community of Nations," in *The Major Addresses of Pope Pius XII*, ed. Vincent A. Yzermans, vol. 1, *Selected Addresses* (St. Paul, MN: North Central Publishing Co., 1961), 272–73.

8. Pius XII, "Religion in the Community of Nations," 276–77; cf. Murray, "Vers une intelligence," 142.

9. John XXIII, *Pacem in Terris*, section 79, in *The Gospel of Peace and Justice*, ed. Joseph Gremillion (Maryknoll, NY: Orbis, 1976), 218.

10. Ibid., 37, 209.

11. The Latin text of *Pacem in Terris* §14 reads: "In hominis iuribus hoc quoque numerandum est, ut et Deum, ad rectam conscientiae suae normam, venerari possit, et religionem privatim publice profiteri," AAS 55 (1963): 260. The English translation reproduced in *The Gospel of Peace and Justice*, 204, reads: "Every human being has the right to honor God according to the dictates of an upright conscience, and the right to profess his religion privately and publicly." In the original "upright" modifies

"norm" rather than "conscience." The language carefully avoids settling the disputed question of whether a sincere but erroneous conscience can be "upright." In the tradition the question had been answered in the negative by Thomists and in the affirmative by Scotus, Suárez, and their followers.

12. Pius XII, radio message, December 24, 1944; AAS 37 (1945): 22; quoted by John Courtney Murray in *The Problem of Religious Freedom* (Westminster, MD: Newman, 1965), 65; cf. Murray, "Vers une intelligence," 141.

13. Pius XII, radio message, 22.

14. John XXIII, *Pacem in Terris*, 12.

15. See *Gaudium et Spes*, sections 4 and 44.

16. "The tendencies to which we have referred, however, do clearly show that the men of our time have become increasingly conscious of their dignity as human persons. This awareness prompts them to share in the public administration of their country, while it also accounts for the demand that their own inalienable and inviolable rights be protected by law. It also requires that government officials be chosen in conformity with constitutional procedures and perform their special functions within the limits of law." *Pacem in Terris*, section 79, in *Gospel of Peace and Justice*, 218.

17. This "Closing Message of the Council to Rulers" was actually read by Cardinal Achille Liénard of Lille; text in Abbott, *Documents*, 730. Murray ascribes it to Paul VI. See *Documents* 693, n. 53.

18. Newman, *An Essay on the Development of Christian Doctrine*, 169–206.

19. Leo XIII, *Immortale Dei* (1885), section 5, in *The Papal Encyclicals 1878–1903*, ed. Claudia Carlen (Wilmington, NC: McGrath, 1981), 107–8.

20. Leo XIII, encyclical *Rerum Novarum* (1891), section 42: "If we turn now to things external and material, the first thing of all to secure is to save unfortunate working people from the cruelty of men of greed, who use human beings as mere instruments for money-making." In *The Papal Encyclicals 1878–1903*, 252.

21. Leo XIII in *Rerum Novarum* distinguished between the dignity that accrues to man as a free and rational creature (6–7) and the added dignity that comes from being called to eternal life thanks to the redemptive work of Christ (21). In *The Papal Encyclicals 1878–1903*, 242–43.

22. Council of Trent, Decree on Justification, canons 4 and 5, in *Enchiridion Symbolorum, Definitionum, et Declarationum de Rebus Fidei et Morum*, 32nd ed., ed. Henricus Denzinger and Adolphus Schönmetzer (Freiburg: Herder, 1963), 1554–55.

23. Vatican Council I, Dogmatic Constitution *Dei Filius*, chapter 3, canon 5, in *Enchiridion*, 3035.

24. Leo XIII, *Libertas Praestantissimum* (1888), section 1: "Liberty, the highest of natural endowments, being the portion of intellectual or rational natures, confers on man this dignity—that he is 'in the hand of his counsel' and has power over his actions." In *The Papal Encyclicals 1878–1903*, 169.

25. Leo XIII, *Immortale Dei*, 36, 115.

26. Leo XIII, *Libertas*, 8, 171.

27. Ibid., 33, 178.

28. Suárez, *De Fide*, disp. 18, sec. 3, no. 6; cf. José Pereira, "Are Ecumenical Councils Infallible?" *Josephinum Journal of Theology* 4 (Summer/Fall 1997): 40–50, at 48.

29. Suárez, *De Fide*, disp. 18, sec. 8, no. 6. See Pereira, "Are Ecumenical Councils Infallible?" 48.

30. Leo XIII, *Immortale Dei*, 14, 110; *Libertas*, 21, 176.

31. Leo XIII, *Immortale Dei*, 13, 110.

32. Ibid., 12, 110.

33. Vatican II, *Acta Synodalia*, II/5:485–95.

34. Cantero, *Acta Synodalia*, IV/1:302–5.

35. Garrone, *Acta Synodalia*, III/2:533–35.

36. Shehan, *Acta Synodalia*, IV/1:396–97.

37. J. Robert Dionne takes note of these interventions but characterizes them as theologically naive, oversimplified, and tendentious. See his *The Papacy and the Church* (New York: Philosophical Library, 1987), 182–89, esp. 183.

38. John Courtney Murray has defended the continuity, especially in his "Vers une intelligence." See also the articles in his *Religious Liberty: Catholic Struggles with Pluralism/John Courtney Murray*, ed. J. Leon Hooper (Louisville, KY: Westminster/ John Knox, 1993), with bibliography. For other defenses of continuity, see Bertrand de Margerie, *Liberté religieuse et Règne du Christ* (Paris: Cerf, 1988); Brian W. Harrison, *Religious Liberty and Contraception* (Melbourne, Australia: John XXIII Fellowship Co-op., 1988); and Aubert, "La liberté religieuse."

39. Schema "De Libertate Religiosa," *Acta Synodalia* III/8: 427–29.

40. Jérôme Hamer, "Histoire du texte de la Déclaration," in *La Liberté religieuse*, 55–110, at 86.

41. De Smedt, final *relatio*, *Acta Synodalia* IV/6: 719.

42. Michael Davies, *Apologia pro Marcel Lefebvre, Part I, 1905–1976* (Kansas City, MO: Angelus Press, 1979), 436. The objections of Archbishop Lefebvre are set forth in his intervention of September 20, 1965, in *Acta Synodalia Sacr. Conc. Oec. Vaticani II*, IV/1, 409–11.

43. Juan Luis Segundo, *Theology and the Church* (Minneapolis, MN: Winston, 1985), 5–6.

44. Daniel C. Maguire, "Moral Inquiry and Religious Assent," in *Contraception: Authority and Dissent*, ed. Charles E. Curran (New York: Herder and Herder, 1969), 143. See also the discussions of Gregory XVI, Pius IX, and the *Syllabus* in Charles E. Curran and Robert E. Hunt, *Dissent in and for the Church* (New York: Sheed & Ward, 1969), 77–80.

45. In addition to the examples already given, see Richard A. McCormick, "Moral Doctrine: Stability and Development," *Proceedings of the Catholic Theological Society of America* 54 (1999): 92; and John T. Noonan, "Development in Moral Doctrine," *Theological Studies* 54 (1993): 662–77, esp. 667–68.

46. Pius IX, Encyclical *Quanta Cura*, section 3, in *The Papal Encyclicals 1740–1878*, ed. Claudia Carlen (Wilmington, NC: McGrath, 1981), 382. The parenthetical (also), not present in the Latin, has been added for clarity in this edition.

47. *Syllabus of Errors*, in *Enchiridion*, 2955, 2977.

48. Leo XIII, *Immortale Dei*, 35, 115.

49. Ibid., 36, 115.

50. On the question of the interpretation of the *Syllabus*, John Henry Newman's chapter in his "Letter to the Duke of Norfolk" still repays reading. He calls the *Syl-*

labus "nothing more than a digest of certain Errors made by an anonymous writer." It has no more authority, he says, than a table of contents. See *Newman and Gladstone: The Vatican Decrees*, ed. Alvan Ryan (Notre Dame, IN: University of Notre Dame, 1960), 150–66, especially 151 and 155.

51. Aubert, "L'enseignement du Magistère," 92.

52. Pius IX, *Quanta Cura* 3, 382.

53. On the difference between the "public peace" and "public order," see Harrison, *Religious Liberty and Contraception*, 102–11.

54. Murray, "Vers une intelligence," 117–39, esp. 125; and *The Problem of Religious Freedom*, 55–60.

55. Murray, "Vers une intelligence," 127.

56. Ibid.

57. Brian W. Harrison, "John Courtney Murray: A Reliable Interpreter of *Dignitatis Humanae?*" in *We Hold These Truths and More*, ed. Donald J. D'Elia and Stephen M. Krason (Steubenville, OH: Franciscan University Press, 1993), 134–65. See also his "Vatican II and Religious Liberty: Contradiction or Continuity?" *Catholic Dossier* 6 (March–April 2000): 21–30. The same issue of *Catholic Dossier* contains several other valuable articles supporting continuity.

58. Ibid., 149, quoting Leo XIII, who writes in his encyclical *Longinqua* (1895): "It would be very erroneous to draw the conclusion that in America is to be sought the type of the most desirable status of the Church, or that it would be universally lawful or expedient for State and Church to be, as in America, dissevered and divorced." *The Papal Encyclicals 1878–1903*, 6, 364–65.

59. Leo XIII, *Immortale Dei* 6, 108–9.

60. Pius XI, encyclical *Quas Primas* (1925), esp. 32: "Nations will be reminded by the annual celebration of this feast that not only private individuals but also rulers and princes are bound to give public honour and obedience to Christ." In *The Papal Encyclicals 1903–1939*, ed. Claudia Carlen (Wilmington, NC: McGrath, 1981), 278.

61. Harrison, "John Courtney Murray," 158.

62. Ibid., 139.

63. Ibid., 155–57.

64. De Smedt, final *relatio*, *Acta Synodalia* IV/6: 719.

65. Harrison, "John Courtney Murray," 157.

66. In the preceding paragraph I have drawn some ideas from Bertrand de Margerie, "Liberté civile et obligation éthique en matière religieuse," *La Vie Spirituelle* 144 (May–June 1990): 355–71.

67. Pius IX, *Quanta Cura*, 3 (quoting from Gregory XVI, *Mirari Vos*), 382.

68. Vatican I, Constitution *Dei Filius*, chapter 3, in *Enchiridion*, 3008, 3010.

69. Murray, "Vers une intelligence," 111–12; Aubert, "Liberté religieuse," 13–20; Harrison, *Religious Liberty*, 33–51.

70. *Libertas*, 19, 175.

71. Ibid., 23–24, 176.

72. Ibid., 21, 175; 30, 178.

73. Murray, "Vers une intelligence," 138.

74. Pius XI, encyclical *Non Abbiamo Bisogno* (1931), 41, *in The Papal Encyclicals 1903–1939*, 453.

75. Pius XII, "Religion in the Community of Nations," 274.

76. Dionne, *The Papacy and the Church*, 148; italics in original.

77. Ibid., 171.

78. This point is powerfully made by Murray in his commentary on *Dignitatis Humanae* in *Documents of Vatican II*, 679, note 5.

79. *DH* states that government must not only abstain from coercion but must also "help create conditions favorable to the fostering of religious life" (*DH*, 6). Harrison, to whom I am indebted for the concept of *ius exigendi*, recognizes only the negative aspect. He calls it "a right of an entirely passive or 'negative' kind: a right simply *to be left alone* by other human beings—'immunity from coercion.'" See his *Religious Liberty and Contraception*, 129; cf. 113–18.

80. Bishop De Smedt in his final *relatio* of November 19, 1965, declared on behalf of the Secretariat: "Nowhere is it affirmed—nor could it be rightly affirmed, as is evident—that there is any right to propagate error," *Acta Synodalia* IV/6: 725; cf. Pius XII, "Religion in the Community of Nations," 274.

81. Vatican II, Decree on Ecumenism (*Unitatis Redintegratio*), 2, in *The Documents of Vatican II*, 343–44.

82. Vatican II, Declaration on Non-Christian Religions (*Nostra Aetate*), 4, in *The Documents of Vatican II*, 663–67.

83. Ibid., 2.

84. It may be a lacuna in *DH* and, in Vatican II as a whole, that the traditional concept of tolerance is nowhere mentioned. But it is not repudiated. On the continuing relevance of this concept, see Max Seckler, "Religionsfreiheit und Toleranz," *Theologische Quartalschrift* 175 (1995): 1–18.

85. Murray, *Problem of Religious Freedom*, 88.

86. Murray, "Vers une intelligence," 138–39.

87. Harrison, "John Courtney Murray," 142–43.

88. Harrison, *Religious Liberty*, 123–30. In the following paragraphs I shall develop Harrison's argument with certain variations of my own.

89. Ibid., 125, with citation from Thomas Aquinas, *Summa Theologiae* 2-2, q. 10, a. 8c.

90 On Paul VI and *DH*, see *Religious Liberty: Paul VI and 'Dignitatis Humanae.' A Symposium Sponsored by The Istituto Paolo VI and The Catholic University of America* (Washington, DC: The Catholic University of America Press, 1993).

91. Avery Cardinal Dulles, "John Paul II on Religious Freedom: Themes from Vatican II," *The Thomist* 65 (2001): 161–78; Herminio Rico, *John Paul II and the Legacy of Dignitatis Humanae* (Washington, DC: Georgetown University Press, 2002).

92. John Paul II, *Centesimus Annus*, 29, in *The Encyclicals of Pope John Paul II*, ed. J. Michael Miller, C.S.B. (Huntington, IN: Our Sunday Visitor Publishing Division, 1996), 618; cf. *Redemptor Hominis*, 12, in *The Papal Encyclicals 1958–1981*, ed. Claudia Carlen (Wilmington, NC: McGrath, 1981), 253–54.

93. John Paul II, *Tertio Millennio Adveniente* (Boston: Pauline Books & Media, 1994), section 35.

94. Newman, An *Essay on the Development of Christian Doctrine*, 188.

Dignitatis Humanae, the Catholic Conception of the State, and Public Morality

Francis P. Canavan, S.J.

$\mathcal{A}$mong certain conservative Catholics there is a nostalgia for the "confessional state," in which the state formally professes a belief in the Catholic religion as the one true faith revealed by God and makes the Catholic Church the established church of the nation. Practical accommodations to the presence of non-Catholic citizens and churches can be made. But that is done on the "hypothesis" that, for the sake of public peace, such citizens and their churches should be granted legal status and protection. On this view, the Catholic "thesis" is that a Catholic people must profess and defend its faith by making it the religion of the state with a privileged position in law that is denied to dissenters.

This "confessionalist" teaching is found in numerous papal documents prior to Vatican II's Declaration on Religious Freedom (*Dignitatis Humanae* [*DH*]). Since *DH*, and its seemingly principled embrace of religious freedom, there has been a debate over the question whether the Declaration constituted a reversal of established Catholic doctrine and is therefore of questionable validity. I will leave that question for theologians to answer and confine myself to three basic points in this essay. First, what the Church actually changed in *DH* was the conception of the state on which the previous "confessionalist" doctrine was based, not its teaching on its own authority or on the duty of its members to uphold and defend that authority. Second, a Catholic defense of limited constitutional government predates *DH*—even if all the political implications of that defense for religious freedom were not developed fully by its proponents. And third (and perhaps as a way of reassuring "confessionalists" to some extent), *DH*'s conception of the state in no way entails an embrace of the liberal view of church-state relations and public morality.

I

I will begin by making the practical point that the confessional state was never an unqualified benefit to the Church. When the teaching or practice of a heretical religion was punished through the imposition of severe legal sanctions, it did not work in the long run. For example, we see that it did not prevent the Protestant Reformation or the Enlightenment. On the contrary, where laws against heresy were enforced by such sanctions, they bred a deepseated hatred of the faith and of the Church. (This was true, by the way, not only in Catholic countries such as Spain but in the Protestant England of Good Queen Bess, where the Act of Supremacy made her the head of the Church and inflicted severe penalties on those who refused to accept her supremacy. It is a nice question whether it was more dreadful to be burned at the stake in Spain or hanged, drawn, and quartered in England. What is clear is that neither one form of punishment nor the other fostered love of the persecuting church but rather a festering hatred.)

Even where the penalties did not involve the infliction of physical pain (for example, the English and Irish penal laws restricting property ownership by Catholic laymen), they bred fear rather than devotion. As someone remarked in the journal *Commonweal* several decades ago, when it became possible to apostasize without suffering civil penalties, millions cheerfully apostasized. It should therefore occur to prudent churchmen that protecting religion through the use of criminal law is counterproductive.

But one need not resort to prudential arguments alone to undercut the "confessionalist" argument. It might also occur to churchmen that the use of criminal law to protect the Catholic faith does not harmonize well with the teachings of Christ. He did indeed present his listeners with a clear-cut choice: either accept his invitation to eternal life or lose it, but he did not advocate civil or criminal penalties for those who rejected the invitation. As Pope John Paul II has said in his apostolic letter "On the Dignity and Vocation of Women (*Mulieris Dignitatem*)," "All of God's action in human history respects the free will of the human 'I.'"[1] Or, as the new *Catechism of the Catholic Church* (quoting *DH*) tells us, "The act of faith is of its very nature a free act."[2] This is not a lesson learned from liberalism and its radically individualist notion of moral autonomy but one implicit in the Christian faith from its very inception: acceptance of the faith has to be a free act.

The union of church and state, then, has not been an unmixed blessing to the Church or to the faith it has taught. Indeed, the very terms "church" and "state" imply the use of a conceptual apparatus that differs greatly from that employed during the Middle Ages, when theologians such as St. Thomas

Aquinas attempted to develop systematic treatments of the proper relationship between the spiritual and temporal spheres. During the Middle Ages, there was but one Christian society, the res publica Christiana, the commonwealth of Christendom. In it there were two distinct jurisdictions, often referred to as *regnum* and *sacerdotium*, the royal and priestly powers. Popes and emperors, kings and bishops, quarreled over the lines between these jurisdictions and over which of the two was ultimately superior, but they took the Christian commonwealth as a given reality.

This distinction of the two jurisdictions within a unified Christian commonwealth (rather than the more recent effort to separate church and state within a fragmented system of sovereign nation-states) nevertheless constituted a marked change from the compact world of the Greek polis or the Roman Empire. In that ancient pagan world, political society was considered to be all-embracing and self-sufficient. For it, society was the polis or, later, the imperium, a compact and undifferentiated unity whose functions were not only those which we today call political but also those which we call religious. The city or the Empire enforced laws and fought wars; it also worshiped the gods, and it saw no reason for regarding priests as being any less civic functionaries than magistrates or generals.

With the rise of Christianity, a new institution arose claiming jurisdiction directly from God within its own sphere. There appeared for the first time a distinct social body that called itself the ecclesia or church. Unlike the people of Israel whom God had made particularly his own, the church was open to all who would accept the faith that it taught and would join it through baptism. Like Israel, it presented itself as having been founded directly by God, and while it acknowledged the authority of governments in temporal affairs, it claimed autonomy in all that pertained to man's relationship with God. Thus began a process of differentiation that narrowed the jurisdiction of the political society by recognizing an authority outside, above, and independent of it. John Courtney Murray describes the political effects of the Christian dispensation in the following way:

> the essential political effect of Christianity was to destroy the classical view of society as a single homogeneous structure within which the political power stood forth as the representative of society both in its religious and in its political aspects. Augustus was both Summus Imperator and Pontifex Maximus; the ius divinum was simply part of the ius civile; and outside the empire there was no civil society, but only barbarism. The new Christian view was based on a radical distinction between the order of the sacred and the order of the secular: "Two there are, august Emperor, by which this world is ruled on title of original and sovereign right—the consecrated

authority of the priesthood and the royal power." In this celebrated sentence of Gelasius I, written to the Byzantine Emperor Anastasius I in 494 A.D., the emphasis laid on the word "two" bespoke the revolutionary character of the Christian dispensation.[3]

Now there were two distinct authorities in society, the political and the religious, the temporal and the spiritual. According to John Courtney Murray, this independent spiritual authority has been the essential element of freedom in the political tradition of the Christian West.

Murray spells out this proposition in chapter 9 of *We Hold These Truths: Catholic Reflections on the American Proposition*, under the title "Are There Two or One?" The basic question, according to Murray, is whether the government of the world is divided between two authorities, temporal and spiritual, each supreme in its own sphere, or whether there is ultimately only one supreme authority, as there was in the classical pagan world, that of the sovereign political state, within which religious bodies exist only as associations of private right. The Christian tradition insists that there are two, with the result that the freedom of the Church is the bulwark of the freedom of all else in a society in which the state is confined to its own limited sphere of jurisdiction and of action.

"Freedom of the church," says Murray, is a "pregnant phrase" that means more than it seems to at first glance.[4] First of all, it naturally denotes the freedom of the Church as a spiritual authority to carry out its divine commission to teach, to rule, and to sanctify. But it also denotes the freedom of the Church as the Christian people "to live within her fold an integral supernatural life," a life with an "inherent superpolitical dignity" that transcends the goals and powers of the state and so founds a claim to immunity from subordination to the state and its temporal ends. Complementary to this are all aspects of the temporal life of man that

> by reason of their Christian mode of existence, or by reason of their finality, . . . transcend the limited purposes of the political order and are thus invested with a certain sacredness. The chief example is the institution of the family—the marriage contract itself, and the relationships of husband and wife, parent and child. Included also are other human relationships in so far as they involve a moral element and require regulation in the interests of the personal dignity of man. Such, for instance, are the employer-employee relationship and the reciprocal relationships established by the political obligation. Sacred too is the intellectual patrimony of the human race, the heritage of basic truths about the nature of man, amassed by secular experience and reflection, that form the essential content of the social consensus.[5]

The centuries since this concept of two sovereignties—and of a corresponding freedom of the Church—emerged have been marked by an unfolding of the implications of this notion of political dualism. They have also been filled with an unending debate, by no means yet concluded, on the proper relationship between these two sovereignties. Here we need only note that the question of that relationship, which in this country we call a separation of church and state, presupposes the distinction between them. If there were only the state, there would be no church to which to relate it or from which to separate it.

Given the reality of both church and state, however, drawing the line between their proper spheres leads ultimately to the idea of constitutional government—that is, government limited in its powers. Underlying this idea is the Christian conception of society as organized in different ways for different purposes. Society is indeed composed of individuals, but not of individuals standing alone opposite the state. The family, for example, is a natural human grouping, and society is made up of families as much as of individuals. As society develops, it articulates itself into a multitude of economic, cultural, and other groups. Society itself is organized as the state but only for certain purposes and for the performance of certain functions relative to those purposes. For the performance of other functions in relation to God, a Christian society organizes itself as the Church or the churches. The state and its organs of government thus come to have limited powers because they have limited goals and functions.

What limits and what functions? The relationship between the two jurisdictions, spiritual and temporal, would change over the centuries, not always to the benefit of the Church (or churches) or to the cause of limited constitutional government.

The definition of the relationships between the two jurisdictions began to change in the thirteenth century with the rediscovery of Aristotle's *Politics* and the emergence of the Thomistic idea that the state was a society in its own right, its origins flowing directly from man's nature as a social and political being. Now it became possible to conceptualize the Church and the state as distinct entities. In the struggle between them, the *regnum* was finally victorious over the *sacerdotium*. After the Reformation, in Protestant countries the king became the head of the Church. (One is reminded of the way in which the English bishops almost unanimously deserted the pope for Henry VIII.) Even in countries that remained Catholic, the king virtually had the power to appoint bishops and thus exercise considerable control over the Church. In short, as a consequence of the Reformation, the Enlightenment, and the rise of militant anticlericalism in Catholic countries, royal protection became a felt need for the Church. The confessional state arose to meet this need, but the Church paid a heavy price for it in subjection to royal control.

What was needed as a consequence of this unfortunate tendency at the practical level toward a Gallicanism that undermined the Church's freedom to carry on its teaching mission and administer the sacraments was a conceptual shift. This shift required a change, not in the Church's understanding of its own nature and mission but in its conception of the nature and function of the state in relation to religion. The intellectual foundations for this shift had already been laid, as noted above, by Thomas Aquinas in his defense of the "naturalness" of political authority. Aquinas's successors (especially theologians such as Francisco Suarez and Robert Bellarmine) expanded upon that defense even if they did not understand fully its historical implications for religious freedom.

II

Francisco Suarez expounds his political philosophy most fully in his *De Legibus*, a work that provides one step along the road toward this shift in the Catholic understanding of the state.[6]

The state, according to Suarez, is an institution purely of the natural order,[7] and it remains such even under the Christian dispensation.[8] It follows from this that the end or purpose of the state is determined by natural law, and will not change even under the law of grace. The proper end of the state is not the eternal happiness of man (*aeternam felicitatem supernaturalem vitae*), since the civil power is merely of the natural order. This is not to deny that one could, when illumined by the light of faith, use civil power for a supernatural end. But this would be merely a relation imposed upon it from without (*per imperium extrinsecum*) and not a relation flowing from its nature.[9]

Even in the order of pure nature, Suarez argues, man's ultimate end, natural happiness in a future life, would not be the goal to which the State is intrinsically ordered. Nor would even the natural happiness of individual men as such in this life be the proper end of the State. The State is concerned only with the natural well-being of the fully developed human society, namely civil society, with whose care it is charged; the welfare of individuals concerns the State only insofar as they are members of this community.[10]

The natural well-being of civil society consists in the fact that men live in an order of peace and justice, with that sufficiency of material goods which is required for the decent sustenance of bodily life, and that moral probity which is necessary for peace, justice, and external welfare. This is the common good of the State, and the end toward which civil power is directed by its nature. The consequence is that the laws which are made in virtue of civil power command and prohibit only in matters pertaining to this end.[11]

Suarez thus saw the power and the jurisdiction of the state as limited to defending and promoting the good of the commonwealth in this temporal life. Its authority, when considered per se, that is, intrinsically and merely in itself, extended no farther. The superior and final end of human life resided in the care of the Church as a body instituted by Christ for that supernatural purpose. The Church's mission is to direct men, by teaching and the administration of the sacraments, to eternal life with God. This conception of the state as limited to securing certain external aspects of the temporal common good while respecting the authority of the Church as a power outside, above, and independent of the state itself marked a further departure from the classical Greek or ancient Roman conception of politics.

Yet while Suarez departed from the Greek and Roman conceptions of politics, he still saw the state as incorporated into the res publica Christiana and endorsed thereby some version of confessionalism.

The citizens of the state were all baptized members of the Church, and so was the king or emperor, to whom the people, the original recipient of the God-given authority of the natural political community, had transferred it. Kings (or the citizens of a democracy, if such there were) were therefore obliged to use their civil power, when necessary to protect the Catholic faith. This obligation was not grounded in a power derived from the nature and purpose of the state as such, but because in a Christian and Catholic society, the state was incorporated into the larger res publica Christiana.

One might fairly conclude that Suarez's "confessionalism," his willingness to subordinate the state to the Church, was not essential to the Catholic notion of the state should conditions obtain under which a unified res publica Christiana no longer exists. The subordination of the state to the Church was not an intrinsic relationship that obtained even in non-Christian countries but an extrinsic one flowing from the inclusion of the state in the larger Christian commonwealth. We see here then a foreshadowing of the aforementioned "thesis-hypothesis" distinction advanced by later confessionalists, but we need to recognize that any defense of confessionalism is predicated, as it was in Suarez, on the actual existence of a solidly Catholic society and does not flow of necessity from the Catholic concept of the state as such.

Still further refinements in the concept of the state remained to be made, and one of the most important of these was made by the twentieth-century Catholic philosopher Jacques Maritain. Maritain distinguishes between community and society on the one hand and, on the other hand, among the nation, the body politic (or political society), and the state.[12]

As Maritain uses the terms, community and society are not synonymous, and neither can be reduced to a mere biological reality. A community is "more of a work of nature and more nearly related to the biological." The family is the most obvious example of a community, but the term could apply to other groupings that grow up "naturally," as it were, without being planned, such as a neighborhood, a workplace, or a common enterprise of some kind. On the other hand, "a society is more of a work of reason, and more nearly related to the intellectual and moral properties of man."[13] It may grow out of a common enterprise, as does a professional association or labor union, but it is chosen, not spontaneously formed.

A community tends to create "a common unconscious psyche, common feelings and psychological structures, and common mores." But a society is formed because of "a task to be done or an end to be aimed at, which depends on the determinations of human intelligence and will and is preceded by the activity—either decision, or at least, consent—of the reason of individuals."[14]

A nation, according to Maritain, is a community, not a society, and does not of itself automatically turn into a political society. Quite distinct nations can form one political society, as in the case of the Austro-Hungarian empire before the First World War (or Canada and Belgium today), and there is no inner necessity or moral obligation that they break apart into distinct bodies politic. On the other hand, a body politic is an entity that in one way or another has institutionalized itself. If a body politic has lasted for a long period of time, it tends to bring into being a national community out of distinct communal parts even if that inchoate sense of oneness needed for there to be a community did not exist when the body politic was originally constituted. For example, Maritain calls the United States a community of communities, a merging of various communities into a national community with its own national psyche and historical experiences and memories.[15]

"The national community as well as all other communities of the nation," he says, is "thus comprised in the superior unity of the body politic." This does not mean that the family or any other institution of what many today would call civil society is caused by or absorbed into the body politic. The family is by nature antecedent to the body politic and has its own rights, freedoms, and purposes, as do the multiplicity of other societies produced through free human initiatives, and should be as autonomous as possible. There is, therefore, an "element of pluralism in every truly political society," and this plural structure of political society must be respected if human beings are to actualize their potentialities within the confines of the temporal common good.[16]

The final distinction worthy of note here is that which Maritain makes between the state and the body politic. The state is "only that part of the body politic especially concerned with the maintenance of law, the promotion of the common welfare and public order, and the administration of public affairs. . . . It is not a man or a body of men; it is a set of institutions combined into a topmost machine. . . ."[17] Therefore, "when we say that the State is the superior part of the body politic, this means that it is superior to the other organs or collective parts of this body, but it does not mean that it is superior to the body politic itself." It is "a part or an instrument of the body politic, subordinate to it and endowed with topmost authority not by its own right and for its own sake, but only by virtue and to the extent of the requirements of the common good." Ultimately, "man is by no means for the State. The State is for man."[18]

Maritain's distinctions, one could argue, are made within the context of the rise of the totalitarian state in the twentieth century. The Catholic Church and those who spoke on its behalf began to see that the Church's freedom from political domination was more important than its establishment by law. They bespeak, therefore, an increasing appreciation of the limitations of state power and an awareness that the plural structures of political society are primarily responsible for advancing the common good of its members. The state's role is juridical; its proper goal is to secure a moral public order within which the common good of political society can flourish. This series of distinctions, or something very similar (combined with an increasing sense of Catholic personalism), is assumed in Vatican II's Declaration on Human Freedom.

III

Those who understand politics only as a struggle for power and influence or who embrace some version of ethical subjectivism often miss the simple fact that the Church sees its mission as teaching a faith in which it really believes. *DH* expressly states: "We believe that this one true [Christian] religion subsists in the catholic and apostolic Church, to which the Lord Jesus committed the duty of spreading it abroad among all men."[19] It is the freedom to teach and practice its faith that is of primary importance to the Church, and any truly Catholic defense of religious freedom is predicated on this assumption of the truthfulness of the One, Holy, Catholic and Apostolic Church.

The Declaration openly acknowledges that its freedom cannot be secured independent of the recognition of a universal principle of religious freedom. The Declaration therefore goes on to say that "all men are to be immune from coercion on the part of individuals or of social groups and of any human power, in such wise that in matters religious no one is to be forced to act in a manner contrary to his beliefs . . ." (*DH*, 2). This freedom, it adds, is founded on "the very dignity of the human person, as this dignity is known through the revealed Word of God and by reason itself" (*DH*, 2). Reason, that is to say, tells us that the nature of man as an intelligent and free creature requires that his pursuit of the most basic and ultimate truths be immune from coercion, including the coercive power of the law.

This idea of the dignity of the human person was not entirely new. In the encyclical *Rerum Novarum*, Pope Leo XIII had said that "no one may with impunity outrage the dignity of man, which God Himself treats with great reverence, nor impede his course to the level of perfection which accords with eternal life in heaven."[20] Leo certainly does not dwell at length on man's personhood, and one should not expect him therefore to follow through on all the political implications of personhood for the Catholic view of the state. The premise of his argument, however, is clear: "Since man by his reason understands innumerable things, linking and combining the future with the present, and since he is master of his own actions, therefore, under the eternal law, and under the power of God most wisely ruling all things, he rules himself by the foresight of his own counsel."[21] Man is by nature rational, therefore free and master of his own actions, but under God's eternal law.

Leo's conception of human nature and Maritain's conceptual distinctions are assumed in the Declaration on Religious Freedom. The freedom of religion written of in that document is an immunity in civil society from coercion in matters of religious belief and practice, within the limits of the temporal common good or, in the terms that the Declaration prefers, "the just requirements of public order, i.e., that part of the common good that is subject to state control."

The search for religious liberty leading up to Vatican II had proceeded historically, not by analysis of an abstract right but by a series of successive delimitations of the power and functions of the state. Vatican II based its declaration on the inherent natural dignity of the human person, but the freedom it proclaimed was based on a refinement, arrived at through historical experience (including experience of the weaknesses of the confessional state) of the concept of the state, its nature, purpose, and powers. Religious liberty, as a civil right, requires that the state remain within the boundaries of its natural jurisdiction. The Declaration states: "This right of the human person to religious freedom is to be recognized in the constitutional law whereby society is governed; thus it is to become a civil right" (*DH*, 2).

Furthermore, although the Declaration asserts religious freedom as a civil right, it also asserts that the right follows from every person's natural obligation as a free and rational being to seek religious truth, to adhere to it when found and to order one's life in accordance with its demands. "Men cannot discharge these obligations in a manner keeping with their own nature unless they enjoy immunity from external coercion as well as psychological freedom" (*DH*, 2).

The Declaration's case for religious freedom thus does not rest on the proposition that human reason or conscience is a law unto itself. On the contrary, it supposes that "the highest norm of human life is the divine law—eternal, objective, and universal—whereby God orders, directs and governs the entire universe and all the ways of the human community" (*DH*, 3).

It is also clear that the Declaration's argument for religious freedom does not imply that religious truth and error are indistinguishable or that one is free to choose truth or error indifferently. The argument depends on the obligation to seek and adhere to the truth, which alone can provide a proper foundation for rights. But, as the declaration notes, "as the truth is discovered, it is by a personal assent that men are to adhere to it" (*DH*, 3).

This argument is very much consistent with the rational, natural-law tradition of Catholic social thought. The document does not use the term "natural law," but it does posit a universal human nature, whose natural tendencies and needs are knowable to the human mind. It further assumes the existence of God, who is truth, and the truth about whom answers to the deepest of human needs. By a rational analysis of the relationship between God and man, and of the intrinsic limits of the constitutional state, it concludes that religious freedom is a natural human right.

Now, if all men sought and infallibly found religious truth, the question of religious freedom would not arise. It is precisely because men's beliefs about religious truth vary so widely and so deeply, and because their consciences are highly fallible, that the coercion of some persons by others in matters religious is possible and, in fact, takes place. In asserting the right of all men to immunity from this coercion, *DH* proclaims neither the right to be wrong nor the impossibility of distinguishing truth from error in religious matters. By a seeming paradox, it guarantees the possibility of being wrong in matters religious, without therefore suffering coercion, as an objective requirement of the nature of free and responsible persons who were made by God to know the truth about Him. Father John Courtney Murray's comment is apposite here: "Neither error nor evil can be the object of a right, only what is true and good. It is, however, true and good that a man should enjoy freedom from coercion in matters religious."[22]

IV

It would be a mistake to think that, in its Declaration on Religious Freedom, the Catholic Church adopted the notion of religious liberty elaborated by the U.S. Supreme Court in its interpretation of the First Amendment to the U.S. Constitution. Since 1947, the U.S. Supreme Court's view of church-state relations has been guided by Justice Hugo Black's dictum that "neither a state not the Federal Government can set up a church. Neither can pass laws which aid one religion, aid all religions, or prefer one religion over another.... In the words of Jefferson, the clause against establishment of religion by law was intended to erect 'a wall of separation between church and state.'"[23] By contrast, the Declaration states its general attitude toward church-state relations in these words: "Government ought indeed to take account of the religious life of the people and show it favor, since the function of government is to make provision for the common welfare. However, it would clearly transgress the limits set to its power were it to presume to command or inhibit acts that are religious" (*DH*, 3).

The Declaration does not proscribe (nor does it favor) the establishment of a particular church or religion as contrary per se to religious freedom. On the other hand, it in no way upholds establishment as an ideal and, indeed, grants it only a rather reluctant recognition as an historical fact. "If in view of particular circumstances obtaining among certain peoples, special legal recognition is given to one religious community in the constitutional order of society, it is at the same time imperative that the right of all citizens and religious communities to religious freedom should be recognized and made effective" (*DH*, 6).

DH argues against the infringement of religious liberty. Far from espousing an "absolute separation of Church and State," the Declaration denies that the state, under the rubric of neutrality in religious matters, has the right to impose on all citizens "a single system of education from which all religious formation is excluded." Indeed, government must not impose "unjust burdens on parents, whether directly or indirectly," that would prevent them from making a "genuinely free choice of schools" for their children (*DH*, 5). At the practical level, this implies a criticism of the American public school monopoly of tax support for elementary and secondary schools. At the level of principle, it indicates that the right to religious freedom accrues not to individuals alone but to families as well.

The Declaration acknowledges that religious freedom, like all other freedoms, can be abused and that government has the right to control such abuse.

But in answering the question about what norm or standard should be employed by the state in distinguishing between the abuse of freedom and the legitimate free exercise of religion, the Declaration makes an important distinction that reflects Maritain's distinction between the more extensive requirements of the temporal common good of political society and the more minimal requirements of public order. Government's action against abuses of religious freedom "is to be controlled by juridical norms which are in conformity with the objective moral order" (*DH*, 7) and which, more specifically, enforce "the just requirements of public order" (*DH*, 3). "These norms," it says, "arise out of the need for effective safeguard of the rights of all citizens and for peaceful settlement of conflicts of rights. They flow from the need for an adequate care for genuine public peace, which comes about when men live together in good order and in true justice. They come, finally, out of the need for a proper guardianship of public morality. These matters constitute the basic component of the common welfare: they are what is meant by public order" (*DH*, 7).

The objective moral order, which is not subject to the will of men, prescribes the protection of rights, public peace, and public morality as public purposes of human society. Realizing and safeguarding these purposes establishes and maintains public order. By enforcing the "just requirements of public order," government in no way violates religious freedom even if it prevents people from doing things that their religious beliefs authorize or even command. (The just requirements of public order, it is clear, should not be construed in liberal, individualist terms.)

DH does not answer the question: who is to determine what the objective moral order is? And it certainly does not spell out in great detail what "the just requirements of public order" entail. At least under a constitutional form of government (which *DH* seems to consider normal), the moral order and the public order derived from it will be effective restraints on government insofar as they are accepted by the collective conscience of the larger and sounder part of society and are upheld by constitutional organs, such as courts of law. There is nothing in *DH* that furnishes grounds for the suspicion that it really contemplates a benevolent Catholic dictatorship repressing heresy under the guise of upholding the "objective moral order." On the contrary, having explained what it means (in general terms) by the public order, it concludes: "For the rest, the usages of society are to be the usages of freedom in their full range: that is, the freedom of man is to be respected as far as possible and is not to be curtailed except when and in so far as necessary" (*DH*, 7).

V

Today, we may safely say that religious liberty in matters of doctrinal faith is not in principle seriously contested in modern Western democracies. The point at issue has shifted from the role of the state in relation to religious doctrine to the state's role in regard to the requirements of public morality. We have replaced religious strife over doctrines such as the Trinity, or the Incarnation, or transubstantiation, with culture wars over issues such as abortion, euthanasia, homosexuality, sex education in schools, population control, pornography, and funding for the arts, all of which arguably can fall within the scope of the temporal common good. Underlying these controversies is a deepening divergence within society about the nature of man and, in particular, the goods that make for human flourishing.

One tactic that secular liberals (or liberal secularists) have used effectively in these culture wars is to turn moral issues into religious issues that, qua religious issues, do not belong in the public square. Any moral belief, it is argued, that is derived from or supported by a religious belief, or taught by a religious institution, must be excluded from any debate over public law and policy. Any law based on such a belief must be declared unconstitutional as constituting an establishment of religion and a denial of the equal protection of the laws, because it imposes the religious beliefs of some members of society on others who do not share those beliefs.

Public issues, the argument goes, must be decided on grounds upon which all citizens, regardless of their religious beliefs or lack thereof, could rationally agree. This argument, however, grants veto power to the most secularized, individualistic (and, perhaps, hedonistic) members of civil society and pretends that only what they would agree to can be taken as an exercise of "public reason." Robert P. George has rightly described this as a liberal victory by default. Once liberals have rejected all views of the temporal common good that contradict theirs on the grounds that they do not enjoy universal consent (or are based on particularistic religious beliefs), liberal secularists' beliefs become "what we can all agree upon."

One could probably make up a list of matters which all reasonable citizens would agree are necessary to a viable and healthy society: police and fire protection, good roads, the settlement of disputes without resort to violence, and so on. But the case being made by secular liberals is that only such matters fall within the jurisdiction of the state, all others being left to voluntary individual or group decision. To argue thus, however, begs the question: when did we all agree that the realm of politics includes only such matters?

Edmund Burke once said that political problems relate primarily to good or evil, not primarily to truth or falsehood. That is as true today as it was when

Burke said it. But we now live in a culture that is increasingly pluralistic in its views about what constitutes the human good and therefore may be part of the common good of society. This is a fact that cannot be wished away. It is also a fact, however, that public law and determinations of public policy inescapably involve the making of moral judgments based on some conception of the human good. Secular liberals wish to be what Justice Oliver Wendell Holmes once described as "the dominant element" in making those determinations while at the same time claiming only to be acting in accord with what "public reason" demands.

It follows that, if public reason is to arrive at public policy determinations, it must arrive at those that enjoy the consent of a large enough part of the public to make the resulting laws and policies workable. This implies the consent, not of a mere and transient majority (or of secular liberals alone), but of what was described during the Middle Ages as the *major et sanior pars*, the larger and sounder part, of the community. One may insist that those views of what constitutes the "just requirements of public order" must concern the temporal common good. But no view of that temporal common good should be excluded simply because it fails to comport with the liberal individualist model of man and society. The aforementioned issues (abortion, euthanasia, et al.) can be raised and resolved within what Suarez described as the "probity of morals that is necessary to the external peace and happiness of the commonwealth and the becoming preservation of human nature."

These issues fit within the Declaration on Human Freedom's "juridical norms," which provide "adequate care for genuine public peace" through "proper guardianship for public morality." They also happen in the United States to coincide with the traditional police power of the states, which is their power to legislate on behalf of the safety, health, welfare, and morals of the people.

It begs the question to assume that the issues mentioned must be resolved on the basis of a radically egalitarian liberalism that levels all social institutions and standards and thereby excludes all considerations derived from traditional morality because that morality is "religious." We may not accept arguments whose only basis is "because the Bible says it's so," but we ought to recognize that reason reflecting on long experience harmonizes to a large extent with traditional (and even biblical) morality.

The role of religious bodies in the political process is to help form the public conscience by means of persuasion. Political decisions are seldom based purely and simply on dictates of conscience (and therefore there is a large part of politics from which the clergy is well advised to abstain). But the most basic ones furnish the moral framework within which civilized and humane people carry on their politics.

If a national community were solidly Catholic, its laws and public policies would naturally reflect a Catholic social conscience. The same would be true of a community that was solidly Calvinist, Jewish, Muslim, militantly secularist like the Third French Republic, officially atheistic like the former Soviet Union, or post-Christian as is much of the Western world today. In every case the laws would reflect the dominant conscience of the body politic, for the idea of a simply neutral state that follows no norms is a deceptive and dangerous myth.

The least-common-denominator political theory advocated by secular liberals is not in fact that upon which we all agree. It is indeed true that politics in a civilized society will in practice be an ongoing process of accommodation on particular issues of law and policy that arise. This by no means implies that we must compromise our moral principles but that, since democratic politics requires a sufficient degree of popular consent, we must often be willing to settle for less than what our principles demand.

Nothing in the idea of religious freedom, especially as that right is conceived by the Second Vatican Council, prevents like-minded citizens who agree on particular public policy matters from building coalitions that can effectuate their views of the temporal common good. Nor is there any reason why such a coalition, even if a minority, may not hold politicians' feet to the fire by showing them the accommodations they must make to get the coalition members' votes. Since this is the way in which the political game is played in a pluralistic society, there is no valid reason why all of us may not play it.

The pluralist game, however, will not be modeled after a football or basketball game in which one team or the other definitely wins. The players in this game, if they are intelligent, will work toward making public decisions that the larger and sounder part of political society can live with, while leaving open the possibility of achieving what they believe to be better decisions that are in greater accord with their moral principles. Abraham Lincoln advocated limiting the spread of slavery in the hope of eventually bringing about its disappearance in the United States. Today, one may advocate the same prudential course in regard to the social-moral evils of our time. And one may do so while advancing a distinctively Catholic view of religious freedom and the type of moral order that best sustains such freedom.

NOTES

1. *Mulieris Dignitatem*. (Boston: St. Paul's Book and Media, 1988), section 4.
2. *Catechism of the Catholic Church* (New York: Catholic Book Publishing Company, 1994), chapter 3, article 1, section III, 160.

3. John Courtney Murray, S.J., *We Hold These Truths: Catholic Reflections on the American Proposition* (New York: Sheed and Ward, 1960), 202.

4. Ibid., 201.

5. Ibid., 203–4.

6. Francisco Suarez, *De Legibus, Opera Omnia*, ed Berton (Paris: Vives, 1856). See also my own "Subordination of the State to the Church according to Suarez," *Theological Studies* XII (September 1951), from which essay the arguments of the next several paragraphs are taken.

7. *De Legibus*, Book III, prologus.

8. Ibid., Book III, chapter 9, section 1.

9. Ibid., Book III, chapter 11, section 4.

10. Ibid., Book III, chapter 11, section 7.

11. Loc. cit.

12. Jacques Maritain, *Man and the State* (Chicago: University of Chicago Press, 1951).

13. Ibid., 2.

14. Ibid., 3.

15. Ibid., 4–9.

16. Ibid., 11.

17. Ibid., 12.

18. Ibid., 13.

19. *Dignitatis Humanae*, section 1. All further references to this document will be taken from the translation supplied by John Courtney Murray in *Religious Liberty: An End and a Beginning* (New York: Macmillan, 1966), 162–89. The document will be cited parenthetically as *DH*, with the section number added, followed by the page number in Murray's book.

20. *Rerum Novarum* (Boston: Daughters of St. Paul), section 57.

21. Ibid., section 11.

22. Murray, footnote 5 to Murray's annotated commentary on *DH* in *Religious Liberty: An End and a Beginning*, 166.

23. *Everson v. Board of Education Of Ewing Township, N.J.*

The Promised Time of *Dignitatis Humanae*: A Radical Protestant Perspective

Thomas Heilke

> The earlier time of that king represented the former age of emperors who did not believe in Christ, at whose hands the Christians suffered because of the wicked; but the later time of that king represented the age of the successors to the imperial throne, now believing in Christ, at whose hands the wicked suffer because of the Christians.
>
> —Aurelius Augustine, Letter to Vincentius, AD 408

Dignitatis Humanae echoes. One hears within it echoes of John Locke ("constitutional limits . . . to the power of government"), Immanuel Kant ("duty" and "freedom of the person"); Max Weber ("quest for values"), and the American Founders ("free exercise of religion"). It seems also to reflect the neo-Thomism of Jacques Maritain.[1] This laundry list of vocabularies seems unfair, an effort at genealogy that is merely a genetic fallacy. The echoes, however, are not merely whimsical parentheses. They seem central as a means to understand the intentions and impact of *Dignitatis Humanae* and of the several related encyclicals that are all the products of the Second Vatican Council (1962–1965). Indeed, this document and its partners have been charged with articulating or even initiating a significant sea change in the Roman Catholic Church that might be described as a crisis or "turning point," a moment of threat but also of promise.[2]

While *Dignitatis Humanae* is a relatively brief document among the more than thirty encyclicals, addresses, decrees, and other writings that emerged directly from the Second Vatican Council, it has become a defining document of that Council. Part of its distinction arises from its articulation of a premise that, in my view, has largely been withheld in the Roman Catholic Church since the late Roman Empire. That premise—toleration as a religious and not exclusively political principle—is surely a substantive aspect of the "promise" of Vatican II. It is a promise sought, but not obtained, by the pacifist branch of the Radical Reformation and by many minority groups dwelling in Christendom and beyond long before and even after Vatican II.

Dignitatis Humanae is a document of theopolitical deliberation. Given that it echoes several modern concepts and given the attendant suspicion that its conceptual apparatus cannot be squared with certain integral elements of the Roman Catholic tradition out of which it emerges, it seems fair to ask: what are the place and occasion of *Dignitatis Humanae*, the space and time of its deliberation? In the context of what an outsider would perceive to be the Roman Catholic tradition, what are we to make of its vocabulary and concerns? After all, the document itself begins with a contemporary problem that it proposes to address in part by harmonizing its claims with previous Roman Catholic tradition.[3] My goal is to consider these questions from the perspective of a radical Protestant history. Place and occasion, I will argue, make too much of a difference here, and that difference renders the final promise of the document ambiguous and insecure.

DIGNITY

"Dignity" seems to be a modern term, an impression made especially strong by its association with Kant, but it has an older lineage as well. The concept of the dignity of man derived from the elevated position of human beings among animate (and inanimate) beings has a venerable history, in which Christian thinkers have traced the idea of dignity to the accounts of creation itself. For example, the Elohim create human beings in their "likeness."[4] The "imago Dei" doctrine of Christianity derives from this episode, according to which human beings enjoy a special status in God's created order.

The content of the "likeness" that gives humans this status and concomitant dignity has, however, been subject to considerable debate. It has generally been held to be "spiritual," not physical, perhaps pertaining to human creativity, or to the possibility of moral perfection, or at least to the imaginative apprehension of such perfection, or, in a more capitalist mode, to "a specific kind of calling, . . . the vocation to be creative, inventive, and intellectually alert in a practical way, in order 'to build up the kingdom of God.'"[5]

The word *dignitas* originally emerged within a sociopolitical context, but it has gradually been expanded beyond the sociopolitical realm to signify an essential attribute of human nature itself. For the Romans, *dignitas* referred to the worth, worthiness, authority, rank, distinction, or majesty that proceeded from one's sociopolitical position or political office. Almost two thousand years later, David Hume knew that the English derivative, dignity, referred to human beings as such, beings who are said to have a specific dignity by dint of their nature as human beings. He also knew that such a form of dignity stood in contrast to the older, comparative term of antiquity, under which dignity was attributed to some persons because of their natural or political superiority over others.[6]

In the Christian tradition, dignity had shifted in meaning from a sociopolitical term to an ontological one, and Hume was skeptical of this shift. While the former meaning has immediate sociopolitical implications—that is, that one's office demands a particular treatment—the latter does not lose this meaning but relocates it in the nature of human beings as such. If such a relocation is at all sustainable, Hume seems to argue, then the "dignity of human nature" distinguishes members of the human species by dint of their traits of curiosity and foresight, by their ability to observe, learn, explore, look backward, etc. They are thus distinct from the members of all other living species, whose mental abilities seem much more circumscribed or even reduced to unthinking instinct.[7] While the "sense of dignity of the human person" in *Dignitatis Humanae* seems always to include the more modest comparative component, it generally carries a more substantial moral significance than even Hume, for example, allows.

Thomas Aquinas, whose ideas are not explicitly cited in *Dignitatis Humanae*, is nevertheless present at a substantive level. He is well aware throughout the *Summa Theologiae* that "dignity" has a conventional, sociopolitical meaning associated with specific social, ecclesiastical, or political offices and that it also has an ontological meaning. The assignation of the title "person" implies or signifies dignity based on high rank, and since "subsistence in a rational nature is of high dignity . . . every individual of the rational nature is called a 'person.'"[8] Accordingly, to contravene the dictates of right reason is to forfeit our dignity,[9] a dignity that resides in our nature as rational beings, not in some sociopolitical convention of office. Aquinas takes care to consider the "natural" dignity of human beings in the order of creation by dint of their reason, but he also considers the limitations of that dignity because of the need human beings have to be completed not by their reason alone but by divine grace.[10]

For Pico della Mirandola, writing within and establishing the Renaissance humanist tradition, it is not the intermediary nature of human beings between God and other creatures, nor is it their rational character as such, that sets human beings apart. Nor is it, as with the later Hume, "the acuteness of [their] senses," the "discernment of [their] reason," or the "light of [human] intelligence [as] interpreter of nature" that sets apart human beings for "the highest admiration."[11] Rather, it is human freedom and the human ability—given by God—of self-determination. It is in the act of choice that human beings find dignity, and it is in the act of choosing well with respect to their ends that they find their highest dignity.[12] Just as Edmund Burke would later famously reflect that we should first see what individuals please to do with their liberty "before we risk congratulations," so Pico does not locate human dignity merely in freedom as such but in a freedom properly exercised. Unlike Aquinas, who argued that "free will" [*voluntas*] was, indeed, a "part of man's dignity,"[13] Pico makes much less of rationality in this regard.

Immanuel Kant, despite his stated skepticism concerning human possibilities for moral rectitude,[14] moves toward dignity as "an intrinsic value."[15] But this dignity remains tied to morality, "the only condition under which a rational being can be an end in himself" and thereby qualify for the dignity that belongs to him as a rational member of the kingdom of ends. "[M]orality, and humanity so far as it is capable of morality, is the only thing which has dignity."[16] This morality, however, is rationally given as universal. It is realized in a liberal regime or kingdom of ends in which all rational members are subject to freely promulgated laws. "Autonomy," by which Kant appears to mean self-legislating, universalizing rationality, is therefore "the ground of the dignity of human nature and of every rational nature."[17]

These various aspects of dignity in Western intellectual history seem to merge in *Dignitatis Humanae*'s understanding of "dignity." Human beings enjoy a special status in creation that is God-given and that manifests itself in their unique intellectual, spiritual, and, especially, reasoning capacities. As a consequence, they are deserving of a special regard and a corresponding treatment from one another that preserves this status and safeguards—indeed, fosters—the human capacities that underlie it.

How central is this understanding of "dignity" to an understanding of *Dignitatis*? On a quick reading, "dignity" seems largely to fall away in the discussion of *Dignitatis Humanae*. On a slower reading, we observe that "dignity" appears ten times in the text, and several of these appearances take place at crucial moments of definition. While much of the argument of *Dignitatis Humanae* seems to rest on standard Roman Catholic theological and philosophical categories, "the right to religious freedom has its foundation in the very dignity of the human person as this dignity is known through the revealed word of God and by reason itself."[18] Dignity so understood seems to combine what Kant would describe as heteronomous elements. First, it reflects Kant's concern for religious freedom and freedom of conscience, and the document calls for a recognition of these freedoms.[19] Second, and at the same time, a Christian/Aristotelian teleology is also at work in the call to such religious freedom. This heteronomous element undermines the intellectual "purity" of

Kant's formulation[20] and undermines thereby a strictly liberal-secular understanding of it:

> It is in accordance with their dignity as persons—that is, beings endowed with reason and free will and therefore privileged to bear personal responsibility—that all men should be at once impelled by nature and also bound by a moral obligation to seek the truth, especially religious truth. They are also bound to adhere to the truth, once it is known, and to order their whole lives in accord with the demands of truth. However, men cannot discharge these obligations in a manner in keeping with their own nature unless they enjoy immunity from external coercion as well as psychological freedom.[21]

Dignity as such does not do the work of securing rights and freedoms; that moral work is the immediate task of that human nature of which dignity is the rightful accompaniment: ". . . the right to religious freedom has its foundation not in the subjective disposition of the person, but in his very nature."[22] Dignity, however, does perform the work of political restraint: "Truth . . . is to be sought after in a manner proper to the dignity of the human person and his social nature."[23]

How can one not support such a declaration? After all, coercion of conscience and restraints on religious belief ostensibly are eliminated by calling attention to the very nature—free rationality—of human beings themselves. Nevertheless, at least three different kinds of difficulty emerge: philosophical, historical, and theopolitical. In the philosophical realm, we have not "a" problem but a thicket of them, including the content and meaning of reason and its connection to human nature; the relationship between reason and moral action; the relationship between reason and political freedom; and the relationship of reason to "revelation." Extensive bibliographies regarding each of these problems exist; but I wish to bracket this entire thicket, as important as it may be, and to focus the brief attention of this essay on the latter two—the historical and theopolitical—as a way of pointing back to the larger philosophical complex of problems.

THE THEOPOLITICAL IN TIME

The theopolitical problem begins with an identification of what is theological—or "religious"—and what is political and what the relationship between them should be. This distinction may or may not itself be specious. In either case, it has a venerable history in Roman Catholic theology and in the Christian tradition generally, dating back to the early church fathers. It also plays a central historical role in the shaping of Western civilization. More importantly, the fact that *Dignitatis Humanae* touches on this distinction is one "echo" of tradition in the midst of the document's modern usages.

The Roman Catholic version of the distinction is stated in succinct form in the Gelasian doctrine of the "two swords." The world, in the AD 494 epistolary formulation of Gelasius, is ruled by two powers—the spiritual, represented in the sacred authority of the Christian priesthood, and the political or worldly, represented in the secular authority of the royal or imperial power. The supremacy of political rule is granted by heaven "in matters affecting the public order," but it remains subordinate to "things divine," or "the sacred mysteries of religion," including especially "the means of . . . salvation."[24] In order to avoid the imposition of anachronistic categories that ultimately make it more difficult to understand the impact of Gelasius's distinction, let us recall that the "secular" in this conception is not understood as a separate realm. Rather, it is a part of a "single community of Christendom, with its dual aspects of sacerdotium and regnum." The medieval *saeculum*, in other words, is "not a space, a domain, but a time," or, as John Milbank would contend, it is the "interval between fall and eschaton where coercive justice, private property and impaired natural reason must make shift to cope with the unredeemed effects of sinful humanity."[25]

Dignitatis Humanae does not retreat from this conception in any important discernible way. The "one true religion" continues to "subsist in the Catholic and Apostolic church," and "all men" are "bound" to seek the truth of this religion, to "embrace it," and "hold fast to it."[26] *Dignitatis Humanae*'s call that men be immune from "coercion in civil society" does not, therefore, have any immediate implications for "traditional Catholic doctrine on the moral duty of men and societies toward the true religion and toward the one Church of Christ."[27]

But surely the authors of *Dignitatis* were not so obtuse as to fail to recognize a salient fact: the relationship between *ecclesia* and *saeculum* is now the inverse of what it was during the time period of medieval Christendom. The emperor Constantine had made every effort to coopt the Christian bishops and to subordinate their concerns to his overriding concern—namely, the stability of the empire.[28] It was the genius of the medieval period to take the two-swords conception of Gelasius and subordinate the ends of the one—*saeculum*—to the ends of the other—*ecclesia*. But this changed radically during the Protestant Reformation. For example, the policies of Zwingli and the separationist theology and post-1525 policies of Luther, the wars of religion, and the birth of the modern nation-state[29] began to reverse this priority, making the state-*saeculum* the superior partner in the arrangement. *Dignitatis* is written in the time and space of a liberal society, after this reversal of the relationship between ecclesia and *saeculum* that ushers in the modern era of the nation-state.

With a careful view to the "signs of the times," *Dignitatis Humanae* addresses itself to "Catholics" on the one hand and to "all men," or "men of the present day," on the other. The new ways of thinking and the consequent demands of "contemporary men" (and not some new, intraecclesial theological debate or development) have driven the need to reconsider the political significance of human dignity from an ecclesial point of view. In that context, *Dignitatis Humanae* recognizes that the ultimateness of the truth of the one true religion that subsists in the Catholic and Apostolic Church requires not coercion but the assent of human conscience in order for this religion to have its proper, genuine, integral effect on the human mind and on human activity. (As an aside, we may note that there is nothing entirely obvious about the need for such assent. One might imagine a circumstance in which following specific behavioral injunctions without the need for complete intellectual assent is unproblematic. For example, such a circumstance might obtain under a conception of religion that poses a set of requirements "concerning beliefs and way of life prescribed by the [revealed] Law" that exist separate and apart from any and all theological and philosophical treatments of the ultimate meaning of such requirements.[30]) The dignity of human beings is upheld so that they may give their genuine assent to those truths that make ultimate claims upon them. In order to be valid, effective, and genuine, assent must have a certain kind of freedom accompanying it or the situation in which it is rendered. Coercion in civil society toward the end of achieving religious consent and proper worship of God is not admissible. Securing proper assent to religious truth makes religious freedom necessary.

According to this argument, the political and social realms remain subordinate to the religious. This subordination, it should be noted, contradicts the liberal teaching of Hobbes, Locke, Mill, and the other luminaries of classical liberalism, which turns the priority of the relationship on its head. Even if one were to be an advocate for human freedom in some generic sense, however, the subordination of some realms of human activity to others would not in and of itself speak against the document. The same classical liberalism that defends religious freedom as a civil right—which the Second Vatican Council "greets with joy"[31]—also places nontrivial restraints on many human activities, including the exercise of religion.[32]

The notion that coercion is an insufficient doorway to truth is not new. It is a common theme among the major theologians of the early church, achieving a careful articulation in Augustine's work. Accordingly, *Dignitatis Humanae* can reasonably claim that religious freedom is not a merely modern doctrine but an ancient one and that it "is one of the major tenets of Catholic doctrine that man's response to God in faith must be free," that "no one therefore is to be forced to embrace the Christian faith against his own will," and that "this doctrine is contained in the word of God and it was constantly proclaimed by the Fathers of the Church."[33] Three of the four figures whom *Dignitatis Humanae* cites for this claim are Lactantius, Ambrose, and Augustine. Their words and deeds illuminate for us the ambiguous place of toleration in the theological canon and the way in which the promise of *Dignitatis Humanae* pays insufficient attention to its own fragility and its own time and place.

TIME, PLACE, AND JUST RULE

Lactantius's *Divine Institutes* is a defense of Christianity against the pagan persecutors of Christians. His purpose is to train those willing to hear and to recall them "from the error in which they are entangled to a better course of life."[34] Lactantius inveighs against the pagans by arguing that, even though they recognize the importance ("excellence") of religious practices, they know neither the true substance of religion nor how it should be defended. Religion, argues Lactantius, cannot be defended "by putting to death, but by dying; not by cruelty, but by patient endurance; not by guilt, but by good faith." To do otherwise is to introduce "evils" into that—religion—which should be defended only by the good. It is to pollute and profane religion, not to defend it.[35] Indeed, as in *Dignitatis Humanae*, so in the Institutes, "nothing is so much a matter of free-will as religion." Without free choice, religion is impossible and mutates into something else. Accordingly, religion can be neither defended nor promulgated by violence, because it requires patient endurance, even unto death. Such a defense of religion preserves faith, pleases God, and "adds authority to religion."[36]

For Lactantius, however, religion is not simply some sort of belief in some sort of divinity (as our contemporary liberal tradition might have it and of which we hear a brief echo, interestingly enough, in §4 of *Dignitatis Humanae*). He contrasts the true religion that worships the one true God with false religions that worship false gods. Unlike the false worshipers of false gods, who persecute the Christians and seek to compel them to false worship, Christians "do not require that any one should be compelled, whether he is willing or unwilling, to worship our God, who is the God of all men; nor are we angry if any one does not worship Him."[37]

Christians, says Lactantius, exercise a longing patience, trusting "in the majesty of Him who has power to avenge contempt towards Himself, as also

He has power to avenge the calamities and injuries inflicted on His servants."[38] This theme of punishment and divine vengeance prevails through the remainder of Book V of the Institutes, which ends with a hope that "wicked princes" and "ravenous and voracious wolves," who may be "ministers of [God's] indignation," will "surely meet with their reward."[39] But those who understand divine vengeance as a future hope for Lactantius should now be surprised, for Lactantius asserts that vengeance is now being realized through the use of temporal power, and he approves of that use.

While there is evidence that Lactantius began writing his Institutes well before the reign of the Emperor Constantine, he dedicated the work to that emperor in the form of a tribute to Constantine's reign of justice by addressing it to "him by whom justice and wisdom have been restored to the affairs of men."[40] The work contains several dedicatory passages, some effusive in their praise of the "mighty Emperor Constantine, who [was] the first of the Roman princes to repudiate errors, and to acknowledge and honour the majesty of the one and only true God."[41] Having restored "justice and wisdom . . . to the affairs of men," Constantine can be sure that he will receive his reward from God, which will include not only blessings in this life but the assurance that the justice and security of his reign and the renewed Empire will continue after him.[42]

The persecutions of Diocletian that preceded the reign of Constantine had been, even by skeptical accounts, severe.[43] Lactantius lived and wrote during those calamities, and he celebrated their end "on that most happy day" when "the Most High God raised [Constantine] to the prosperous height of power."[44] Urging patience in the face of the persecutions, he forged a description of such patience that deserves recognition for concise accuracy.[45] It is not clear, however, that the "violent prejudice"[46] Lactantius displays in "Of the Manner in which the Persecutors Died," or, for that matter, in passages in the *Divine Institutes*, exhibits such patience. These lapses would be nothing more than peccadilloes were it not for the sharp contrast between his vituperative prose regarding the general activities of one particular ruler on the one hand and his exultations regarding the happy reign of his successor— Constantine—on the other.[47] It is impossible to agree with Coxe that Lactantius's remarks concerning the reign of Constantine indicate a certain degree of "distrust" or merely "modest tribute."[48] Lactantius seems to be a whole-hearted supporter of Constantinian policies that include an intricate mingling of the affairs of imperial rule with the affairs of the Church.

The Emperor Constantine had indeed ended persecutions of Christians and restored to them the properties that many had lost during the reign of Diocletian: some earlier emperors had done likewise, especially Gallienus after the persecutions of his father, Valerian.[49] It is only natural to celebrate a benefactor who restores peace and security, especially for oneself and one's own. Celebration gives way to theopolitical collusion, however, when the reign of God and the reign of the emperor begin to overlap. For example, in another of his encomiums, Lactantius celebrates Constantine's reversal of the "evil policy of others," his restoration of safety and stability, and his removal "from the commonwealth" of "the malefactors whom the Lord has delivered into [his] hands," thereby demonstrating to everyone "the nature of genuine sovereignty."[50] Moreover, Constantine is no normal statesman: "By an inborn sanctity of character and with a recognition of truth and God, in everything you consummate the works of justice," so that, "in the task of ordering human affairs, divine power should have employed you as its agent and minister."[51]

Lactantius was certainly not alone among his contemporaries in his praise. The church historian Eusebius, for example, sees Constantine as "invested . . . with a semblance of heavenly sovereignty" so that the emperor "directs his gaze above, and frames his earthly government according to the pattern of that Divine original, feeling strength in its conformity to the monarchy of God," who "decrees that all should be subject to the rule of one."[52] Constantine has received "as it were, a transcript of the Divine sovereignty," and he therefore "directs in imitation of God himself, the administration of the world's affairs."[53] In his hands, the power of imperium brings "those whom he rules on earth to the only begotten Word and Saviour, [and] renders them fit subjects of his kingdom." He is a friend of God who, "graced by his heavenly favor with victory over all his foes, subdues and chastens the open adversaries of the truth in accordance with the usages of war."[54] Constantine's rule is a form of evangelism and of church discipline.

The entangling motives for such praise move far beyond relief at the cessation of deadly persecution, and I have addressed that problem elsewhere.[55] Thankfulness for peace does not justify a segue into declaring that imperial rule conforms with a heavenly pattern that all rational human beings naturally understand.[56] To declare with the Apostle Paul that a ruler is a "minister" or a servant" of God who "bring[s] wrath" upon malefactors is to say much less than to say that he or she reveals a "genuine sovereignty" and a consummation of justice, and whose earthly rule imitates the rule of heaven. Lactantius and Eusebius seem to have little problem making the segue.

Several distinct themes are commingled in these encomiums, of which three are directly tied to the concerns of *Dignitatis Humanae*: Christian witness through patient teaching and potential suffering, desire for God's vengeance on one's persecutors, and the justice of good political rule or public order.[57] According to the encyclical, Jesus Himself demonstrates with highest clarity how it is that "God calls men to serve Him in spirit and in truth," which binds us in conscience but does not put us "under compulsion." Because "God has regard for the dignity of the human person whom He Himself created," we are free to make our own judgments. Therefore, Jesus used patience in His teaching, attracting disciples at times by the use of miracles to "illuminate His teaching and to establish its truth." He sought to arouse or confirm faith but never to coerce anyone. He denounced unbelief, but He left vengeance to God. Moreover, He refused the temptation of political rule, and He seems to have called for patient toleration in His parable of the wheat and the tares. At the same time that He rejected rule by force in every respect, however, He also "acknowledged the power of government and its rights," even while clearly "warning that the higher rights of God are to be kept inviolate."[58]

We can legitimately doubt whether Lactantius or Eusebius made a clear distinction between celebrating peace and seeking to participate in political rule in their praise of Constantine. We can also doubt whether they maintained a clear grasp of Christian patience. And we should not be entirely surprised that they have failed to do so. Having come into possession of the truth of existence, it is difficult not to want to express it politically, which includes imposing it by force or at least celebrating the imposition of a seeming facsimile thereof. This temptation makes fragile the premise of *Dignitatis* concerning toleration.

TIME, PLACE, AND AUGUSTINE'S PRAGMATICS OF TOLERATION

Augustine never precisely made the move of Lactantius and Eusebius, but he did become impatient and he ultimately failed to eschew ecclesiastical entanglement with political authority. With those moves, he established a precedent for the creation of a Christendom that historically compromised the claim of *Dignitatis Humanae* §12 that "the doctrine of the Church that no one is to be coerced into faith has always stood firm."

Ambrose, Augustine's teacher and bishop of Milan, preceded him in these steps. Along with Gregory, the sixth-century bishop of Rome, Ambrose is another author *Dignitatis Humanae* calls upon as a proponent of the tradition of toleration. Both Ambrose and Gregory—with considerable ability and living in two quite different eras—were deeply enmeshed in the imperial and local politics of their day, and both on occasion advocated the use of force against those with whom they disagreed theologically. For both, the theological and political conflicts overlapped, as they did for Augustine.[59]

Like Lactantius fifty years before him, Augustine faced persecution. The source of that persecution, however, had changed significantly. Augustine feared not the pagan rulers but Christians who were using violence against other Christians. These Christians whom Augustine opposed were not merely a divisive ecclesiastical movement, especially in the North African church. Their arguments with the "mainstream," nascent Catholic Church (whose membership the Donatists outnumbered in some areas of North Africa) were overlaid with socioeconomic and nationalistic identities (as was the Arian controversy that engaged Augustine's teacher, Ambrose).

Every policeman dreads a call to a domestic dispute: these are often the most volatile and violent of any. The Donatist schism was a periodically violent domestic dispute in which the "police"—the imperial authorities—were taking and even switching sides. As opportunity had arisen, both religious sides had taken to hand the means of violence afforded by the local and imperial political authorities, with whom they were variously and closely allied.

The dispute was indeed domestic, and it had a distinctly "worldly" nature, as Rebecca West has noted. "[O]nce a Church acquires property and takes over administrative duties from the State to the extent to which Christianity had done during the fourth century," West points out, "schism becomes not only a difference of opinion about ecclesiastical organization but an attempt at malversation." Such a dispute "is as little a matter for tolerance as an attempt of certain shareholders in a company to take out their capital and seize part of the company's plant."[60] All hostile exaggerations of their misconduct notwithstanding, "there can be no denying that many of [the Donatists] thieved, burned churches, beat people with clubs, threw vitriol over bishops, and murdered their opponents; and the standard of civil order was so low that they could do these things with impunity."[61] Augustine himself had suffered significant physical abuse at their hands.

At first, in a letter recounting a debate with a Donatist bishop, Augustine denied that the persecution of various Christians by other Christians or of Christians and pagans by each other could ever be justified. With what I take to be some hesitation, Augustine argued that Christians cannot oppose schism and heresy by force: "toleration for the sake of peace" and nonviolent persuasion are the properly prescribed Christian means for dealing with disagreements.[62] But such toleration within the Church seemed nearly impossible, despite the theological proximity of the two disputants on nearly all essential questions.[63] The Church had gradually become a political player and hence a preserver of sociopolitical order, so that the Donatist offenses against that order seemed increasingly, by the logic of power, to demand a forceful response.

In letters that follow, we see Augustine developing a response that, as West observes, "was in no way different from the spirit in which his father, or any other good Roman citizen, would have waged war against rebels who had risen against the Empire."[64] In the language of *Dignitatis Humanae*, Augustine had to determine how to discharge the obligation of adhering to the truth and living in accord with it on the one hand with securing, on the other hand, immunity from external coercion and the psychological freedom needed to adhere to that truth.[65] At the same time, he assumed responsibility for maintaining social order from the point of view of the political authorities of the Empire. (*Dignitatis Humanae* seems to enjoin no less.[66]) To accomplish these tasks, Augustine confronted three specific problems: the nature and effects of coercion, the nature of the times, and the reasons for rejecting his former argument concerning patient toleration.

In a letter written seven years later to another Donatist "brother," Emeritus, Augustine moves from a policy of patient nonviolence toward the policies of his later life. When schism within the Church includes the use of violence, Augustine argues, political authorities are free—and, indeed, obligated—to use force and violence against the schismatics. Christians should, no less than anyone else, expect to be physically secure from the violence of those who disagree with them. To ensure such security, Christians, no less than anyone else, are privileged to call in political authorities to use force against other, "schismatic" Christians who have themselves deployed violence. Perhaps Christians "ought not to persecute even the wicked," but it is a reasonable step to avail oneself of properly constituted authorities who are ordained as "ministers of God to execute wrath upon those that do evil" and who possess the means of violent force ("the sword") for a reason. Should the political wielders of the tools of justice not be rallied to employ power in a good cause? After all, the office-holders under this authority are now themselves Christians. Schism, moreover, is an evil work, and those who commit it and resist "the powers that be in a good cause and not in an evil work . . . bring judgment" on themselves.[67]

In two further letters, Augustine draws on four examples from the Old Testament and three from the New to reverse his earlier opinion that "no one should be coerced into the unity of Christ, that we must act only by words, fight only by arguments, and prevail by force of reason." Augustine completes the logic of coercion, arguing that we must first discern the merits of each particular case to determine whether and when the use of force is justified: "when good and bad do the same actions and suffer the same afflictions, they are to be distinguished not by what they do or suffer, but by the causes of each." In the present case, Augustine's (Catholic) Church, in fact, "suffers persecution through the pride and impiety of those carnal men whom it endeavours to correct by afflictions and terrors of a temporal kind."[68]

Augustine recommends that the Church follow the righteous disciplinary example of Moses in contrast to the unrighteous, oppressive disciplinary example of Pharaoh: "Whatever . . . the true and rightful Mother does, even when something severe and bitter is felt by her children at her hands, she is not rendering evil for evil, but is applying the benefit of discipline to counteract the evil of sin, not with the hatred which seeks to harm, but with the love which seeks to heal."[69] Parallel acts of force must be distinguished by the intentions of the agents. In the one case, the agent seeks to destroy; in the other, the agent seeks the welfare of those whom he disciplines. Augustine persecutes, we might say, to preserve human dignity. He recalls those whom he coerces to the fullness of their dignity: being persecuted for righteousness's sake is not equivalent to being punished for a crime.[70] And for the same reason, admonishment in a good cause is generally less severe than when the Christian religion was outlawed and coerced in pagan times.[71]

Augustine's argument for applying coercion with religious intent is ultimately pragmatic. First, New Testament examples to the contrary notwithstanding, coercion, at least among Christians, works. It secures ecclesial unity and assures social harmony, the two having come increasingly to coincide. Second, times have changed. In Augustine's shorthand, the writings of the New Testament contain no examples to help us understand how rulers should defend the Church in (his) contemporary times, because at the time of those writings, there were no rulers willing to defend the Church. But now there are "successors to the imperial throne . . . believing in Christ, at whose hands the wicked suffer because of the Christians."[72] They do not punish crime in this case, but admonish heretics "to depart from evil."[73] The object is always to deliver heretical coreligionists from error "by the help of the terror of judges and laws," not to avenge oneself or to kill one's foes[74] or even to treat them as though they were common criminals.[75]

Augustine pleaded for clemency even toward pagan persecutors of Christians.[76] Some Donatists—perhaps disingenuously—complained that "the apostles never sought such measures from the kings of the earth." Augustine retorted that such claims neglect to consider "the different character of that age and that everything comes in its own season." Rulers were now Christians, and Christianity had become a widespread, respectable religion and an institutionalized source of social order. In Augustine's present time, a king should serve the Lord "by preventing and chastising with religious severity all those acts which are done in opposition to the commandments of the Lord,"[77] as only those in positions of political authority can do.

The character of these changed times and Christian responses to them in the decaying Western empire influence how we should read and respond to the call of *Dignitatis Humanae.*

MODERN TIMES: DIGNITY AFTER CHRISTENDOM

A millennium and a half or more separates us from Augustine, Lactantius, and the other Christian writers that *Dignitatis Humanae* draws upon as representatives of toleration in the Roman Catholic tradition. Much water, mingled with no small amount of blood, has flowed under the bridge since they wrote. That is not an indictment of the Roman Catholic tradition per se: many Christian traditions have blood on their hands. And when it calls upon Ambrose, Augustine, Lactantius, and Gregory as participants and anchors in a long tradition, one must note that their time is not the time of *Dignitatis Humanae*. But if the Church wishes to make appeal to religious freedom and toleration, it cannot do so purely on the basis of a historical record that includes both toleration and coercion, freedom and betrayal, opposition to and collusion with unjust rulers. It must explain why some aspects of its record merit precedence over others.

Equally importantly, *Dignitatis Humanae* seems in several important respects to hearken back to the time of preestablishment, pre-Constantinian Christianity in the West, to a time when its occasionally sanguinary record had not yet been established. As Christianity became the religion of the Empire and then of the various political units that inherited political authority during the decay and dissolution of the western Empire, the Church became "in a word . . . a compulsory society in precisely the same way as the modern state is a compulsory society."[78] Outsiders, be they Jews, heretics, or unbelievers, were often treated with bare toleration, receiving minimal rights and protection when they weren't being coerced, banished, or executed.[79]

To be fair, Ambrose, Augustine, and Gregory did, in correspondence and published writings, advocate forbearance. They also implicitly and explicitly sought to diminish the severity of the political and religiously motivated violence of both those with whom they were allied and those to whom they were opposed. During their time and beyond, however, the Church developed what I have called a patterned set of relationships between two complex entities: itself and the political authorities of the *saeculum*. The major features of this set of relationships include a mutually supportive, symbiotic relationship between *ecclesia* and secular authority. Perhaps because of this symbiotic relationship, Thomas Aquinas, who lived during the full maturity of Christendom, was much less tolerant than Augustine in the matter of heresy. He was concerned, it seems, for societal and political order, and it was not possible to consider such order apart from ecclesial cohesion, which implied a certain degree of violent sociopolitical coercion to produce religious conformity. This effort to produce religious conformity would become much more intense in the early modern era.[80]

Theoretical and practical distinctions between these two realms of Christendom are sustained in clear ways, and they are of no small consequence. Their relationship can be described from a variety of perspectives—political, ethical, anthropological, sociological, even "civilizational." Developments in this latter category receive the most praise in those circles where the integration of Christian ideas with pagan philosophical ones (as are evident in those aspects of the discussion in *Dignitatis Humanae* that include references to natural reason, for example) is considered a civilizational achievement of the first order.[81]

We may conceive of the Church as carrying or exemplifying the substance of Christ. Administering such substance to the surrounding society can be accomplished in at least two basic and distinct ways. On the one hand, Christian believers may find themselves to be members of a unique religious minority. Under this status, their ethical claims may be addressed to each other, without immediate claims on the surrounding society even while the Church bears witness to that surrounding sphere. This community of Christian believers would be a concrete, visible entity with visible differences in behavior (for example, gathering together to practice unusual rites on a particular day of each week, or providing extensive welfare to its poorest members, or not exposing its infants) that clearly distinguish it from the surrounding society in concrete, visible, and ethically nontrivial ways.

Politically, such an assembly of believers might doubt that one could directly see the reign of God in history (as Lactantius and Eusebius had implied one could). It might generally deny that any civil authority could claim to speak transhistorically on behalf of God (as later emperors and monarchs did),[82] even while the group itself would claim to represent the rule of God and the Lamb.[83] Joining such a group, especially in a society in which proper care of the gods (which the Christians reject) is taken to be instrumental for ensuring civic survival and maintaining political order, would require courage. The risks might include economic and social (or even personal physical) harm. The choice to join would imply "taking a decision of a genuinely ethical kind."[84]

On the other hand, in the establishment Church after Constantine, times have changed:

> Up to then, it had required courage to join the church; but from now onwards, this quality was needed, rather, in refusing to join. To profess the Christian faith began to serve as a testimonial to one's suitability for worldly affairs, and for an official career. Large numbers in good society laid emphasis on church activity—in short, the church grew into an essential element of public life, an element forming part of the very world which she had combated up to that point.[85]

Under such circumstances, the Church was gradually made up not of an assenting minority but of everyone. This fact meant, first, that efforts of various kinds arose to distinguish "true" believers, who were now invisible or nearly so within the larger churchly society, from everyone else within the Church.[86] Second, ethical claims came to be divided into two levels, one being addressed to an upper caste of religious professionals, while a lower set was developed for everyone else (the "laity"). As the two realms of *saeculum* and *ecclesia* developed further in their interrelationships, even secular rulership could become one of the "spiritual gifts" or charismata that are displayed in individual members of the Church and that together make up the inward and outward activities of that body of believers known as the Church.

Does the "traditional Catholic doctrine on the moral duty of men and societies toward the true religion and toward the one Church of Christ"[87] imply the renewal of this latter possibility, which had once before become the case by the ninth century?[88] Or is it rather the case that the Church manifests its gifts before a watching world in such a manner that it never assumes that the overlap between *ecclesia* and *saeculum* could be such that charismatic manifestations and secular participation would be one and the same? For example, is it possible to think of the Church as a "people of God . . . called to be today what the world is called to be ultimately?"[89] What time perception of what overarching truth would this claim entail? Whither the knowledge in our time that human dignity should be upheld, and, more specifically, whither the knowledge that such an upholding includes allowing men to "act on their own judgment," not coercing them, and leaving them to enjoy and make use of "a responsible freedom"?[90]

I have, of course, emphasized only one aspect of the knowledge that Augustine, Lactantius, and the others furnish us—namely that, under appropriate circumstances, religious persecution and the abrogation of freedom are permissible and sometimes even laudable, even if simultaneously regrettable. Whither this knowledge? How, for example, do we know what is "just public order,"[91] or what the "just demands of public order" imply, or what is the link between such order and the "external expression" of "internal acts of religion," these latter being "those internal, voluntary and free acts whereby man sets the course of his life directly toward God"?[92] How—in terms of the Gospel— do we know when we should abrogate these freedoms? For *Dignitatis Humanae*, the source of our knowledge is the same as the source for the positive claims concerning human dignity, namely, a combination of both "the sacred tradition and doctrine of the Church—the treasury out of which the Church continually brings forth new things that are in harmony with the things that are old"[93]—and the demands of the times.

But what time is it? It is the time to realize that the dignity of the human person, his "inviolable rights," are linked to "the constitutional order of society." It is the time, in other words, of the liberal regime. It is also the time—roughly a century now—in which more civilians have died at the hands of their own governments than at the hands of foreign powers. This makes it, most urgently, a time to "demand . . . that constitutional limits be set to the powers of government" as was done in varying ways for varying reasons in the past. It is also the time in which the Constantinian sun of Christendom—heralded by Lactantius and Eusebius and established in its heaven by Augustine and his successors—has finally set. It may be, at the same time, the hour of a new, bright noon that Nietzsche proclaimed even while he expressed shock and dismay at the setting of that old, bright Constantinian star.[94] Is there amidst all these times a yet broader epochal time, a time that spans all the others?

Two such times emerge from *Dignitatis*: the time of "the sacred tradition" and the time of "the doctrine," both of the Church. But are there other times of the Church available, or does the Church itself as an institution, as a body of believers, instantiate such a time? The sacred tradition and doctrine of the Church seem temporally compromised, containing conflicting contents that seem to depend on the times. One time has implied or even demanded a mode of political violence that another time has not. One such overlapping time, *Dignitatis* notes, is a prudential time: freedom from coercion is, however valid, freedom "within due limits," a circumscribed freedom. The source of such prudential reasoning is natural law, which derives from the timelessness of an eternal law that transcends all temporal reckonings. A second time that *Dignitatis* makes available to us is the time of human nature, a time that spans all epochs but is subordinate to the time of the Church, which is immortal. This nature is a nature of "reason and free will," by dint of which we are "privileged to bear personal responsibility" and "impelled . . . and also bound . . . to seek the truth, especially religious truth."[95] In light of these two times, and we may put the question yet again: what time is it? Is there a third time?

The claim that patterns of Church life are to be patterns of "human socialness as a whole" establishes a very different time relationship between Church and political authority from that exhibited in the writings of *Dignitatis Humanae*. Our clues for direction in ethical practice would be found more strongly in the time of the Church and its practices and less strongly in dictates of some natural law or the principles of some extraecclesial philosophical anthropology. Our clues might include the practice, say, of "binding and loosing," of baptism, and of breaking bread (Eucharist). In such time, it would be anachronistic to engage in a debate, inspired by the categories of philosophy, that is concerned with the "definition of what happens to the 'emblem'" in the sacrament of communion "when (and only when) the right words are spoken by the priest." This debate was not a part of the first-

century context of the institution of what we now call Eucharist, and it is a
debate that allows us to ignore the economic implications of the Eucharistic
practice of that time. In our time, as we reach for the beginning time of the
Church, we note that "the synthesis of Christianity and empire beginning in
the fourth century" necessarily replaced "the economic meaning of breaking
bread together with something else."[96]

Our post-Christendom time echoes pre-Christendom time, and with
that move we have broken the charmed claim that natural law, for example, is
less particularistic than Church practice. Instead, natural law has become a
particular (not universal) expression of human reason, embodied in a particular (not universal) philosophical tradition, and it is confronted by the particular claim, "so scandalous for many of us," that "biblically the meaning of history is carried first of all, and on behalf of all others, by the believing
community."[97] Because "the particular content of what we find in our particular history" and "the ways we celebrate in our continuing liturgical narration"
are neither "esoteric" nor "provincial" but expressions of a missionary story
that is "defined not by race, nor by geographic isolation, but only the story itself," a story "that by its very nature must be shared, and which invites into its
celebration all who hear it," the story is not more "provincial," say, than a doctrine of natural law.[98]

The content of this ethic guards against provincialism, because the ethic
"forbids itself either to impose its identity or desires on others coercively or to
withhold it from any as a privilege." "The content of the ethic of this community includes at its heart an affirmation of the dignity of the outsider and
the adversary in such a way that while the dangers of arbitrary narrowness can
never be totally banned, they can at least be warded off."[99] If the Gospel is for
everyone, and if the contents of this Gospel message are sufficient for life and
practice, then those contents are no more—and perhaps a great deal less—
particularistic than any other set of universal claims. "[T]he story God has
chosen to have us tell is the story of some people more than others, of Abraham and Jesus," and the doxological telling of this story, replete with meanings, teachings, and concrete, practical implications for the present, is no
more—and perhaps significantly less—particularistic than the dictates of natural law, and no more—and perhaps less—"determinative in dictating what
the method of the witness must be."[100]

The example of the concretely practiced Eucharist might be more accessible to most readers of *Dignitatis Humanae* than is the vague and abstract
concept of a "just public order," or even the dictates of natural law. A key
problem with *Dignitatis Humanae* is that it assumes, except in section 11, that
a modern vocabulary is more adequate for illuminating the truth of the
Gospel than is the Gospel itself. Insofar as *Dignitatis Humanae* speaks of just

political order, and not, say, of the Eucharist (a concern that, on its face, would seem to be a distraction in this context), it uses the language of "rights," "duty," "reason," and "justice." This language assumes Constantinian priority in that it remains the language of establishment. It asks what is the best form of government, and it presumes to have good knowledge of the answer from the perspective of those who rule. The answer, moreover, is found not in the example either of Jesus or even of the Church but of political discourse and philosophical inquiry that originates elsewhere and under axioms or assumptions of generalizability that the pre-Constantinian, pre-Christendom Church did not assume.[101]

If we were to return to the Eucharist as an embodied example of just political order, we might ask how that embodiment speaks to the world in a mutually intelligible way without the immediate intervening overlay of language containing terms like justice, dignity, and rights—terms that are themselves contested within the Roman Catholic tradition. We might reach to a long span of distant time—the tradition of Jewish Passover—a long span of less distant time—the tradition of Christian Eucharist—and to the present—the meaning of Eucharist in the context of its Passover roots as a vision of hope for this present time—to find in the Eucharist a witness to the watching world, concerning just political order and the preservation of human dignity. (We don't eat, for example, while others go hungry.)[102]

The same argument can also apply to baptism and to other practices of the Church. Originally a rite by which one entered into the Church—the new people of God—with a full assent that transcended all prior ascribed or chosen identities, baptism retained important aspects of these characteristics in the era of Christendom, but it also gained new, less happy ones. Whereas "the primary narrative meaning of baptism" prior to Constantine "is the new society it creates, by inducting all kinds of people into the same people," baptism in Christendom after Constantine takes on a primarily sacramental meaning that adopts concepts from a Greek philosophical tradition and with which it defines salvation in terms of "an 'original' sinfulness linked to being born in a human body." Baptism becomes "a symbolic washing with consecrated water" that saves us from this original sin. Within this meaning there is no reason to address "the breaking down of barriers between classes of people. It does not mean a new age breaking in. There is no clear reason not to do it to a newborn infant who does not ask for it. There is no reason it was wrong to do it coercively to whole tribes in the Middle Ages."[103] The newer conception of baptism is thereby—the temporal irony should not escape us—less linked to modern ideas of human dignity than is the older baptismal practice.

The point of these two examples—and we could multiply them—is to ask what kinds of language—conceptual and actualized in time—are available to the Church to engage the concerns of its time and place, as *Dignitatis Humanae* intends. The point of my argument has been to consider if the Church's tradition regarding the everyday political concerns that *Dignitatis Humanae* addresses has an enacted language that is adequate to the task. My provisional answer, based on a brief examination of the historical authorities *Dignitatis Humanae* prescribes, is that it does, but that this is not the language that *Dignitatis Humanae* chooses. Insofar as this conclusion is warranted, I would suggest that how we speak to the world both in our vocabulary and in our claims can be shaped in significant part by which one of two positions we believe ourselves to be occupying—a minority community of faith or a ruling position in society.

My claim is not unique: it is a common understanding of structural realists that where you stand depends on where you sit. In other words, one's ethical formulation, perspective, and understanding are susceptible to one's place in the world.[104] This fact does not make "truth" relative or determined by position, but it does relativize claims about the truth with respect to one's position.[105] It might be the case, for example, that speaking of "rights" or "reason" or "common welfare of society" imposes a new kind of coercion by asserting a privilege to "dictate what the common language is," just as "classical 'natural law'" or another form of "reason" did in the past. This move might be a kind of "epistemological tyranny"[106] that we circumvent only through a language developed directly out of Church practices themselves.

I take this to be one thrust of Vigen Guroian's call to "rediscover the ecclesial context of Christian ethics." That context, as Guroian and others have so powerfully argued in the decades after Vatican II, is a post-Christendom one.[107] In specific Church practices, we would hear dignity echo as we combine old practices and stories and terms with new vocabulary. *Dignitatis* has combined venerable but tainted concepts with new vocabulary, which is a less accessible mode than the one I have suggested here.

The kind of common ground that classical liberal and contemporary neoconservative concepts and strategies can establish and that are evident throughout much of *Dignitatis Humanae* (but happily not all of it) are deeply subversive of this effort to recover practices peculiar to the Church and yet accessible to a watching world. We need to do translation regardless of the "timelessness" we choose to embody, whether natural law or a two-millennium-long tradition of Church practices. There is no direct mention of human dignity in Aquinas's account of natural law, which does not obviate its translatable presence there. So, too, Eucharist, baptism, and other Church practices may preserve human dignity, even if that term was not a part of the original articulation of those practices. Dignity is present underneath the language of the activities, waiting for the time for it to appear to conceptual consciousness.

The argument here concerning practices of persecution and the language of establishment in the tradition to which *Dignitatis Humanae* directs its readers should in no way be understood as an attempt at ad hominem criticism. The times and their particular trials can blur and distort our vision of the past, the present, and the future. Restoring the integrity of the authoritative tradition upon which *Dignitatis Humanae* calls requires a recovery of the gold from its surrounding dross. This call raises the possibility of many resources that the Church has available to display before the watching world. Foremost among them is redeeming the time by means of the Christian practices of confession and repentance.

NOTES

1. See especially Jacques Maritain, *Man and the State* (Chicago: University of Chicago Press, 1951).
2. Richard P. McBrien, *Catholicism: Study Edition* (San Francisco: Harper and Row, Publishers, 1981), 3, 5.
3. *Dignitatis Humanae*, §1.
4. Genesis 1:26.
5. Michael Novak, "The Judeo-Christian Foundation of Human Dignity," *Journal of Markets and Morality* 1 (October 1998), 2, 108.
6. David Hume, "On the Dignity or Meanness of Human Nature," in *Essays: Moral, Political and Literary*, ed. Eugene F. Miller (Indianapolis: Liberty Fund, 1985), 80–86.
7. Hume, "Dignity," 183. Hume's position is typical of British philosophical anthropology of the time: cf. Eric Voegelin, "Ought in Kant's System," in *The Collected Works of Eric Voegelin*, vol. 8, *Published Essays, 1926–30*, trans. Miroslav Hanak and Jodi Cockerill and ed. (with introduction by) Thomas Heilke and John von Heyking (Columbia and London: University of Missouri Press, 2003), 181–83.
8. Thomas Aquinas, *Summa Theologiae*, I.29.a.iii; cf. *S.T.*, II.II.102.a.ii.
9. Aquinas, *S.T.*, II.II.147.a1.
10. Aquinas, *S.T.*, III.4.a1.ii; *S.T.*, III.7.a1.ii, and *S.T.*, III.89.a3.
11. Pico della Mirandola, "On the Dignity of Man," in *The Renaissance Philosophy of Man*, ed. Ernst Cassirer, Paul Oskar Kristeller, and John Hermann Randall (Chicago: University of Chicago Press, 1948), 223–25.
12. della Mirandola, "Dignity of Man," 227.
13. Aquinas, *S.T.*, I.59.a.iii; cf. *S.T.*, II.II.64.a.2.
14. Immanuel Kant, "Speculative Beginnings of Human History," in *Perpetual Peace and Other Essays*, trans. and ed. Ted Humphrey (Indianapolis: Hackett Publishing Company, 1983), 51n5; cf. Voegelin, "Kant's System," 289.
15. Immanuel Kant, *Groundwork of the Metaphysic of Morals*, trans. H. J. Paton (New York: Harper and Row, Publishers, 1964), 102.

16. Kant, *Groundwork*, 102.

17. Kant, *Groundwork*, 103.

18. *Dignitatis Humanae*, §2.

19. *Dignitatis Humanae*, §2.

20. Voegelin, "Kant's System," 183–86; 187–88.

21. *Dignitatis Humanae*, §2.

22. *Dignitatis Humanae*, §2.

23. *Dignitatis Humanae*, §3.

24. Gelasius, "Letter to Emperor Anastasius," [AD 494], in *Readings in European History*, ed. J. H. Robinson (Boston: Ginn, 1905), 72–73.

25. John Milbank, *Theology and Social Theory: Beyond Secular Reason* (Oxford: Blackwell Publishers, 1990), 9.

26. *Dignitatis Humanae*, §1.

27. *Dignitatis Humanae*, §1.

28. See Harold Allen Drake, *Constantine and the Bishops: The Politics of Intolerance* (Baltimore: Johns Hopkins University Press, 2000).

29. William Cavanaugh, "The City: Beyond Secular Parodies," in *Radical Orthodoxy: A New Theology*, ed. John Milbank, Catherine Pickstock, and Graham Ward (London and New York: Routledge, 1999), 182–200.

30. Compare with Ralph Lerner and Muhsin Mahdi, "Introduction," in *Medieval Political Philosophy: A Sourcebook*, ed. Ralph Lerner and Muhsin Mahdi (New York: The Free Press, 1963), 12–13.

31. *Dignitatis Humanae*, §15.

32. The most obvious example here, of course, is Thomas Hobbes, whose bourgeois credentials are secure, even if his "liberal" ones are not entirely (see Hannah Arendt, *The Origins of Totalitarianism* [New York: Harcourt Brace Jovanovich, 1973], 139–47). For the sake of peace, Hobbes would have the sovereign—whether a single person or an assembly of legislators—determine all public theological truth (Thomas Hobbes, *Leviathan*, chapters IV, XXXIII, and XXXVI). John Locke also places restrictions on religion, not only in banishing atheists from his polity but also in establishing a particular (and somewhat peculiar) theology by means of which religious practice can be tamed (John Locke, *A Letter on Toleration*, ed. James Tully [Indianapolis: Hackett Publishing Company, 1983], 30, 48–51). Finally, we see in John Stuart Mill a similar desire to tame religion and find a distinct social niche for it that it can inhabit without causing too much trouble (John Stuart Mill, *On Liberty*, ed. Elizabeth Rapaport [Indianapolis: Hackett Publishing Company, 1978], 46–49). Contemporary debate on this matter has not subsided. See Ashley Woodiwiss, "Rawls, Religion, and Liberalism," in *The Re-Enchantment of Political Science: Christian Scholars Engage Their Discipline*, ed. Thomas Heilke and Ashley Woodiwiss (Lanham, MD: Lexington Books, 2001), 65–83; Robert Audi and Nicholas Wolterstorff, *Religion in the Public Square: The Place of Religious Convictions in Political Debate* (Lanham, MD: Rowman & Littlefield, 1997).

33. *Dignitatis Humanae*, §10.

34. Lactantius, "The Divine Institutes," trans. William Fletcher and ed. Alexander Roberts and James Donalson, *Ante-Nicene Fathers: The Writings of the Fathers Down to*

A.D. 325, vol. 7, *Lactantius, Venantius, Asterius, Victorinus, Dionysius, Apostolic Teaching and Constitutions, Homily, and Liturgies* (Grand Rapids, MI: William B. Eerdmans Publishing Co., 1975 [1886]), I.i (p. 10).

35. Lactantius, "Divine Institutes," V.xx (157).

36. Lactantius, "Divine Institutes," V.xx (157).

37. Lactantius, "Divine Institutes," V.xx and V.xxi (157–58).

38. Lactantius, "Divine Institutes," V.xxi (158).

39. Lactantius, "Divine Institutes," V.xxiv (161).

40. Lactantius, "Divine Institutes," V.xxiv (161). There is some evidence that Constantine was personally familiar with this work (cf. Hans Lietzmann, *A History of the Early Church*, vol. III, *From Constantine to Julian*, trans. Bertram Lee Woolf [Cleveland: Meridian Books, 1961], 158.)

41. Lactantius, "Divine Institutes," I.i (10).

42. Lactantius, "Divine Institutes," I.i (10).

43. See, for example, A. H. M. Jones, *Constantine and the Conversion of Europe* (New York: Collier Books, 1962), 49–58.

44. Lactantius, "Divine Institutes," I.i (10).

45. Lactantius, "Divine Institutes," V.xxiii (159); cf. Thomas Aquinas, *Light of Faith: The Compendium of Theology* (Manchester, NH: Sophia Institute, 1993), sec. 227, 290–91; Aquinas, *ST*, II I. 55, a. i and iv.

46. Jones, *Constantine*, 7. Lietzmann speaks of the "fierce hatred" of Lactantius for the emperors (*Constantine to Julian*, 60).

47. Contrast, for example, Lactantius, "Of the Manner in Which the Persecutors Died," VII, trans. William Fletcher and ed. Alexander Roberts and James Donalson, *Ante-Nicene Fathers: The Writings of the Fathers Down to A.D. 325*, vol. 7, *Lactantius, Venantius, Asterius, Victorinus, Dionysius, Apostolic Teaching and Constitutions, Homily, and Liturgies* (Grand Rapids, MI: William B. Eerdmans Publishing Co., 1975 [1886]) with Lactantius, "Divine Institutes," I.i, II.i, and V.xxiv.

48. A. Cleveland Coxe, "Introductory Notice," in *Ante-Nicene Fathers*, ed. Alexander Roberts and James Donalson, 10n.1.

49. Jones, *Constantine*, 46.

50. Lactantius, "Divine Institutes," VII.26, quoted in Charles Norris Cochrane, *Christianity and Classical Culture: A Study of Thought and Action from Augustus to Augustine* (New York: Oxford University Press, 1957), 186. An alternate translation may be found in Lactantius, "The Divine Institutes," trans. Fletcher and ed. Roberts and Donalson, Lactantius, at 456–57.

51. Lactantius, "Divine Institutes," VII. 26.

52. Eusebius, "Oration in Praise of Constantine," III, 584, in *A Select Library of Nicene and Post-Nicene Fathers of the Christian Church*, 2nd series, ed. Philip Schaff and Henry Wace, vol. 1, *Eusebius* (Grand Rapids, MI: William B. Eerdmans Publishing Co., 1952), 584.

53. Eusebius, "Oration," I, 583.

54. Eusebius, "Oration," II, 583.

55. "Yoder's Idea of Constantinianism: An Analytical Framework toward Conversation," in *A Mind Patient and Untamed: Assessing John Howard Yoder's Contributions to*

Theology, Ethics, and Peacemaking, ed. Gayle Gerber Koontz and Ben C. Ollenburger (Scottdale, PA: Cascadia Publishing House, 2004), 89–125.

56. Eusebius, "Oration," III, 584.

57. *Dignitatis Humanae*, §2 & §4.

58. *Dignitatis Humanae*, §11.

59. Hans Lietzmann, *A History of the Early Church*, vol. IV, *The Era of the Church Fathers*, trans. Bertram Lee Woolf (Cleveland: Meridian Books, 1961), 57ff; James Barmby, "Prolegomena," in *A Select Library of Nicene and Post-Nicene Fathers of the Christian Church*, 2nd series, ed. Philip Schaff and Henry Wace, vol. XII, *Leo the Great and Gregory the Great* (Grand Rapids, MI: William B. Eerdmans Publishing Co., 1956), vi–xvi.

60. Rebecca West, *Saint Augustine* (Chicago: D. Appleton and Company, 1933), 136–37.

61. West, *Saint Augustine*, 137–38.

62. Aurelius Augustine, *The Confessions and Letters of Augustine*, vol. 1 of *The Nicene and Post-Nicene Fathers*, series 1, ed. Philip Schaff (Grand Rapids, MI: William B. Eerdmans Publishing Co., 1952) (Letter XLIII), 518–38.

63. Augustine, Letter CLXXV. This letter is reproduced as "The Correction of the Donatists," in *The Nicene and Post-Nicene Fathers*, series 1, ed. Philip Schaff, vol. 4, *The Writings against the Manichaens, and against the Donatists* (Grand Rapids, MI: William B. Eerdmans Publishing Co., 1952), 1193–1230.

64. West, *Saint Augustine*, 138.

65. *Dignitatis Humanae*, §2.

66. *Dignitatis Humanae*, §7 and §8.

67. This is the letter reproduced as "The Correction of the Donatists" in Schaff.

68. Augustine, *Letters*, XCIII, 758.

69. Augustine, *Letters*, XCIII, 750.

70. Augustine, *Letters*, XCIII, 751–52.

71. Augustine, *Letters*, XCIII, 753. The capital punishment of the "Priscillianists" in late Roman Spain would be the first of many exceptions to this rule (Lietzmann, *Church Fathers*, 72–73).

72. Augustine, *Letters*, XCIII, 752.

73. Augustine, *Letters*, XCIII, 753.

74. Augustine, *Letters*, C, 808.

75. Augustine, *Letters*, CXXXIII, 934–35.

76. Augustine, *Letters*, CXXXIX, 974.

77. Augustine, "Correction of the Donatists," 1208. Augustine's examples, of course, are entirely from the Old Testament, a matter of no small consequence for subsequent Christian political thought.

78. R. W. Southern, *Western Society and the Church in the Middle Age*s (Harmondsworth, England: Penguin Books Ltd., 1970), 17.

79. Southern, *Western Society*, 17.

80. Aquinas, *ST* II.II. 12, art. 3 and 4.

81. See Eric Voegelin, *Renaissance and Reformation*, ed. David Morse and William Thompson (Columbia: University of Missouri Press, 1998), 140–41; and

David Walsh, *After Ideology: Recovering the Spiritual Foundations of Freedom* (San Francisco: HarperCollins Publishers, 1990).

82. John Howard Yoder, *The Priestly Kingdom: Social Ethics as Gospel* (Notre Dame, IN: University of Notre Dame Press, 1984), 130.

83. John Howard Yoder, *The Royal Priesthood: Essays Ecclesiological and Ecumenical*, ed. Michael G. Cartwright (Grand Rapids, MI: William B. Eerdmans Publishing Co., 1994), 128ff.

84. Lietzmann, *Church Fathers*, 97.

85. Lietzmann, *Church Fathers*, 97–98.

86. Lietzmann, *Church Fathers*, 98–100.

87. *Dignitatis Humanae*, §1.

88. Voegelin, *Renaissance and Reformation*, 141.

89. John Howard Yoder, *Body Politics: Five Practices of the Christian Community before the Watching World* (Scottdale, PA: Herald Press, [1992] 2001), ix.

90. *Dignitatis Humanae*, §1.

91. *Dignitatis Humanae* §2.

92. *Dignitatis Humanae*, §3.

93. *Dignitatis Humanae*, §1.

94. Friedrich Nietzsche, *Die Fröhliche Wissenschaft*, §125, in *Friedrich Nietzsche: Sämtliche Werke; Kritische Studienausgabe in 15 Bänden*, ed. Giorgio Colli and Mazzino Montinari, *Bd. III* (Berlin: Deutscher Taschenbuch Verlag de Gruyter, 1980), 480–82; and Friedrich Nietzsche, *Götzendämmerung* iv ("Wie die 'wahre Welt' endlich zur Fabel wurde"), in *Friedrich Nietzsche: Sämtliche Werke; Kritische Studienausgabe in 15 Bänden*, ed. Giorgio Colli and Mazzino Montinari, *Bd. VI* (Berlin: Deutscher Taschenbuch Verlag de Gruyter, 1980), 81.

95. *Dignitatis Humanae*, §2.

96. Yoder, *Body Politics*, 14–15. For a similar perspective from within the Roman Catholic tradition, see Monika K. Hellwig, *The Eucharist and the Hunger of the World* (Mahwah, NJ: Paulist Press, 1976).

97. Yoder, *Royal Priesthood*, 118.

98. Yoder, *Royal Priesthood*, 115.

99. Yoder, *Royal Priesthood*, 115.

100. Yoder, *Royal Priesthood*, 115; cf. Yoder, *Priestly Kingdom*, 40–44. Yoder argues convincingly that Aquinas's use of natural law was "to distinguish that things that everyone (including Christians) need to obey from those elements of divine moral guidance from Scripture which can be left to the Hebrews," so that "[t]he appeal to 'nature' was an instrument of *less* rather than *more* commonality with non-Christians" (p. 42). Accordingly, none of Thomas's distinctions concerning "law" in questions 90–108 of Pt. II of Pt. I of his *Summa* has "the purpose of enabling 'ecumenical' discourse in the realm of the positive determinations of civil law (or moral law in the public arena) with persons rejecting Thomas's world view" (198–99, n. 13).

101. Yoder, *Priestly Kingdom*, 154–55.

102. I Corinthians 11:20–22, 33–34.

103. Yoder, *Body Politics*, 32.

104. Thucydides, *The Peloponnesian War*, vol. 84–116; Robert Kagan, *Of Paradise and Power: America and Europe in the New World Order* (New York: Vintage Books, 2004).

105. Yoder, *The Original Revolution: Essays on Christian Pacifism* (Scottdale, PA: Herald Press, 1971), 148–82.

106. John Howard Yoder, "'Patience' as Method in Moral Reasoning," in *The Wisdom of the Cross: Essays in Honor of John Howard Yoder*, ed. Stanley Hauerwas et al. (Grand Rapids, MI: William B. Eerdmans Publishing Co., 1999), 34. For a further elaboration, see Yoder, *Priestly Kingdom*, 114–16.

107. Vigen Guroian, *Ethics after Christendom: Toward an Ecclesial Christian Ethic* (Grand Rapids, MI: William B. Eerdmans Publishing Co., 1994), 11–28.

· 6 ·

Persuaded, Not Commanded: Neo-Calvinism, *Dignitatis Humanae*, and Religious Freedom

David T. Koyzis

$\mathcal{A}$t the time of the Reformation none of the fragments of the splintered Western church, except for a number of Anabaptist bodies, was explicitly committed to what we would now call religious freedom. The near-universal assumption was that, much as the Old Testament kings were held responsible for suppressing idolatry within the Israelite or Judahite kingdom, so the rulers of the various Christian commonwealths of Europe were responsible for supporting the true religion as they understood it within their realms. Those churches explicitly labeling themselves Reformed or Presbyterian did not depart from this consensus, as can be seen in the writings and confessional documents they produced in the first century or so following the Reformation.

It was not until the nineteenth and twentieth centuries that at least some of these churches, under the influence of Abraham Kuyper's principle of sphere sovereignty, or what has more recently been called differentiated responsibility, began to move toward a conception of society recognizing the distinctive tasks of the institutions of church and state. Since then there has been a remarkable convergence on issues of religious freedom between the Roman Catholic and Reformed churches, as exemplified by the Second Vatican Council's *Dignitatis Humanae* (*DH*)[1] and the writings and practical efforts of neo-Calvinists, particularly in North America.

CALVIN AND THE REFORMED CONFESSIONS

A survey of the confessional documents of the Reformation era makes it clear that the reformers, particularly those within the Calvinist movement, were guided by two political commitments: they regarded the status of the civil

115

magistrate as a confessional matter, and they ascribed to the civil magistrate the authority to advance the true religion within his jurisdiction. The degree of unanimity on both points is remarkable. John Calvin himself, though taking care to distinguish between the respective duties of civil and ecclesiastical authorities, nevertheless insists that "civil government has as its appointed end, so long as we live among men, to cherish and protect the outward worship of God, to defend sound doctrine of piety and the position of the church."[2] Indeed, he also argued that civil government had an obligation to prevent "idolatry, sacrilege against God's name, blasphemies against his truth, and other public offenses against religion from arising and spreading among the people."[3] This view is shared by the great Calvinist political theorist Johannes Althusius. Although seeming to anticipate later developments by affirming that "[f]aith must be persuaded, not commanded, and taught, not ordered,"[4] Althusius nevertheless charges the magistrate with the responsibility for upholding true religion.

The French Confession of 1559 (also known as the Confession of La Rochelle) avers that God "has put the sword into the hands of magistrates to suppress crimes against the first as well as against the second table of the Commandments of God" (art. 39, 382).[5] The first table of the Decalogue concerns the relationship between God and human beings, while the second table treats the relationship among human beings themselves. Thus, the authors of the French Confession, one of whom was Calvin himself, understood the political authorities to have a legitimate role in protecting and supporting true worship of God.

In similar fashion the Scots Confession of 1560 declares that the civil magistrate is responsible "for maintenance of the trew Religioun, and for suppressing of Idolatrie and Superstitioun whatsoever" (art. 24, 476). The unaltered Belgic Confession (1561), the principal standard for the Dutch Reformed churches, claims that magistrates must "protect the sacred ministry, and thus . . . remove and prevent all idolatry and false worship; that the kingdom of antichrist may be thus destroyed, and the kingdom of Christ promoted" (art. 36, 432). With normative status in the Swiss and Hungarian Reformed churches, the Second Helvetic Confession of 1566 maintains that the magistrate shall "advance the preaching of the truth, and the pure and sincere faith, and shall root out lies and all superstition, with all impiety and idolatry, and shall defend the Church of God." He is to "suppress stubborn heretics (who are heretics indeed), who cease not to blaspheme the majesty of God, and to trouble the Church, yea, and finally to destroy it" (art. 30, 305, 306).

The first half of the seventeenth century saw an increase in religious tensions in both the British Isles and the European continent. Nevertheless, even as it distinguished between the functions of church and state, the Westmin-

ster Confession of Faith, ratified by the English Parliament in 1647 during
the brief period of the Puritan Commonwealth, failed to depart fundamentally from the near-universal view of the civil magistrate's authority prevalent
during the previous century. "The civil magistrate," it declared,

> may not assume to himself the administration of the Word and Sacra-
> ments, or the power of the keys of the kingdom of heaven: yet he hath au-
> thority, and it is his duty to take order, that unity and peace be preserved
> in the Church, that the truth of God be kept pure and entire, that all blas-
> phemies and heresies be suppressed, all corruptions and abuses in worship
> and discipline prevented or reformed, and all the ordinances of God duly
> settled, administered, and observed.

Following the Emperor Constantine's precedent in convening the first Council of Nicaea in 325, the Confession concludes: "For the better effecting
whereof he hath power to call synods, to be present at them, and to provide
that whatsoever is transacted in them be according to the mind of God"
(chapter 23.3, 653).

While the French, Belgic, and Helvetic confessions possess authoritative
status within the various continental Reformed churches and their North
American transplants, the Westminster standards, including the Confession
of Faith, are in some sense normative within the Presbyterian churches of the
British Isles and other Anglo-Saxon countries. Yet all of these churches,
whatever their national setting, hold that government is responsible for supporting the teaching authority of the institutional church and suppressing
false religion.

PUTTING ASIDE THE CONFESSIONAL STATE

For a number of reasons, this "constantinian" position did not effectively survive the turbulent years of the seventeenth century. In England, the Commonwealth came to an end in 1660, two years after the death of Oliver
Cromwell, and by 1688 both parliamentary supremacy and the nation's
Protestant identity had been securely established. During this period, however, the secularizing liberal ideas associated with Thomas Hobbes and, more
moderately, John Locke, exercised an increasingly influential force in English
public life.

In Europe, the devastating Thirty Years' War finally ended in 1648, with
general agreement that the competing Christian confessions must find a way
of coexisting. This did not immediately lead to an outright abandonment on

the Reformed side of a commitment to what might be described as the confessional state. In fact, to this day Reformed and Presbyterians have largely maintained their confessional documents intact (with two notable exceptions), while in practice relinquishing the earlier approach to political authority. In North America, most Reformed Christians are committed to a full measure of religious freedom.

Why did this occur? To begin with, although the confessions might indeed charge government with supporting true religion, it seemed no longer possible to secure a popular consensus as to which form of Christianity is true. With dissidents on both sides willing to go to their deaths to defend their understanding of, say, Christ's presence in the sacrament, it seemed inadvisable for government to determine dogmatic issues not immediately connected to the administration of public justice. Thus, the impetus behind the abandonment of the confessional state was in part a practical one, a recognition of the fact that a government presiding over a confessionally divided population would find it gravely difficult to keep civil peace if it favored one confession over another, much less suppressed the latter.

A second factor responsible for the decline of the confessional state was the gradual weakening of belief in the doctrines of the Christian faith among intellectual elites, if not the general public. By the end of the eighteenth century, under the influence of the Enlightenment, increasing numbers of Europeans were openly expressing doubt in the cardinal tenets of what was once assumed to be a common faith. By the nineteenth and twentieth centuries, even prominent ecclesiastics in the Protestant churches were expressing a similar skepticism, almost going so far as to see it as an expression of a kind of virtue. Particularly in the wake of the Kantian project, those who were firm in their belief in God and deferring to the authority of his Word were now portrayed as immature and unwilling to think for themselves. In such a context it seemed a small step to move toward an overtly secular state embracing what the French call *laïcité*. The major strand of political theorizing extending from Machiavelli through Hobbes and Rousseau up to Marx reflected an increasing hostility toward traditional theistic religion.

In today's North America all mainline Protestant bodies believe in religious freedom but often for distinctly secularist reasons incompatible with their own confessions. In such bodies, where the effort to maintain confessional identity has often been dangerously compromised, at least at the synodical level, there is naturally little inclination to push for a confessional state, even if it were feasible. Here religious freedom is affirmed, not so much out of principle, as out of a lack of conviction that *any* religion can be known to be true. And if so, then such freedom is likely to be a severely constricted freedom, largely limited to the private realm and certainly excluded from the public square, where uncontested propositions accessible to universal reason must be held to have clear priority.

In this context, it is perhaps worth noting that two groups of Reformed Christians in North America continue to maintain much more than a nominal allegiance to the confessional state. One of these is the Reformed Presbyterian Church in North America, a body tracing its roots to the Covenanter tradition in Scotland.[6] On at least one occasion, its members have proposed an amendment to the United States Constitution acknowledging not only a theistic basis to the country's laws but also the Lordship of Jesus Christ.[7]

The second group is of more recent vintage and variously goes by the names of theonomy and reconstructionism. Theonomy is characterized by the assumption that the civil precepts of the Old Testament law, understood in a fairly literal way, are still valid for today. As spokesman Greg L. Bahnsen puts it, "We should presume that Old Testament standing laws continue to be morally binding in the New Testament, unless they are rescinded or modified by further revelation."[8] The further assumption is that contemporary political rulers are bound to follow the letter of the law as laid down in Scripture, including, most notably, upholding and advancing true (read: Reformed) religion. Tolerance of religious pluralism is explicitly repudiated by theonomists as tantamount to the acceptance of relativism. Theonomists are found in some of the smaller Presbyterian denominations, especially the Orthodox Presbyterian Church, although the movement does not by any means dominate this body.[9]

ABRAHAM KUYPER AND "ARTICLE 36"

In the Netherlands during the nineteenth century, the Reformed churches that had once dominated the country's cultural and political life developed an alternative to not only the traditional "constantinian" position but to the embrace of religious liberty on either purely pragmatic or secularist grounds. Although in the aftermath of the French Revolution and the tumultuous Napoleonic years, secularization was sweeping through Europe, at the same time a far-reaching revival of Christian piety was occurring, especially in the world of continental Protestantism. In the years after 1815 many European countries found themselves divided between the heirs of the Revolution, along with its ideologies, and observant believers in a more traditional Christianity. In France this pronounced cleavage led to nearly two centuries of political instability (as evidenced by the frequent changes in regime throughout this period) as the two subcultures fought for supremacy, sometimes at the ballot box but often in less civil fashion.

In some of the smaller countries of Europe, however, the leaders of the rival spiritual communities, after initial decades of political antagonism, devised ways of working together for concrete political purposes, even as they continued to compete within the larger culture and as their followers lived fairly separate lives. The Netherlands was one such country. In many respects, this modus vivendi developed almost accidentally and for quite practical reasons. The simple fact was that by this time Reformed and Catholic populations had come to exist as distinct and largely independent subcultures. Something similar was well on the way to happening regarding secularism. At the same time, each of them wished at last to live in peace. The result was a quest for a new view of church and state that would allow the Netherlands to avoid religious conflict. It followed that some alternative must be chosen to avoid the turmoil of the sixteenth and seventeenth centuries.

Rather than following the French Republic by embracing *laïcité*, or the secularization of the public realm, the Dutch opted for a kind of power-sharing arrangement *within the public realm itself*, however, among the leaders of the spiritual communities. This would have the net effect, not of excluding traditional religion from, but of allowing each religion its own voice in, the public square. The resulting political arrangement in the Netherlands has come to be known among political scientists as consociationalism, or elite accommodation, the classic period of which lasted from 1917 to 1966.[10]

One of the implications of this move, although perhaps not originally intended by either Kuyper or Guillaume Groen van Prinsterer, his predecessor in the leadership of the Reformed community, was the abandonment of the confessional state.[11] This affected both the configuration of political parties in the Netherlands and, somewhat surprisingly, an outright modification of one of the confessional documents in the Reformed Churches in the Netherlands (*Gereformeerde Kerken in Nederland*), the formation of which Kuyper had himself instigated in 1892.

Kuyper had established the Anti-Revolutionary Party (ARP) as the first organized political party in the Netherlands, although this party was based on the much earlier movement founded by Groen van Prinsterer, styling itself as antirevolutionary and Christian historical in character.[12] The movement and subsequent political party were based on a traditional understanding of Reformed Christianity animated by the effort to combat the monopolistic pretensions of a secularism stemming from the French Revolution. By the end of the century, however, a dispute between Kuyper and one-time Free University colleague P. J. Hoedemaker (1839–1910) led to the latter's formation of a group that subsequently joined the new Christian Historical Union (CHU), the second Reformed Christian political party in the Netherlands.[13] The latter sought to maintain allegiance to the confessional state as articulated in article 36 of the Belgic Confession.

Despite the CHU's origins as a splinter from the ARP, the two parties proved able to cooperate, along with the Roman Catholic State Party (the RKSP), in broad *Christian* democratic coalition governments throughout much of the twentieth century.[14] These governments did not attempt to enforce confessional uniformity on the Netherlands but in practice protected the religious freedom of their citizens, whatever their confession. In fact, they pursued a robust form of confessional pluralism that allowed the different religious communities considerable leeway in living out their ultimate convictions in both private and public.

Within the *Gereformeerde Kerken* themselves, Kuyper succeeded in persuading the Synod of Utrecht in 1905 to remove the section from article 36 requiring the government to suppress false religion, arguing that this was a holdover from the by-then obsolete medieval position that the Church could be embodied in only a single institutional form within a given territory.[15] As Peter S. Heslam points out, Kuyper's own position underwent modification during his life.[16] Kuyper held to his own motto, "a free church in a free state," on principled, not merely pragmatic, grounds. Yet he seems to have changed his mind on whether civil government could take its bearings from only the natural knowledge of God ostensibly available to all or whether it was permitted to invoke God's explicitly revealed will in pursuing its purposes.

Heslam concludes that, by the time Kuyper delivered his Stone Lectures at Princeton in 1898, he had come to reserve "a place once again for God's revealed will in the judgments of the state, but insisted that this was to be mediated through the consciences of government officials and not through the dictates of any church."[17] In short, Kuyper was in effect arguing that the state has an integrity in its own right under God's sovereignty. The state's jural task is derived immediately from God and not in mediated fashion through the institutional church.[18]

This at least potentially freed government from the necessity of determining which ecclesiastical confession is the true religion and which is not. Kuyper's principle of *soevereiniteit in eigen kring*, translated as "sovereignty in its own sphere" or simply "sphere sovereignty," is not the same as separation of church and state, as that phrase has come to be interpreted in American constitutional jurisprudence in recent decades.[19] Tragically, in this jurisprudence it has come to be interpreted in a manner reminiscent of the French understanding of *laïcité*, as requiring the body politic to be stripped of particular spiritual content and as mandating what Richard John Neuhaus famously labeled a naked public square.[20] Kuyper's understanding, by contrast, recognizes that, although state and church are distinct institutions with their own normative tasks in God's world, religion cannot by any means be excluded from the body politic, whose very constitutional and legal framework presupposes the foundation of a particularizing spiritual vision of the good life. To be sure, government ought to be evenhanded in its treatment of the various confessional communities within its jurisdiction, but it cannot be neutral with respect to its own foundational vision.

NEO-CALVINISM AND RELIGIOUS FREEDOM

Kuyper's followers and heirs, who are often labelled neo-Calvinists, have by now become ardent proponents of religious freedom. The contemporary neo-Calvinist view is ably captured by H. Henry Meeter's injunction that "freedom of conscience and, hence, freedom of religion should be guaranteed to all citizens, including unbelievers. No one should be molested by the state because of his religious convictions unless the authority of the state in its own proper sphere is transgressed."[21] So thoroughly has this come to be accepted that Meeter, writing in 1939, could assume with confidence that his Reformed Christian reading audience would accept his assessment as a matter of course. Indeed, even if all citizens shared the same religious loyalty, he argues that the principle of sphere sovereignty would still make it wrong for the state to establish a church. It would be wrong because church and state have distinct mandates from God. To declare a state-church would be "a step backward, a retrogression" and even a decline to a "lower level of religion."[22] If Meeter is perhaps too quick to ascribe a commitment to full religious freedom to Calvin and the early Reformed Christians, he is nevertheless correct in pointing out the relative tolerance of religious diversity in the Netherlands and, one might add, Switzerland, both of which accepted refugees from other, less tolerant countries in Europe.

It might well be argued, in fact, that much of neo-Calvinism's political agenda nowadays is centered on the quest for religious freedom; understood not merely as the liberty to follow one's ultimate convictions in private and certainly not as the separation of church and state but as a much more comprehensive liberty mandating an open public square accommodating a variety of religious communities. This has been called confessional pluralism or, to underscore its distance from a merely pragmatic approach, principled pluralism.[23]

To be sure, there is considerable overlap between the concerns of neo-Calvinists and other proponents of religious freedom, both *Christian* and non-Christian. Paul Marshall's *Their Blood Cries Out* is a good example of a book written by a professed neo-Calvinist calling attention to an issue that could appeal even to secular liberals otherwise uncomfortable with the capacious public square championed by neo-Calvinists.[24] When it was published, Marshall's book received an encouraging degree of mainstream attention and acclaim, because he focused on an obvious injustice that virtually all his readers could recognize as such: millions of Christians around the world are being persecuted in quite tangible and egregious ways for their beliefs.

Although Marshall's ongoing work with the Center for Religious Freedom at Freedom House underscores the considerable common ground between neo-Calvinists and especially other Christians, neo-Calvinists are perhaps most associated with the struggle to gain official acknowledgment of the priority of parental rights in education. They have also come to be associated with movements pushing for electoral reform, especially the adoption of some form of proportional representation (PR) in place of the current first-past-the-post (FPTP) system operative in most Anglo-Saxon democracies.[25] Yet even here support for PR is motivated by the desire to open up the public square to a diversity of confessionally based viewpoints—yet another manifestation of the concern for religious freedom. They are also among the leading advocates of what has come to be known as charitable choice, that is, the establishment of policies securing faith-based organizations equal access to governmental funds in the area of social services.[26]

These are issues on which there is hardly unanimity among Christians, unlike situations where outright persecution takes place. Not all Christians, even evangelical Protestants, are inclined to support school choice, and some continue to support the notion of an ostensibly nonconfessional common public school on principle. Similarly, many, if not most, North American Christians have no position whatever on their country's electoral system, failing to see a connection between the issue and the secularizing implications of a public square artificially closed to minority religious communities by FPTP. Others either oppose or support the welfare state in general without attending to the religious freedom issues related to public-private sector partnerships.

DH: CATHOLICISM'S PARALLEL PATH

Much as neo-Calvinism's emphasis on sphere sovereignty served to move Reformed Christians beyond the confessional state to embrace religious freedom, the Second Vatican Council (1962–1965) moved the Roman Catholic Church in a similar direction. In fact, it might well be said that, from the middle of the nineteenth century, Roman Catholicism and Reformed Christianity moved along strikingly parallel paths in a similar direction.[27] As Kuyper was working out the social and political implications of Calvinism in the Netherlands, Pope Leo XIII was publishing his groundbreaking social encyclicals, the most famous of which is, of course, *Rerum Novarum* (1891).[28] Much as Kuyper's principle of sphere sovereignty was a way of accounting for complexity in God's world, including the pluriformity of human society, successive popes were doing the same thing with subsidiarity, a term coined by Pope Pius XI in *Quadragesimo Anno* (1931) but already implicit in Leo's writings and arguably in the philosophy of Thomas Aquinas himself.

A major difference between the two movements is that, while Catholic social teachings, along with the neo-Thomist revival sparked by Leo's *Aeterni Patris* (1879), would come to exert significant influence throughout Europe and Latin America, neo-Calvinism's influence, at least in the beginning, was largely restricted to the Netherlands. Indeed, only in the middle and later years of the twentieth century, after its influence in the Netherlands had begun to wane, would neo-Calvinism move beyond its native soil and exert an influence in places like South Africa, North America, Australia, and New Zealand. In these locales, through the efforts of Dutch Reformed immigrants, neo-Calvinism regained some of its original vigor, although its influence hardly rivals that which it exercised in the Netherlands.

Yet the demands of civil peace compelled both neo-Calvinism and Catholicism to rethink their approach to the whole question of religious freedom in the light of the newfound religious pluralism that became a basic fact of social life after the sixteenth century. Rather than clinging to a clearly obsolescent paradigm or embracing religious freedom on pragmatic or secularist grounds, furthermore, both traditions renewed themselves by articulating a fresh approach that was simultaneously faithful to their respective traditions and adapted to the new social realities of modern times.

On the Catholic side, this rethinking crystallized in *DH*, the Second Vatican Council's Declaration on Religious Freedom. In the face of the growing demand for religious liberty, *DH* avows, the Council has searched "into the sacred tradition and doctrine of the Church" in order to bring "forth new things that are in harmony with the things that are old" (*DH*, 1). In this case, the "new" thing consists in the affirmation "that the human person has a right to religious freedom" encompassing a right not "to be forced to act in a manner contrary to his beliefs," as well as a right not "to be restrained for acting in accordance with his own beliefs, whether privately or publicly, whether alone or in association with others" (*DH*, 2) so long as "the just requirements of public order are observed" (*DH*, 3). The parallels between the approach that emerges in *DH* and that which informs contemporary neo-Calvinism are striking.

In the first place, *DH*'s embrace of religious freedom is rooted in principle, rather than merely pragmatic considerations. The right to religious freedom, it affirms, has its "foundation" in the "very dignity of the human person as this dignity is known through the revealed Word of God and by reason itself" (*DH*, 2). At the same time, *DH* is at pains to make clear that its commitment to religious freedom is not a function of some type of religious relativism. On the contrary, it affirms that its embrace of religious freedom "leaves untouched traditional Catholic doctrine on the moral duty of men and societies toward the true religion and toward the one Church of Christ" (*DH*, 1). Catholic and Reformed Christians, of course, disagree as to the institutional identity of that church, but they are at one in acknowledging that God's image-bearers are responsible for seeking the truth, embracing it and living accordingly.[29] ("It is," *DH* affirms, "in accordance with their dignity as persons . . . that all men should be . . . impelled by nature and . . . bound by a moral obligation to seek the truth, especially religious truth. They are also bound to adhere to the truth, once it is known, and to order their whole lives in accord with the demands of truth" [*DH*, 2]).

In these traditions, therefore, the desire to protect religious freedom within the body politic in no way alters their overriding commitment to the truth. Indeed, it is the truth that constitutes religious freedom's ultimate foundation—if we cannot affirm that human beings truly possess the dignity both traditions attribute to them, then we can no longer affirm the inviolability of the rights that flow from this dignity.

Secondly, like neo-Calvinism, *DH* recognizes that religious freedom cannot be reduced in liberal fashion to the mere right of *individuals* to worship as they please. Affirming that "religious bodies are a requirement of the social nature of both man and religion itself," it concludes that "the freedom . . . from coercion in matters religious which is the endowment of persons as individuals is also to be recognized as their right when they act in community" (*DH*, 4). If this freedom extends to individuals acting "alone," it also extends to their acting "in association with others" (*DH*, 2). Indeed, religious communities "have the right not to be hindered in their public teaching and witness to their faith," to "govern themselves according to their own norms," to "establish educational, cultural, charitable, and social organizations, under the impulse of their own religious sense," and to attempt "to show the special value of their doctrine in what concerns the organization of society and the inspiration of the whole of human activity" (*DH*, 4).

Religion, in short, is by its very nature manifested and expressed socially, not merely a private predilection with no social consequences. Precisely because humans are intrinsically social beings, it follows that they must be given the opportunity to express externally their internal religious orientation. "The social nature of man," as *DH* affirms, "itself requires that he give external expression to his internal acts of religion; that he should participate with others in matters religious; that he should profess his religion in community" (*DH*, 3). *DH*'s teaching thus affirms that religion inescapably has a public side. The liberal attempt to relegate religion to the private realm is nothing less than a denial of something integral to the very meaning of religion. Official efforts to secularize the public square amount to at least an infringement if not an outright denial of religious freedom. Convinced that justice itself requires that people be allowed a wide latitude to manifest publicly their religious convictions, both *DH* and neo-Calvinism advocate policies that would establish and maintain an open public square, a public square accessible to all.

This means, in the third place, that religious liberty requires freedom for the Church as an institution. "The Church," as *DH* observes, "should enjoy that full measure of freedom which her care for the salvation of men requires," the full measure of "independence . . . necessary for the fulfillment of her divine mission" (*DH*, 13). Because the Church has a unique God-given role in human society, its ability to function in this role must be protected by the civil authorities. Far from implying the sort of throne and altar arrangement championed by nineteenth-century restorationists after 1815, the independence of the Church must be respected and protected by the state. Indeed, this independence "is the fundamental principle in what concerns the relationship between the Church and governments and the whole civil order" (*DH*, 13).

Quite naturally, *DH*'s focus is on the Roman Catholic Church as the repository of the Christian faith. Neo-Calvinism, with its more plural understanding of the institutional church, is more explicit in calling for the independence of the several churches and for preventing government interference in their institutional activities, although even this can be seen as implicit in the logic of *DH*. Religious freedom, it affirms, "is to be recognized as the right of *all* men and communities" (*DH*, 13), of not just the Catholic Church but of all "religious bodies" (*DH*, 3).

Finally, parallels exist between neo-Calvinism and *DH* on the whole question of education. At least since the time of Plato and Aristotle, it has been widely assumed that the *polis* is primarily responsible for the education of children. According to Aristotle, for example, the character of the citizenry —its possession or lack of specific virtues—inevitably impacts the ethos of a given *polis*. The political authorities, therefore, must undertake to maintain this ethos by inculcating in the citizenry the virtues necessary to support it. This requires in the first place framing good laws, since law is a teacher of virtue. But it also entails more direct efforts at education of the young.

Contemporary states have understood this to call for the establishment and upkeep of a comprehensive system of schools funded from the public purse. To be sure, in North America such public schools are administered by local governments, although state/provincial and federal governments inevitably make policy with respect to education. In most jurisdictions on this continent, furthermore, these public schools enjoy a monopoly of funds raised through local property taxes. The rationale behind this monopoly, particularly in the United States, is that, in order to avoid the excessive entanglement of church and state, government can support only "nonsectarian" schools, that is, those not explicitly based on a particular religious confession.

Many, if not most, Christians in North America simply accept this favored treatment of public schools without question, assuming that it is necessary to secure social unity. A number of Christian communities have effectively been dissidents from this apparent consensus. The most prominent of these is the Roman Catholic Church, which maintains a network of parochial schools across the continent, established soon after Catholic immigrants arrived in the two countries from their European or Latin American homelands. Lutherans of the Missouri and Wisconsin Synods also maintain their own systems of primary and secondary schools oriented around their distinct confessional identities. Seventh-Day Adventists and increasing numbers of evangelical Protestants operate their own day schools, the latter in particular due to a perceived moral decline in the public schools. Finally, Calvinists in especially the Christian Reformed Church operate an extensive school system not under the auspices of a church denomination but of parentally controlled boards federated into a larger organization, Christian Schools International.

Government recognition and funding of such schools vary among the several provinces and states. Up until the 1960s, the vast majority of schools within Québec were Catholic schools controlled by ecclesiastical authorities, while the British North America Act and the Constitution Act of 1867 mandated the maintenance of a Protestant system as well for particularly the English-speaking non-Catholic minority. Until the mid-twentieth century the Ontario public schools were generically Protestant, while a system of "separate" Catholic schools received partial and eventually full provincial funding, as provided for once again in section 93. Alberta provides full funding for the public schools and partial funding for independent schools. Newfoundland fully funded four denominational school systems until 1997, when they were taken over by the provincial government. The states of the United States vary less in their treatment of confessional schools, although the Supreme Court has recently judged as constitutionally permissible efforts at implementing voucher systems in several states.[30]

DH insists that religious freedom demands parents' control over the education of their children. "Since the family is a society in its own original right," it declares, it has the right to live its own domestic religious life under the guidance of parents. Parents, moreover, have the right to determine, in accordance with their own religious beliefs, the kind of religious education that their children are to receive. Government, in consequence, must acknowledge the right of parents to make a genuinely free choice of schools and of other means of education, and the use of this freedom of choice is not to be made a reason for imposing unjust burdens on parents, whether directly or indirectly. Besides, the rights of parents are violated, if their children are forced to attend lessons or instructions which are not in agreement with their religious beliefs, or if a single system of education, from which all religious formation is excluded, is imposed upon all. (*DH*, 5)

With perhaps minor emendations, this statement could have been written by any one of the neo-Calvinist heirs of Kuyper, as it well summarizes the position of both Catholic and Reformed traditions. Education, on this view, is fundamentally a parental responsibility, and the right of parents to choose where to educate their own children is one that must be respected by government, both legally and financially.[31] That this would entail an end to the monopolistic claim of the public schools over tax revenues would seem to place this stance outside the mainstream of public opinion in large parts of both the United States and Canada. Nevertheless, it is a view that increasing numbers of North Americans of whatever religious tradition are coming to embrace. Undoubtedly, the most important factor in play here is pragmatic in nature: the failure of the public schools to provide an adequate education. But there are other factors as well, such as the Universal Declaration of Human Rights' affirmation that "parents have a prior right to choose the kind of education that shall be given to their children" (art. 26[3]).[32]

One of the most important factors in this change of heart is the heightened understanding, among both Catholics and Protestants, that religion is not so easily excluded from education of any kind, that, when all is said and done, "nonsectarian" education is impossible. Biology or chemistry textbooks pointedly omitting any reference to God are based, after all, on the religious assumption that creation can be understood apart from the Creator who brought it into being. Social studies texts lacking such references will inevitably communicate, if only tacitly, that human social formations, in all their complexity, answer to no order higher than ourselves and are thus infinitely malleable in accordance with our own autonomous aspirations for them.

If the public schools cannot ultimately be devoid of a religious worldview, then for government to privilege them above other more overtly confessional schools is tantamount to establishing a nontheistic religion and penalizing parents who wish their children to be educated in a more explicitly theistic worldview. By privileging these schools, in short, the state is infringing upon the right of the human person to the free exercise of religion. For this reason, Catholics and neo-Calvinists alike, along with increasing numbers of Christians from other traditions, persevere in making the case for more equitable funding of a variety of schools, whether they be labeled public or independent, nonsectarian or confessional.

THE PROMISE OF RELIGIOUS FREEDOM

Until recently, many North Americans might have been tempted to assume that religious freedom was yesterday's issue, at least within the domestic context. After all, the United States in particular was built by successive waves of settlers, many of whom were fleeing religious persecution in their former homelands. Canada's prairies were peopled by such communities as Mennonites, Hutterites, and Doukhobors, who sought the liberty to practice their respective faith commitments in a new land. Inasmuch as many North Americans assumed that their countries were already generically Christian in some sense, they may not have been aware of the long-standing efforts of political authorities to grapple with the fact of religious plurality within their own and other countries. Indeed, it might not have appeared to be a significant issue at all.

In recent years, however, a number of developments have brought the issue back to the forefront of public consciousness. The terrorist attacks on the United States of September 11, 2001, raised awareness of the nature of radical Islamism as a movement capable of mobilizing huge numbers of adherents of the world's third great monotheistic religion. The rule of the Taliban in Afghanistan was regarded as especially egregious in the West insofar as it systematically denied the religious liberties of those within the territory under its control. Samuel Huntington's *The Clash of Civilizations* has drawn attention to the role of religion in fomenting potential conflict among the world's great civilizations, particularly between the post-Christian West and Islam.[33] Finally, there is the French Parliament's enactment of a controversial law prohibiting the wearing of headscarves, yarmulkes, oversized crosses, or other obvious religious symbols in public buildings.

While the secular media often cynically portray the Christian churches as little more than institutional concentrations of self-serving power, it is almost certainly true that historically Christians have more often been the victims of persecution than its perpetrators. Philip Jenkins has estimated that, at the height of medieval Christendom, there were probably many more Christians living in Spain, northern Africa, and what we would today call the Middle East under political authorities hostile to their faith than were living in the relatively sparsely populated lands of Western Europe, where Christianity was officially favored.[34]

Today, moreover, huge numbers of Christians in Africa, Asia, and the Middle East continue to be persecuted for their faith. Even in the historically Christian lands of the West, Christians are often confronted with some measure of official hostility, as the claims of their religion are conspicuously at variance with liberal political culture's exaltation of individual autonomy. If Christians are not facing outright persecution in the contemporary West, there are increasing efforts to mute Christianity's witness, particularly within the public realm. Against this backdrop, it is perhaps not surprising that Catholics, neo-Calvinists, and a number of other Christian communities are at the forefront of efforts to safeguard religious freedom throughout the world and across the entire range of human activities.

NOTES

1. For purposes of convenience, *Dignitatis Humanae* will be abbreviated as *DH*, and citations will be given parenthetically by section number.

2. John Calvin, *Institutes of the Christian Religion*, ed. John T. McNeill, trans. Ford Lewis Battles, 2 vols. (Philadelphia: Westminster Press, 1960), book 4, chapter 20, section 2, 1487.

3. Ibid., 4, 20, 3, 1488.

4. Johannes Althusius, *Politics*, trans. Frederick S. Carney (Boston: Beacon Press, 1964), chapter XXVIII, 167. Althusius is perhaps unusual in appealing for an end to the religious persecutions then taking place in so much of Europe and embracing tolerance of confessional diversity: "Where there are no persecutions, there everything is peaceful, even though there are different religions" (168).

5. Unless otherwise indicated, this and subsequent references to the various Reformed confessions are taken from Philip Schaff, *The Creeds of Christendom*, vol. III, *The Evangelical Protestant Creeds* (Grand Rapids, MI: Baker Book House, 1983; reprint, New York: Harper & Row, 1931). The article number in the creed will be followed by the page number of this volume. I have employed the English translation of the Helvetic confession found at www.ccel.org/ccel/schaff/creeds3.v.ix.html. Accessed August 23, 2006.

6. For a defense of the confessional state from a Covenanter position, see William Edgar, "The National Confessional Position," in *God and Politics: Four Views on the Reformation of Civil Government*, ed. Gary Scott Smith (Phillipsburg, NJ: Presbyterian and Reformed, 1989), 176–99.

7. Edgar, "The National Confessional Position," 189.

8. Greg L. Bahnsen, "The Theonomic Position," in *God and Politics*, 24.

9. The Orthodox Presbyterian Church (OPC) was founded in 1936 by a group, led by J. Gresham Machen, that had left the former Presbyterian Church in the

United States of America over the perceived increasing liberalism in the parent body. The OPC represents a rigorous form of Reformed confessionalism rooted in "old school" Presbyterianism and nineteenth-century Princeton orthodoxy, with an admixture of Dutch Reformed influence via the Christian Reformed Church. For a collection of essays treating the history of the OPC, see *Pressing toward the Mark: Essays Commemorating Fifty Years of the Orthodox Presbyterian Church*, ed. Charles G. Dennison and Richard C. Gamble (Philadelphia: The Committee for the Historian of the Orthodox Presbyterian Church, 1986).

10. For treatments of consociationalism in several different contexts, see Arend Lijphart, *Democracy in Plural Societies* (New Haven: Yale University Press, 1977); Kenneth McRae, *Consociational Democracy: Political Accommodation in Segmented Societies* (Toronto: McClelland and Stewart, 1976); *Party Elites in Divided Societies: Political Parties in Consociational Democracy*, ed. Kurt Richard Luther and Kris Deschouwer (London: Routledge, 1999); and Jeffrey L. Obler, Jürg Steiner, and Guido Dierickx, *Decision-Making in Smaller Democracies: The Consociational "Burden"* (Beverly Hills, CA: Sage Publications, 1977). Lijphart's name is probably most associated with consociationalism, although in recent years his work has broadened somewhat to cover a number of comparative institutions, particularly electoral and party systems. For the classic treatment of consociationalism in the Netherlands, see Lijphart, *The Politics of Accommodation: Pluralism and Democracy in the Netherlands* (Berkeley: University of California Press, 1968, 1975). For an interpretation contrasting with Lijphart's, see Harry Van Dyke, "Groen van Prinsterer's Interpretation of the French Revolution and the Rise of 'Pillars' in Dutch Society," in *Presenting the Past: History, Art, Language, Literature*, ed. Jane Fenoulhet and Lesley Gilbert (London: Centre for Low Countries Studies, 1996), 83–98.

11. For the definitive account of Groen's life and work, see Harry Van Dyke, *Groen van Prinsterer's Lectures on Unbelief and Revolution* (Jordan Station, ON, Canada: Wedge Publishing Foundation, 1989). Included in this volume is an abridged English translation of his best-known work, *Unbelief and Revolution (Ongeloof en Revolutie)*.

12. See McKendrie R. Langley, "Emancipation and Apologetics: The Formation of Abraham Kuyper's Anti-Revolutionary Party in the Netherlands, 1872–1880" (Th.D. dissertation, Philadelphia: Westminster Theological Seminary, 1995).

13. The dispute between Kuyper and Hoedemaker is recounted in John Bolt, *A Free Church, A Holy Nation: Abraham Kuyper's American Public Theology* (Grand Rapids, MI: William B. Eerdmans Publishing Co., 2001), 321–32. The Free University of Amsterdam had been founded in 1880 by Kuyper and others as an explicitly Christian university in the Reformed tradition.

14. Between 1977 and 1980 the three parties, including the ARP, the CHU, and what had by then become the Catholic People's Party (KVP), merged to form a single party, the Christian Democratic Appeal.

15. Bolt explicitly observes the similarity between this development and the position embraced by *DH* decades later. See Bolt, 321.

16. Peter S. Heslam, *Creating a Christian Worldview: Abraham Kuyper's Lectures on Calvinism* (Grand Rapids, MI: William B. Eerdmans Publishing Co., 1998), 161–66.

17. Ibid., 164. Kuyper's lectures were subsequently translated into English and published as Abraham Kuyper, *Lectures on Calvinism* (Grand Rapids, MI: William B. Eerdmans Publishing Co., 1931).

18. The Christian Reformed Church's Synod of 1958 not only followed the example of the GKN and similarly excised the section mandating a confessional state but went so far as to substitute in its place the following: "[The civil rulers should govern] in order that the World of God may have free course; the kingdom of Jesus Christ may make progress; and every anti-Christian power may be resisted." *Acts of the Synod 1958* (Grand Rapids, MI: Christian Reformed Church in North America, 1958).

19. For Kuyper's treatment of this principle, see his "Sphere Sovereignty," delivered at the opening of the Free University of Amsterdam in 1880 and subsequently translated and published in *Abraham Kuyper: A Centennial Reader*, ed. James D. Bratt (Grand Rapids, MI: William B. Eerdmans Publishing Co., 1998), 461–90.

20. Richard John Neuhaus, *The Naked Public Square: Religion and Democracy in America* (Grand Rapids, MI: William B. Eerdmans Publishing Co., 1984).

21. H. Henry Meeter, *The Basic Ideas of Calvinism*, 6th ed., rev. Paul A. Marshall (Grand Rapids, MI: Baker Book House, 1990), 136.

22. Ibid., 135.

23. For an excellent introduction to this conception of pluralism and its relevance to contemporary American public life, see James W. Skillen, *Recharging the American Experiment: Principled Pluralism for Genuine Civic Community* (Grand Rapids, MI: Baker Book House, 1994). Insofar as religious communities are directed by their divergent ultimate commitments to follow different paths or ways, Richard Mouw and Sander Griffioen also speak of "directional diversity." See Mouw and Griffioen, *Pluralisms and Horizons: An Essay in Christian Public Philosophy* (Grand Rapids, MI: William B. Eerdmans Publishing Co., 1993), esp. 87–109.

24. Paul Marshall, *Their Blood Cries Out: The Untold Story of Persecution against Christians in the Modern World*, with Lela Gilbert (Dallas: Word Publishing, 1997). See also *Religious Freedom in the World: A Global Report on Freedom and Persecution*, ed. Paul Marshall (Nashville: Broadman & Holman, 2000).

25. See, for example, Nick Loenen, *Citizens and Democracy: The Case for Proportional Representation* (Toronto: Dundurn Press, 1997); and David T. Koyzis, "Voter Turnout and Competitive Politics," *Public Justice Report* 23, no. 23 (2000): 3.

26. For a collection of essays on this topic, see *Welfare in America: Christian Perspectives on a Policy in Crisis*, ed. Stanley W. Carlson-Thies and James W. Skillen (Grand Rapids, MI: William B. Eerdmans Publishing Co., 1996). This issue was an important part of George W. Bush's original policy agenda but has effectively taken a back seat to the ongoing war on terrorism. Carlson-Thies himself served in the White House in the Office of Faith-Based and Community Initiatives in 2001–2002.

27. For a comparison and contrast of two traditions, see David T. Koyzis, *Political Visions and Illusions: A Survey and Christian Critique of Contemporary Ideologies* (Downers Grove, IL: InterVarsity Press, 2003), especially 215–43; and M. C. Smit, *Toward a Christian Conception of History*, trans. and ed. H. Donald Morton and Harry Van Dyke (Lanham, MD: University Press of America, 2002), 189–201.

28. For an in-depth exploration of the relationship between Kuyper's thought and Leo XIII's social teaching, see the symposium on "A Century of Christian Social Teaching: The Legacy of Leo XIII and Abraham Kuyper," in *Markets & Morality* 5, no. 1 (Spring 2002); and Harry Van Dyke, "How Abraham Kuyper Became a Christian Democrat," *Calvin Theological Journal* 33 (1998): 420–35.

29. For a Reformed understanding of ecclesial unity, see Herman Bavinck, "The Catholicity of Christianity and the Church," trans. John Bolt, *Calvin Theological Journal* 27 (1991): 220–51. Bavinck tends to confuse the fissiparousness occasioned by multiple schisms in which nothing less than doctrinal truth is at issue with legitimate institutional pluriformity. Yet he would appear to be correct in judging that denominational pluralism historically contributed to the acceptance of religious freedom.

30. This was decided in *Zelman v. Simmons-Harris* (June 27, 2002).

31. For neo-Calvinist statements on education, see, e.g., Rockne McCarthy et al., *Society, State, and Schools: A Case for Structural and Confessional Pluralism* (Grand Rapids, MI: William B. Eerdmans Publishing Co., 1981); James McCarthy, W. Skillen and William A. Harper, *Disestablishment a Second Time: Genuine Pluralism for American Schools* (Grand Rapids, MI: Christian University Press, 1982); and *The School Choice Controversy: What Is Constitutional?*, ed. James W. Skillen (Grand Rapids, MI: Baker Book House, 1993).

32. "United Nations Universal Declaration of Human Rights," in *The Human Rights Reader*, rev. ed., ed. Walter Laqueur and Barry Rubin (New York: Meridian, 1990), 197–202.

33. Samuel P. Huntington, *The Clash of Civilizations and the Remaking of World Order* (New York: Simon & Schuster, 1996).

34. Philip Jenkins, *The Next Christendom: The Coming of Global Christianity* (Oxford: Oxford University Press, 2002), 22–25.

On Proposing the Truth and Not Imposing It: John Paul's Personalism and the Teaching of *Dignitatis Humanae*

John F. Crosby

$\mathcal{W}$riting[1] just after Vatican II, John Courtney Murray observed that, though the teaching of *Dignitatis Humanae* (*DH*) on the right to religious liberty is "clear, distinct, and technically exact," the philosophical and theological foundations of this right are not equally clear and distinct. He thought in fact that the Council had left unfinished the "more difficult question of how to construct the argument—whether derived from reason or from revelation—that will give a solid foundation to what the Declaration [on religious freedom] affirms."[2] What I propose to do here is to examine how the Christian personalism of John Paul II might assist us in securing the foundations of the right to religious freedom.

DH affirms that this right is rooted in the dignity of the human person, saying in one place, "The Declaration of this Vatican Council on man's right to religious freedom is based on the dignity of the person, the demands of which have become more fully known to human reason through centuries of experience."[3] John Paul was deeply indebted to, indeed was deeply formed by this growing awareness of man as person and of the dignity of persons, and in fact through his writings and teachings made himself an agent of this growing awareness, a full participant in the event of this growth. We would therefore expect that his deep and original reflections on the human person, which have proved to be so fruitful in different areas, as in the area of personal embodiment and human sexuality (theology of the body), will also prove fruitful for completing the work that Father Murray thought needed completing. In this paper I will not limit myself to what John Paul in fact said directly about the teaching of *DH* but will also consider what his personalism, beyond the letter of his writings and pronouncements on *DH*, implies for the right to religious freedom.

FREEDOM VERSUS TRUTH?

"The people of our time prize freedom very highly and strive eagerly for it. In this they are right."[4] But Christian believers of all times have prized the truth about God and man very highly and have striven eagerly for it. In this they were also right. How does the modern esteem for freedom cohere with the traditional Christian zeal for truth?

In the hurly-burly of human history, the respect for freedom and the zeal for truth have not always enjoyed a peaceful coexistence and in fact have again and again been antagonistic to each other. So let us begin by trying to understand the root of this chronic antagonism between them. It lies in the objective and binding character of the truth by which Christians live and for which they are ready to die. They think that the Nicene Creed is not just true *for Christians*, is not just an objectivization of the inner experiences of Christians, but that it is literally true, really true, not true for some and not others, but true *simpliciter* and therefore true for everyone. In fact, they think that it is a truth that non-Christians need no less than Christians, a truth that non-Christians ought to come to acknowledge, a truth that has a claim to be received and venerated by every human person. They think the same thing about the moral law by which they live; it is valid for and binding on all human persons.

If truth could be relativistically dissolved, if moral affirmations had nothing more than emotive meaning, then of course truth would not seem to be antagonistic to freedom. Or if truth were nothing more than William James makes it out to be in his *Lectures on Pragmatism* it never would have occurred to anyone to speak of an antagonism between freedom and truth. Or if moral and religious truth constituted an optional realm of valid requirements, a realm which one were free to enter or not, like the world of a game and its rules, then of course such truth could easily cohere with the boldest demands of freedom. What makes for conflict with the freedom for which so many people aspire is the objectivity and universal validity that Christians claim for the truth by which they live, and not only the universal validity but also, as we could put it, the *universal destination* of this truth, that is, the fact that it is meant for every human person.

Let us distinguish two ways in which such truth can seem to be antagonistic to freedom. Some will say that if we acknowledge truth in this strong Christian sense we will be oppressed by what Kant called *heteronomy*. Since this truth originates outside of our freedom, descending as it were from above, it will inevitably remain something foreign to our freedom; if we are told that we ought to live by it, then we are oppressed by a foreign law, a law not our own, not appropriate to us, and hence we are crippled by heteronomy. Only that which is born of my freedom, only that in which I recognize my self, only that of which I am the measure, can enter into my existence without any threat of heteronomy; and only in this way can I live the autonomy that is my birthright as person. From this point of view Christian revelation and Christian morality, claiming as they do to originate in God and to bind all human persons, can only seem to be a grave threat to our freedom.

Now whereas this threat arises internally, in the encounter of each person with the Christian claims, there is a related threat to our freedom that arises in a more external way. This one arises in the political community when the state, acknowledging the obligation to uphold Christian truth for the common good of the political community, uses its powers of coercion to prevent non-Christians from expressing their religious commitments in the public sphere. It is not as if the state tried to coerce them into becoming Christians, for the futility and wrongness of such coercion has long been understood. Rather, Christian rulers of a state may well think that they should prevent Christians from defecting from their faith and joining a non-Christian religious community, or prevent that community from governing itself according to its own self-understanding, or block the efforts of that community to gain new adherents or to exercise influence on the life of the larger society in which it is situated. The Christian rulers in a state may well say that error has no rights to assert itself in any of these public ways and that they in fact have the duty to secure for Christian truth a privileged place in the political community. Once again truth has come into conflict with freedom, but this time not in the form of a Kantian heteronomy but in the form of coercion authorized against non-Christians.

Those who insist on the antagonism of freedom and truth commonly see these two levels of the antagonism as being interrelated, as when they think that the coercion practiced against nonbelievers is simply heteronomy transposed into the political order; that coerced nonbelievers are oppressed by a foreign law in the same way in which Christian truth oppresses the consciences of those to whom it is proposed. It is as if the act of coercion just articulates what is already given in the strong truth claims of Christianity. There is a remarkable paper of the Austrian jurist, Hans Kelsen,[5] in which he argues for a close correspondence between philosophical realism and political tyranny. He says that just as the tyrant oppresses those who are subject to his power, so the object of knowledge, understood in realism as something in its own right and as being independent of the act of knowing, tyrannically oppresses the knower. Kelsen even thinks that this realism lends support to authoritarian regimes. Thus, he concludes that the knower can recover his freedom only by doing what people do when they depose a tyrant and take responsibility for their political life: the knower has to depose the object of knowledge, deny that it has any being of its own, and assert himself as the norm and measure of the object of knowledge. Kelsen thinks that this turn to an idealist or subjectivist understanding of knowing helps to lay the foundation for a democratic regime. Thus do the two antagonisms between freedom and truth flow together in Kelsen's legal theory.

Now many of our contemporaries are like Kelsen in thinking that there is only one way to secure themselves against the threats of heteronomy and of coercion: they have to get rid of the strong truth claims of Christian faith and morals, they have to relativize them and to hold with Protagoras that each man is the measure of his own truth. Only in this way is the threat of heteronomy struck at its root. And only in this way is every pretext removed for coercively upholding Christian faith and morals; if there is no universally binding truth about God and man, if each person forms his own truth, then rulers will not even be tempted to uphold one man's truth and to suppress another's, and it will be easy and natural for them to govern according to the principle of "live and let live." In other words, in the conflict between freedom and truth, truth should give way and yield to freedom; the conflict should be resolved by sacrificing truth to freedom.

But the Catholic Church at Vatican II found an entirely different way of dealing with the antagonism of freedom and truth. In its Declaration on Religious Liberty it acknowledged freedom in a way in which the Church had never acknowledged it and yet did this without ceasing to profess Christian faith and morals and without in any way withdrawing the strong truth claims inherent in them. Thus, instead of sacrificing truth to freedom, *DH* found a new way of harmonizing freedom and truth. The Declaration taught that every person "should be immune from coercion on the part of individuals, social groups and every human power so that, within due limits, nobody is forced to act against his convictions in religious matters in private or in public, alone or in associations with others" (*DH*, 2). Even rulers committed to the truth of Christian faith and morals are bound to abstain from coercively restraining the public activities of non-Christians; their task is to uphold the religious liberty of Christian and non-Christian alike and not to privilege the position of Christians and of Christian revelation in the body politic.

But by swearing off all coercion in the support of truth, the Church by no means swears off allegiance to the demanding truth claims of Christian faith and morals. She continues to announce to all people the truth entrusted to her by Christ. But she knows that the spiritual "space" created by the immunity from coercion is just right for the reception of the moral and religious truth that she bears, for she knows that "truth can impose itself on the mind of man only in virtue of its own truth, which wins over the mind with both gentleness and power" (*DH*, 1). Coercion interferes with this gentle power, which can act upon the mind only in the absence of all coercion. So when the Church renounces coercion she is far from betraying the truth that she bears: she renounces coercion for the sake of this truth, for the sake of letting it enter unobstructed into the hearts of those to whom it is addressed.[6]

And now we ask the central question of this paper: what can the personalism of John Paul II contribute to the understanding and the grounding of this new attempt at reconciling freedom and truth? What is it about persons that repels all coercion in making religious commitments? Is there a way in which persons can be related to objective truth so that it does not oppress them but liberates them?

THE SUBJECTIVITY OF THE HUMAN PERSON

I begin with Wojtyla's understanding of personal subjectivity. I doubt whether any previous pope ever spoke of subjectivity, but John Paul speaks of it constantly, and he does so just when he is speaking out of his personalism. And though *DH* never speaks of subjectivity, it does speak of the growing sense that persons have of their dignity, and what John Paul says about subjectivity helps us understand why persons have this dignity and why they should be given that immunity from coercion that was proclaimed by *DH*.[7]

St. Augustine is well-known for describing the danger of losing ourselves in the world outside and for admonishing us to turn within, to enter into the "inner man." He explores the interiority of man like no one before him did. In our time this rich theme has been taken up and developed by existentialists and personalists, among others. Now Karol Wojtyla, too, has from the beginning been fascinated with the interiority of persons. He announces one of the great themes of his personalist philosophy when he writes: "We can say that the person as a subject is distinguished from even the most advanced animals by a specific inner self, an inner life, characteristic only of persons. It is impossible to speak of the inner life of animals."[8] This interiority of which Wojtyla speaks is nothing other than personal subjectivity; the two terms are interchangeable for him, though he clearly prefers the term subjectivity.

Let us consider the way in which we know the world around us— plants, rocks, clouds, stars, houses, animals, and other human beings. We know them all as *objects* of our experience, that is, as standing in front of us, as outside us. But ourselves we know in a fundamentally different way; we do not just stand in front of ourselves, looking at ourselves from outside ourselves, but we first experience ourselves in the more intimate way of *being present to ourselves*; that is, we first experience ourselves not from without but from within, not as object but as subject, not as something presented to us but as a subject that is present to itself.[9] Now this self-presence is the interiority or subjectivity of a human person. And it is not just a way in which persons experience themselves, it is a way in which they exist: the more present they are to themselves, the more alive they are as persons and the more capable of acting as persons.

This interior self-presence, in which each person dwells with himself, is easy to overlook. When we think about something, give attention to it, or talk about it, we put it in front of ourselves, and so it comes naturally to think that this is the way we experience even ourselves. Of course, we can make an object of ourselves and of our inner life, as when we say that all human beings, ourselves included, have an inner life, but our primary experience of ourselves is not from without as object, but from within as subject, and so this self-experience is in a way hidden from our view.

Wojtyla asks what kind of activity most of all reveals our subjectivity, and he answers that we show ourselves as subjects in acting through ourselves, acting in our own name, owning our acting. He contrasts this acting through ourselves with passively being acted upon, or in other words, passively enduring what befalls us. If someone manipulates or coerces us, then that person interferes with our subjectivity. Such a person makes us passive at the very point at which we as subjects want to act through ourselves; such a one makes us an object of his own acting instead of letting us exist as a subject of our own acting. Already now we can begin to detect the bearing of Wojtyla's thought about subjectivity on the teaching of *DH*, but we are not yet quite ready to explore this connection.

Wojtyla teaches that we can do justice to ourselves as persons only by taking account of our subjectivity. He says that for too long philosophy tried to understand man without sufficiently consulting the evidence of subjectivity. Even Aristotle looked at man mainly from the outside, as one being among others, examining man in the same objective way in which he examined plants and animals. He used the same categories for explaining man and the other beings in nature, categories such as substance or matter/form. He was with his "cosmological" approach to man, as Wojtyla calls it, still able to see that man ranks higher than plants and animals, but he was not able to do justice to man as person. Only the exploration of subjectivity that begins with St. Augustine discloses the mystery of each human being as person. Thus, it is that Wojtyla distinguishes a cosmological image of man, based on understanding man from without, from a personalist image of man, based on understanding him from within.[10] We saw that *DH* speaks of the growing awareness that people have of their dignity as persons; we can now explain this growing awareness as an awakening of personal subjectivity. People are increasingly aware that they exist not as objects but as subjects, and through this awareness they come to themselves as persons.

It may seem that Wojtyla, at least as I am presenting him, inclines dangerously to a view of the human person as a being enclosed in himself, or even closed in on himself. Such a view seems to be implied in the idea that man as person comes to evidence to the extent that he turns within and turns away from what is outside him. In response, Wojtyla says that

> it is just because of his inner being, his interior life, that man is a person, but it is also because of this that he is so much involved in the world of objects, the world "outside," involved in a way which is proper to him and characteristic of him. *A person . . . as a definite subject has the closest contacts with the whole (external) world and is more intimately involved with it precisely because of its inwardness, its interior life.*[11]

There is then a self-transcendence of us human persons that is correlated to our subjectivity.[12] This means that the personhood that comes to light by consulting the evidence of subjectivity is a transcendent personhood, a world-open personhood.[13] Our participation in the world becomes a source of estrangement for us only when it is lived at the expense of our subjectivity, when it draws us off ourselves or interferes with our self-presence and the exercise of our freedom. Augustine is right to admonish us to break away from this kind of world-experience and to return to ourselves. But if we relate ourselves to the world as personal subjects acting through ourselves, we can safely live in the length and breadth of the world; far from losing ourselves, we give evidence of our subjectivity and we thrive as persons.

It is important to see that Wojtyla does not propose that the personalist perspective should replace the cosmological perspective. Man is not exclusively a being of subjectivity but exists as an embodied person and hence also offers the aspect of an object. The cosmological perspective retains for Wojtyla its own truth; it is true that each human person also exists as one among many. The human person in fact lives in the tension of existing as a subject who faces the whole world and yet at the same time existing as one being among others within the world.[14]

Now we are in a position to anticipate how these personalist themes will frame Wojtyla's understanding of the right to religious liberty proclaimed by *DH*. It is not enough that believers profess what is objectively true and act according to what is objectively right; their subjectivity must be in order, they must profess the truth *as persons*, they *must act through themselves* in doing what is objectively right. Sometimes thinkers lose sight of subjectivity in their zeal for the true and the right. William James approvingly quotes Huxley as saying "let me be wound up every day like a watch, to go right fatally, and I ask no better freedom."[15] But if you are "wound up" like a watch in your right acting, you just passively endure your rightness. As a result, you are not the subject of it, you do not own it, it just unfolds in you, over your head; it is a completely depersonalized, objectivized rightness and hence not really a rightness at all. And if instead of being wound up like a clock, you are coerced by others into right profession and practice, you are no less bypassed in your personal subjectivity.

To fully appreciate the contribution the subjectivity of the human person makes to grounding the right affirmed by *DH*, we need to explore the nature of the person's encounter with truth as it emerges in the personalism of Wojtyla.[16]

THE APPROPRIATION OF THE TRUTH

In his book *Love and Responsibility*, Wojtyla makes the following significant statement:

> Truth is a condition of freedom, for if a man can preserve his freedom in relation to the objects which thrust themselves on him in the course of his activity as good and desirable, it is only because he is capable of viewing these goods in the light of truth and so adopting an independent attitude to them. Without this faculty man would inevitably be determined by them: these goods would take possession of him and determine totally the character of his actions and the whole direction of his activity. His ability to discover the truth gives man the possibility of self-determination.[17]

Wojtyla speaks here to our issue of truth and freedom. But whereas many thinkers set them at odds with each other, as we saw, Wojtyla speaks of a truth that does not interfere with freedom but rather awakens and elicits freedom.

If we interpret this passage in the light of the work to which it belongs, then we can say that a value like the value of the feminine can capture the interest of a man in a way that does not engage his freedom; a man finds himself being affected and drawn in a certain direction, being acted upon by a value before he acts through himself toward it. Wojtyla speaks here in fact of a kind of "moral determinism," meaning that the factor that constrains a person's freedom is not some factor of environment or heredity but is rather the very good that attracts the person. Now Wojtyla recognizes another value that the man can discern in the woman, her value or dignity as person. This value does not affect the man so immediately as does the value of the feminine, which can instantly engender attraction without the least effort on the part of the man; the dignity that the woman has as person is more hidden and shows itself only to one who looks in a deeper way at the woman. When it is discerned, it acts on the man with a greater reserve, for it gives rise to a sense of moral ought, a sense that the woman as person ought to be shown respect. This sense of ought grounded in the dignity of the person is the "truth" of which Wojtyla speaks in the passage just quoted. And Wojtyla says that I am never so free as when I open myself to the ought and act to fulfil it; the freedom that is inhibited by the pull of certain values (which are of course not limited to sexual values) is revived and elicited by the call of this truth.

Now one might still have one's doubts as to whether this truth based on the moral ought is really so friendly to our freedom. One might say that many people seem to be constrained and oppressed by all of the oughts that they hear ringing in their conscience. Thus, people who say, "I don't really want to do this but I know I ought to do it," do not sound as if they were enjoying any great freedom as a result of acting in accordance with moral truth. Wojtyla is aware that moral truth can sometimes be oppressive to our freedom. In one place he explicitly acknowledges "the tension arising between the objective order of norms and the inner freedom of the person." But in the same place he indicates what it is that can relieve this tension. Here is the extremely significant sentence in Wojtyla's major philosophical work, *The Acting Person*: "The tension arising between the objective order of norms and the inner freedom of the person is relieved by truth, by the conviction of the truthfulness of good. But this tension is, on the contrary, intensified and not relieved by external pressures, by the power of injunction and compulsion."[18]

It is at first not easy to make out just what the "conviction of the truthfulness of good" is supposed to be. But if we interpret it in contrast with "external pressures" and "the power of injunction and compulsion," then we can take Wojtyla to be saying that we have to understand a norm in terms of the good or value in which it is grounded. For example, the norm directing us to respect persons has to be understood as the truth *about the human person*, as expressing what is due to persons *in virtue of their dignity*. Then the norm becomes intelligible to us, and we are enabled to take the norm into ourselves and to make it our own. It is as if we would ourselves enact the norm if it did not already exist; since it already exists, we ratify it for ourselves so that we now own it so intimately that we want nothing more than to act in accordance with it. This means that we are free in acting, and we are free because the truth that binds our acting is a truth about some good or value, that is, a truth that we see growing out some good or value as the natural requirement of the good or value.

A tension arises between norms and freedom only when the norm is detached from goods and values, when it demands a kind of blind obedience from those whom it addresses; then it becomes an oppressive burden, and those who are committed to the norm are tempted to resort to coercion for the sake of upholding it. But the way to relieve the tension and to avert the recourse to coercion is not to abolish the norms, the binding truth, but rather to come to understand the goods and the values on which the truth is based. Then the truth gains the "gentle power" over us of which *DH* speaks, binding us even as it respects our freedom. And then our obedience is not a blind but a seeing obedience; it is an obedience that coheres with freedom, since we ourselves are enabled to want what the norm requires. We see, then, how Wojtyla refines his initial affirmation that persons are never so free as in responding to normative truth; his fully articulated teaching is that they are never so free as in responding to the normative truth that is intelligible to them in terms of the goods and values that give rise to it.[19]

In the passages just quoted, Wojtyla is speaking of moral truth, which forms a part of the proclamation of the Church, but what he says holds in its own way for the doctrines that make up the rest of her proclamation, such as the doctrines about the person of Christ. Here too we find that what seems foreign to our freedom on first being proposed to us can be embraced in all freedom if it is in some way made "intelligible" to us, not indeed intelligible in the eminent way in which moral truth is made intelligible with reference to goods and values, but still somehow really relieved of every aspect of threatening foreignness. Wojtyla recognizes this other kind of intelligibility or congeniality, for example, in the attempt to show how "Christ the Lord . . . in the very revelation of the mystery of the Father and of his love, fully reveals man to himself and brings to light his most high calling."[20] One way in which Christ reveals man to himself is by revealing the mystery of the love existing between Himself and His Father; when human beings see themselves in the light of this mystery, they discover that man, "who is the only creature on earth that God has wanted for its own sake, can discover his true self only in a sincere giving of himself."[21] The truth which Christ has heard from His Father and shared with us ceases to seem foreign to us or to be in any way threatening to us, as soon as we see how it reveals us to ourselves.

It is not as if the mystery of the inner life of the Trinitarian God becomes entirely transparent to our understanding as soon as it illumines our existence; it is rather the case that even while remaining impenetrable and mysterious it illumines our existence, not unlike the sun which, though it blinds those who look directly at it, provides us with the beneficent light and warmth by which we live. As the sun is life-giving, so is the revealed truth that explains man to himself. And no one can suspect such truth of oppressing the freedom of those who embrace it.[22]

At this point, I submit, we have responded to the first claim mentioned above about the antagonism of freedom and truth by showing how, in the light of Wojtyla's personalism, truth—for all its objectivity and binding power—can be entirely congenial to our subjectivity and freedom, how it can be owned by the one who is bound by it. We must now address the second claim, namely that those who hold to objective truth are sure to resort to co-ercion in announcing it to others.

PERSONALISTIC VALUES

How does John Paul go about announcing revealed truth? He sees of course his first task as announcing this truth unabridged, in all its objectivity and universality, with all its demands. In the most important single utterance of his moral magisterium, the encyclical *Veritatis Splendor*, he defended this normative truth against those who undermine it. For instance, in the encyclical he deals with those who interpret conscience as having a creative power with respect to moral truth, as if the judgment of conscience could make our actions right; against this he affirms that the judgment of conscience is under the truth, subject to the truth, and so quite capable of being an erroneous judgment.[23] Conscience, he insists, *finds* a truth not of our making. In his social encyclicals he affirms the social importance of acknowledging an objective "truth about good"; if people cannot appeal to a higher law known to them all, then they have no other way of negotiating their disputes than resorting to violence.[24] The pope has also taken account of the postmodernist relativism of our time, in response to which he has affirmed the universality of truth, that is, the fact that it is the same for all human beings at all times. In these and other ways, John Paul has affirmed and reaffirmed objective moral truth as the norm for our freedom.

But then he acknowledges a second task, namely the task of making "intelligible" the truth entrusted to the Church, of connecting it with the deepest aspirations of people, of showing it to be the fulfillment of the moral insights that they already have, of showing how it "reveals us to ourselves" as persons, of showing the richness of the existence of believers. It is this pastoral strategy of John Paul that lets truth be proposed without threatening the freedom of those to whom it is proposed. For truth is here proposed without coercion; it is proposed in such a way that, in the expressive words of *DH*, it "imposes itself only in virtue of its own truth which wins over the mind with both gentleness and power ~~if the truth~~" (*DH*, 1). The same gentle power that the believer experiences in accepting revealed truth becomes the basis for his way of communicating this truth to others; he proposes this truth to them so that they too feel its gentle power. This is why John Paul renounces all coercion in drawing people to truth and resolves to use only persuasion. For he knows that the resort to coercion will "close the space" in persons in which they can encounter the truth in its gentle power; he knows that it will lead to a profession of revealed truth that is not personally owned by those who profess it.

This negative judgment on coercion is reinforced by something in Wojtyla's personalism that we pointed out above, namely, his distinction between a cosmological image and a personalist image of man. As Wojtyla points out, when man is understood cosmologically, he is "reduced to the world," that is, viewed as too "embedded" in the world, as too "continuous" with subpersonal beings. But when man is understood through his subjectivity and interiority, then he stands forth as person. And in standing forth as person, he appears as "incommensurable" with the world, as altogether other than it. As long as one thinks within the frame of a cosmological anthropology, I would suggest, one will expect much from the exercise of coercion among human beings. When one thinks within a personalist framework, a framework that does justice to the irreducibility of man to the world, on the other hand, one will expect less from coercion. The more one enters into the interiority and subjectivity of persons, the more one will have to acknowledge that the deepest acts and commitments of persons are very little amenable to the instruments of coercion.

It is all-important to understand that the pope does not prefer persuasion over coercion simply on the grounds that people arrive at truth more reliably by way of persuasion—as if persuasion were simply a better means than coercion for achieving the real end, the possession of truth, as if persuasion simply had the practical advantage of not provoking the resistance that is typically provoked by coercion. John Paul is in fact far from thinking that the appeal to freedom in persuasion is an instrumental means for coming into possession of the truth. He does not think that by relying on the gentle power of truth the Church will strengthen more of her faithful or make more new converts to the Church than by relying on the heavy hand of coercion. He would probably say that the two approaches cannot even be compared in terms of their fruits, since the faith resulting from persuasion is so different from the faith resulting from coercion. In any case, he would be neither surprised nor troubled to find that the way of persuasion is less efficacious than coercion in drawing numbers of people into the Church; his commitment to persuasion is not means based on results. He thinks that we should work with persuasion and with appeals to freedom not for the sake of achieving better results *but for the sake of achieving an entirely new order of goods proper only to the freedom of persons.* We need to reflect more closely on this important idea.

It is explained memorably by Kant in a passage in which he asks why we human persons are endowed with "practical reason," which is what Wojtyla means by freedom. Kant[25] thinks that reason in man need not have been practical; we might have possessed reason but have been so constituted that our behavior was governed by instinct and not by reason. It is only natural, then, for him to be puzzled over why reason in man is practical. He rejects the answer that with practical reason we are in a better position to satisfy our everyday needs and to survive the dangers that threaten us in our environment; Kant thinks that for this purpose instinct would have served us better than freedom, for in acting in the self-consciousness of freedom we act more awkwardly and clumsily than if we were governed by sure-footed instinct.

What then is the raison d'être of freedom, or practical reason? He answers that through freedom we can participate in an entirely new order of value, the order of good and evil, and that we can realize values of a magnitude entirely different from that of the values of surviving in our environment; we emerge from the biological and the vital and take our place in the realm of reason and spirit, in the kingdom of ends. Kant goes so far as to say that we can achieve through freedom values that *justify our very existence*, a concept that has no place in the environment. In the end, Kant says, the awkwardness we experience as free beings in the environment is a small price to pay for being capable of moral goodness, which is a goodness without qualification, that is, a worth that surpasses every other worth.[26]

One sees the parallel with John Paul. He would grant that there is an awkwardness and even an occasional waywardness of belief that result when the Church invites each person whom she addresses really to own his or her faith; the social stability of more traditional and authority-bound modes of belief gives way to the instability of believers who, just awakening to their personal existence, go in different directions, some of them in bad directions that would not even have even occurred to them in more stable times. This confusion has some analogy with the awkwardness and confusion of human beings emerging from instinctive solidarity with their environment and learning to negotiate the environment by means of reason and freedom. But John Paul thinks that this is a reasonable price to pay for the new values of belief that become possible when each believer believes in all freedom and so really owns his faith and really believes in his own name.

Karol Wojtyla has in fact given philosophical attention to these new values. He calls them "personalistic values" and distinguishes them from moral values.[27] Whereas moral values are based on the moral norms to which our actions should correspond, personalistic values are based on the structure of the person that our actions should express and perfect. If an action is performed in all freedom, if it is not performed in a conventional or conformist way or under coercion or under the inordinate influence of another, but if it is performed as my own, so that I fully act through myself and fully determine myself in performing it, then it has a high personalistic value.

As described up to this point, we can not tell how morally sound the action is, whether it fulfills the moral law or not. We cannot do so because the moral evaluation of the action goes in a different direction; our description assures us only of the personalistic value of the action. On the other hand, Wojtyla says that personalistic value acts on moral value in the sense of perfecting it. If the action just described was in accordance with the moral law, then its moral value is greatly enhanced by its personalistic value, just as its moral value would be greatly reduced if it lacked personalistic value (for example, if I do the right thing but with an action strongly molded by a spirit of conformism, then the moral value of the action is a very modest value). It is very characteristic for John Paul as pastor to be mindful of personalistic values and to adapt the whole of his pastoral activity to cultivating them, for he wants to see in believers not just any moral value, not just any objective rightness of action and of faith; he wants to see moral commitment and faith brought to perfection by personalistic value.

And so we say that the persuasion that the pope advocates is not meant as a more effective means than coercion for leading people to the truth; it is meant as the only right way to address persons in matters of religious truth. Though freedom is conceived by John Paul with constant reference to the gentle power of truth, it is by no means set in an instrumental relation to the possession of truth.

It might be worth recalling here what I recently pointed out in a study of the implications of Wojtyla's personalism for issues of bioethics.[28] I placed particular stress on the importance of the widely accepted norm according to which doctors should solicit the "informed consent" of a patient before treating the patient. This norms demands that a patient should as far as possible understand the advantages and risks of a given treatment as well as the alternatives to the treatment, including the alternative of nontreatment, and that doctors should wait for the consent of a patient before proceeding with a particular course of treatment. Wojtyla, I contended, would enthusiastically embrace this norm while rejecting the "paternalistic" model of medicine wherein the physician assesses the advantages and risks of a treatment for the patient and makes the decision for him, while the patient for his part trusts the judgment of the physician in a manner similar to the way a child trusts a parent. For it follows from Wojtyla's personalism that a patient should not just passively undergo a beneficial treatment but should, as far as his illness allows, be the responsible subject of his illness and of his treatment, taking responsibility for the decisions concerning treatment.

Indeed, Wojtyla would say that the ideal of informed consent stands in the service of protecting and cultivating the subjectivity of the patient. And even if patient choices based on informed consent did not always lead to better medical results for patients than paternalistically motivated physician choices, Wojtyla would still, as I interpret him, hold firmly to the ideal of informed consent and would do so on the grounds that it is in some ways more important to respect patients as persons than to restore the health of patients. And in a somewhat similar way, it is for Wojtyla more important to take searchers after God seriously as persons than to put a true profession of faith into their mouths that they cannot make their own. We take them seriously as persons by making them immune from coercion as we announce the Gospel to them.

AD INTRA AND *AD EXTRA*

One of the advantages of John Paul's personalist reading of *DH* is that he makes *DH* relevant to our understanding of renewing the Church from within. Though *DH* concerns in the first place the appropriate way of announcing revealed truth to those outside the Church, it also implies something important for the way in which the pastors of the Church should build up the faith of those who already believe what the Church teaches. This is why in one place Wojtyla distinguishes between the teaching of *DH* considered *ad intra* and considered *ad extra*:

> If the right to religious freedom appears from the text of the Declaration to present itself *ad extra*, in relation to secular public order, at the same time the postulate of conscious faith becomes clear on reading the Declaration *ad intra*, i.e. in relation to believers and to the Church seeking its own self-realization. This postulate must above all be understood as a postulate of the enrichment of faith on the part of the subject: an enrichment corresponding to the subject's nature, which is personal . . .[29]

The phrase "postulate of conscious faith" may not be entirely clear on first reading, but taken in context it seems to mean "requirement that faith be fully owned by believers." For the same reason that John Paul is concerned that nonbelievers come to own personally the faith of the Church, he is also concerned that already existing believers come to own it more personally. He thinks that pastors who strive with persuasion to deepen the faith of Catholics are acting in the spirit of *DH*.

Wojtyla explains further this "postulate of conscious faith" in a well-known passage where he explains the kind of renewal of the Church that was intended by Vatican II:

> The question, "What does it mean to be a believing member of the Church?" is indeed difficult and complex, because it not only presupposes the truth of faith and pure doctrine, but also calls for that truth *to be situated in human consciousness* and calls for a definition of *the attitude, or rather the many attitudes, that go to make the individual a believing member of the Church.* . . . A purely doctrinal Council would have concentrated on defining the precise meaning of the truths of faith, whereas a pastoral council proclaims, recalls or clarifies truth for the primary purpose of *giving Christians a life-style, a way of thinking and acting.* . . . In the present study . . . we shall concentrate on the consciousness of Christians and the attitudes they should acquire.[30]

This concern with consciousness, attitudes, and lifestyle should be familiar to us by now, for it is nothing other than a concern with what Wojtyla calls personalistic values. Thus, the very personalistic values that Wojtyla discerns and admires in *DH* were also discerned by him as being central to the renewal of the Church from within that was intended by Vatican II. This means that Wojtyla's personalist approach to the teaching of *DH* reveals the special affinity between *DH* and the project of the Council as a whole.[31]

Here is an example of how John Paul also applies *DH ad intra*. Everyone knows how deeply committed he is to the teaching of the Church on the moral disorder of contraception, as set forth in the encyclical *Humanae Vitae*. But he has not tried to uphold this teaching simply by "laying down the law," by demanding obedience, by threatening punishments, and the like. He thinks that that is just the approach to give people the impression that the moral law cramps their freedom. He has throughout his pontificate taken a different approach. On one occasion he said: "it is not enough that this encyclical be faithfully and fully proposed, *but it also is necessary to devote oneself to demonstrating its deepest reasons.*"[32]

He himself goes to very great lengths to show its deepest reasons, for his strikingly rich and original theology of the body, which he presented to the Church in his Wednesday audiences between 1979 and 1984, was developed precisely with a view to showing how the Church's teaching about married love and procreation is rooted in the truth about man and woman.[33] He thinks that, if Catholic spouses do not understand this truth, then the Church's teaching on contraception will seem to be outside them and will feel burdensome. However, if they understand this teaching in the personalist way he has presented it, they can internalize it, that is, make it their own and so can become really free in living it, even when it requires considerable sacrifice from them. By the way, we have here one reason for the unusual length of John Paul's encyclicals and of his other magisterial utterances; he is trying not only to deliver the doctrinal "bottom line," not only to declare unambiguously what it is that Catholics believe, but he is also trying, good personalist pastor that he is, to find links between Church teachings and the personal existence of believers, to make these teachings resonate in their existence, so that they can be free in living them.

All of this shows, just how seriously John Paul takes believers *as persons*. I almost want to say that he takes them not only as objects but as subjects of the faith of the Church, whereas pastors who are content just to lay down the law and demand the obedience of the faithful invert this order, treating the faithful more as objects than as subjects of the faith of the Church. What I mean is that this faith enters more intimately into those believers who are led by the pastoral approach of John Paul to make this faith their own, whereas it remains in some sense outside those who are simply told what to believe and what to do.

I am reminded here of what St. Thomas Aquinas says about the two different ways in which creatures are subject to the eternal law. Plants and animals are subject to it in one way by *being directed* to their ends, and rational beings are subject to it in another and more excellent way *by understanding their end and directing themselves* to it. The more passive subjection to the natural law in the first case gives way to the more active owning of it in the second.[34] We see something similar in John Paul's pontifical style, where the faithful are no longer governed in a passive way but are increasingly led to make the faith of the Church their own, or as we could also say, where the obedience expected of believers is becoming more and more the *rational obedience* of which St. Paul speaks.

But one has to take care in applying *DH ad intra*. The pope certainly does not mean that the entire governance of the Church has to be carried out by persuasion alone, as if there were some kind of suspicious coercion in defining the faith of the Church in a binding way, authoritatively excluding error, withdrawing the *mandatum* from unsound teachers, applying the sanctions provided in canon law, refusing to ordain men of questionable orthodoxy, imposing certain obligations on the faithful, etc. Nor does the pope countenance a personalist right to dissent from authoritative Church teaching, as if any Catholic, as soon as he is unable to make his or her own some teaching of the Church, had to be at liberty to contest the teaching and, in the case of a moral teaching, to be at liberty to ignore the teaching in the conduct of his or her life (as if Catholic spouses unconvinced by the reasons for the teaching of *Humanae Vitae* were at liberty to practice contraception). On the contrary, John Paul acknowledges, as every pope must, that there is real authority in the Church. It goes without saying that the exercise of this authority must not be identified with the coercion in religious matters against which *DH* wants to protect all citizens of the political community.

Most of these uses of authority simply aim at the preservation of the objective content of revelation. To grasp the importance of preserving this content, one need only reflect on Alasdair MacIntyre's analysis of the effects of ethical emotivism on contemporary American culture. As he points out, in our culture persuasion often degenerates into manipulation because of the widely shared emotivist subjectivism about truth and goodness.[35] This means that, if we are really going to be able to give reasons to each other so as to engage in genuine persuasion rather than relying on coercion and manipulation, we have to encounter each other on the basis of norms and values that we take to be objectively valid. It should never be forgotten that the gentle activity of persuading presupposes the stern reality of objective truth, which for its part is preserved intact by various acts of ecclesial authority.

It should also be recalled that *DH* not only aims at protecting individual believers and nonbelievers but also aims at protecting religious communities such as the Church. It affirms the right of religious communities to organize themselves as they see fit and to uphold their own distinctive identities.[36] *DH* is as concerned with the rights of the Church as it is with the rights of individual believers. Only a perversely individualistic interpretation of *DH* would so exalt the rights of individuals as to make it impossible for a religious community to constitute itself, to prescribe a common way of life for its members, and even to identify who is authorized to teach in its name and who is not.

We touch here on a vast, complex subject that it is impossible to do justice to here. Suffice it to say that, when we have acknowledged all that needs to be acknowledged about religious authority in the Church, it remains true that there are certain ways of exercising this authority, especially certain paternalistic ways, that tend to prevent the faithful from becoming full subjects of the faith of the Church and other ways of exercising authority that tend to foster this. John Paul clearly sought to exercise authority in this latter way. His way of governing the church *ad intra* was akin to his commitment *ad extra* to the immunity from coercion affirmed by *DH*.

CONCLUDING REFLECTIONS

One might ask whether what we have drawn from Wojtyla really amounts to a full justification of that immunity from coercion. We have of course sufficiently justified the thesis that persons must never be coerced to profess some religious belief that they do not hold, but *DH* takes this for granted; the real novelty of *DH* lies rather in affirming that persons must not be coercively restrained from expressing erroneous beliefs in public ways and from trying to share these erroneous beliefs with others. In other words, *DH* renounced even the limited coercion usually involved in a "confessional state," that is, a state in which the Catholic Church is legally established and non-Catholic persons and bodies are subject to various legal disadvantages. And one might ask whether Catholic truth is necessarily prevented from imposing "itself on the mind of man only in virtue of its own truth," winning over "the mind with both gentleness and power" (*DH*, 1) within the setting of the legal establishment of the Church and of the more restrained coercion that this typically implies.

Wojtyla would answer, speaking out of his personalism, that even this kind of coercion interferes with the gentle power of truth. He would say, or in any case someone empowered by his personalism might say, that to protect Catholics from hearing the errors of non-Catholics is to protect them in too paternalistic a way; it is to treat them as children whose eyes have to be shielded from certain sights. Catholics have to own their faith in such a way that they stand firm in it for better reasons than that they are kept from ever hearing its critics of their faith; if only they grow in the "consciousness, lifestyle, attitudes" of which Wojtyla spoke above, then they will not be so easily unsettled by the existence of non-Catholic voices around them. On the basis of Wojtyla's personalism, one might add that Catholics who as Catholics enjoy special legal privileges, such as eligibility for public office, acquire an interest in remaining Catholic that has nothing to do with the gentle power of the truth of Catholicism and may interfere with this gentle power. And, of course, the pressure on non-Catholics to join in with the established religion makes it harder for them to feel the gentle power of truth and to convert to Catholicism out of honest conviction.[37]

Wojtyla's personalism implies that the civil law performs a greater service to the truth by letting it speak in the consciences of those who hear it than by actively taking the side of truth and trying to uphold and enforce it. The civil law should content itself with "securing the space" in which persons encounter truth and in which the Church undertakes her work of persuasion. What this means concretely is that the law should grant to all citizens the immunity from coercion of which *DH* speaks.

At the same time, this personalism works at an even more fundamental level in supporting this immunity. It has to be considered that the immunity is difficult to support on the basis of the ancient Greek conception of the way in which human beings are present in the polis. I refer to the conception according to which individual citizens are present with their whole being in the polis, as if they never stepped out of the political frame of reference to perform actions belonging to another, higher frame of reference. On this view even religion is situated within the polis, and a religious cult is a political act. It follows that the coercive methods that are appropriate to ordering life in the polis are also appropriate to ordering religious activities.

But Wojtyla, who as we saw explores personal subjectivity in such a way as to undermine the older cosmological image of man by showing that man is not snugly embedded in the cosmos but exists in a way that is incommensurable with all other beings in nature, undermines as well the older idea of human existence being completely embedded in the polis. For it follows from his teaching on subjectivity and truth that human persons are not only incommensurable with nature and the cosmos but are also incommensurable with the political community. As they are not entirely "contained" in the cosmos, so they are not entirely "contained" in the polis. But then the coercion that is natural to the ordering of the polis is put into question; it may no longer be appropriate to human persons insofar as they surpass the frame of reference of the polis.[38]

One might object that there is at least one part of the proclamation of the Church that John Paul is willing to uphold by coercion, namely, certain moral teachings of the Church. In *Evangelium Vitae* he said that the criminal law should treat abortion as a crime and should use all the resources of law and state to prevent abortions and to punish abortionists. He does not think that abortion should be resisted only on the level of persuasion, though this level should not be underrated; he is quite willing to resort to coercion as well and not just the indirect coercion that is typically involved in a confessional state. It is then, according to this objection, not all of Catholic teaching, but only large parts of it, that John Paul is ready to entrust to the way of persuasion. One critic of John Paul has in fact alleged that in *EV* he departs from the teaching of *DH* and seems to be hankering after at least a residue of the earlier arrangements whereby Catholic teaching was legally privileged.[39]

Wojtyla, however, knows well that women coercively prevented from having an abortion are not thereby morally improved, just as doctors coercively prevented from performing abortions are not thereby morally improved; he knows well that real moral improvement in them cannot be achieved by coercion at all. He favors coercion *as a way of protecting the victim of abortion*. It is an overly moralizing view that sees in the criminalization of abortion an attempt to impose morality.[40] Wojtyla wants to see abortion criminalized, not in order to enhance anyone's moral state but to establish elementary justice and to prevent the shedding of innocent blood. The coercion he advocates does not even enter the area in which persuasion works with the gentle power of truth. It is in no way meant to substitute for such persuasion, even though he wants to see it complemented by efforts to persuade those who are tempted to have recourse to abortion (cf. *EV*, 82). In fact I would venture to go further and to say that for Wojtyla the criminalization of abortion and of all other forms of killing the innocent is as fundamental an act of human law as the act of securing the religious freedom of all citizens. A just legal order is no less concerned with the right to life than with the right to religious liberty.

What Wojtyla's personalism contributes to the unfinished work described by John Courtney Murray, then, is a fuller account than *DH* gives of the immunity from coercion which *DH* affirms. *DH* argues that human persons have the obligation to seek religious truth and to embrace it when found, and that coercion interferes with fulfilling this obligation. Wojtyla takes the argument further by showing that coercion works its interference at a more fundamental level. Coercion, he shows, tends to prevent people from even encountering the gentle power of truth; it blocks the sight of the values out of which moral truth arises and hinders people from understanding how Christ reveals man to himself; it tends to close the space in which the believer must exist if he is to grow in personalist value and really own his profession of faith. This space must be kept open for believer and nonbeliever alike, for in no other space can a human being be addressed as a person by Christian truth and in no other space can he come to accept it in all freedom.

NOTES

1. I wish to thank the Earhart Foundation for a generous grant supporting the researching and writing of this paper. I also wish to thank Derek Jeffreys for his very helpful critical comments on an earlier draft of this paper.

2. John Courtney Murray, "Arguments for the Human Right to Religious Freedom," in *Religious Liberty: Catholic Struggles with Pluralism/John Courtney Murray*, ed. J. Leon Hooper (Louisville, KY: John Knox Press, 1993), 230.

3. *Dignitatis Humanae*, section 9. I will be employing Laurence Ryan's translation of this document which appears in *Vatican II: The Conciliar and Post-Conciliar Documents*, ed. Austin Flannery, O.P. (Collegeville, MN: The Liturgical Press, 1975). Further citations of this document will be given parenthetically by section number with the title abbreviated as *DH*.

4. *Gaudium et Spes*, section 17. I am employing the translation that appears in *Vatican II: The Conciliar and Post-Conciliar Documents*.

5. Hans Kelsen, "Relativism and Absolutism in Politics and Philosophy," in his collection *What Is Justice?* (Berkeley: University of California Press, 1957).

6. One recent study of *DH* shows how easy it is to upset the balance of freedom and truth in the teaching of the Declaration. In his *John Paul II and the Legacy of* Dignitatis

Humanae (Washington, DC: Georgetown University Press, 2002), Herminio Rico, S.J., writes: "The mission of the church in the service of the truth was, thus, recentered [by *DH*] and became, primarily, a commitment to promote the free development of responsible persons" (219). He says that after *DH* "first and foremost in the rank of its [the Church's] preoccupations no longer is the defense of objective truth, but the promotion of persons in their dignity" (84). Rico speaks of the "decentering of the church's primary attention from transcendental truth in favor of the concrete person" (85). Rico speaks as if freedom had been exalted by *DH* above truth and misses entirely the respect in which freedom is esteemed for the sake of truth, that is, for the sake of giving truth the space it needs to make its "gentle power" felt. For an excellent critique of Rico's book, see Kenneth L. Grasso, "Freedom Through Truth," review of *John Paul II and the Legacy of* Dignitatis Humanae, *Review of Politics* 66 (Spring 2004): 339–42.

7. In the next few pages I use a few paragraphs from my paper, "Karol Wojtyla on Treating Patients as Persons," in *John Paul II's Contributions to Bioethics*, ed. Christopher Tollefson (Dordrecht, the Netherlands: Springer, 2004), 151–68.

8. Karol Wojtyla, *Love and Responsibility*, trans. H. W. Willetts (New York: Farrar, Straus & Giroux Inc., 1981), 22.

9. I draw here on the discussion of consciousness found in Wojtyla's *The Acting Person*, trans. Andrzej Potocki, ed. Anna-Teresa Tymieniecka (Dordrecht, the Netherlands: D. Reidel Publishing Company, 1979), 25–59. But the term self-presence is my own; I find it more accessible than "the reflexive function of consciousness," which is the way Wojtyla refers to what I call self-presence.

10. See Wojtyla's seminal paper, "Subjectivity and the Irreducible in the Human Being," in *Person and Community: Selected Essays/Karol Wojtyla*, trans. Theresa Sandok (New York: Peter Lang, 1995), 209–17.

11. Wojtyla, *Love and Responsibility*, 23. The italics are from Wojtyla.

12. Drawing on Wojtyla among others, I have explored this correlation of apparent opposites in my *The Selfhood of the Human Person* (Washington, DC: Catholic University of America Press, 1996), chapter 5, especially 161–73.

13. This finding too breaks out of the horizon established by the cosmological perspective. For looked at cosmologically, or from the outside, each human being is "one of many," "one among others," whereas looked at subjectively each person, facing as he does the whole world, exists in a way as if the only person.

14. This tension is admirably characterized by Robert Sokolowski in his *Introduction to Phenomenology* (Cambridge: Cambridge University Press, 2000), 112–19.

15. Quoted by James in *Pragmatism and Other Essays* (New York: Washington Square Press, 1963), 54.

16. Notice that up to this point Wojtyla's personalism has been explained without recourse to any theological premises. Indeed, the main source of his personalism, his treatise *The Acting Person*, is a remarkably "secular" work in the sense that it contains no references to God and no citations from Scripture. But instead of calling it a secular work, we should call it an eminently phenomenological work, probing as it does the experience available to every person. There are of course theological dimensions of Wojtyla's personalism, and these are in evidence when, for example, Wojtyla explains how it is that Christ reveals man to himself. But he is quite capable of going deep into

the mystery of the person without theology. This important feature of Wojtyla's personalism is completely lost on Herminio Rico, S.J., who, in his *John Paul II and the Legacy of* Dignitatis Humanae, complains that the pope's entire discourse about freedom and truth is theological and that this interferes with the reception of *DH* in the secular world (127–35). One of the principal weaknesses of Rico's work is his complete ignorance of the rich philosophical corpus that underlies John Paul II's teaching on freedom and truth. He would have to read John Paul's teaching very differently if only he were acquainted with Karol Wojtyla's personalist philosophical vision.

17. *Love and Responsibility*, 115. On this point, see *The Acting Person*, 135–39, 143–48, and 158–62.

18. Wojtyla, *The Acting Person*, 166.

19. Wojtyla is here in the debt of Max Scheler, who articulated a relentless critique of Kant's ethical formalism. Wojtyla studied closely Scheler's protest against the freestanding moral imperatives of Kant as well as Scheler's insistence that all obligation must ultimately go back to experienced values. Though Wojtyla thought that Scheler went too far in his reaction against Kant and failed to do justice to the moment of obligation in the moral life, he completely agreed with Scheler on the necessity of some value foundation for moral obligation. I have discussed this debate between Scheler and Kant, as well as Wojtyla's stance toward it, in my paper "Person and Obligation: Critical Reflections on the Anti-Authoritarian Strain in Scheler's Personalism," *American Catholic Philosophical Quarterly* 79, no. 1 (2005): 89–117.

20. *Gaudium et Spes*, 22.

21. Ibid., 24.

22. Perhaps another way in which revealed truth becomes intelligible is through the human beings whose existence is completely formed by it. I mean that, when we experience abundant life and rich, real humanity in an ardent Christian and when we see that this abundance and richness come from his existence being formed by his faith in Christian revelation, then we can hardly keep thinking of revelation as something foreign to man, as a heteronomous imposition on human freedom. It is nothing foreign in the existence of this ardent believer. We might even appropriate the expression just used, namely, that Christ reveals man to himself and say that the ardent believer shows us what our humanity might become. In such a believer revelation becomes in a way intelligible, it stands forth as something proper to man, and we see how it can be embraced without drawing man heteronomously off himself. I am not saying that this ardent believer constitutes decisive evidence for the truth of Christianity, but only that he is evidence for the power of Christian belief not to disfigure but to enhance the humanity of the believer. Although it seems to be entirely consistent with the spirit of his work, I have not come across this line of thought in Wojtyla's writings.

23. See *Veritatis Splendor*, sections 54–64.

24. Among many other places, John Paul makes this point in his encyclical *Centesimus Annus*, section 44.

25. It is entirely appropriate to bring Kant into a study of Wojtyla, since Kant was one of Wojtyla's main interlocutors in his courses at the Catholic University of Lublin. After St. Thomas and Scheler, no one is more prominent as interlocutor for Wojtyla

than Kant. It was not just that Wojtyla had to study Kant in order to study Scheler; he had other reasons for taking Kant seriously, such as the nascent personalism in Kant's moral philosophy. He certainly knew well the passage of Kant to which I refer in the text. On the other hand, the claim of Robert Kraynak's ~~claim~~ in *Christian Faith and Modern Democracy* (Notre Dame, IN: University of Notre Dame Press, 2001) that John Paul II is too reflective of a "Kantian Christianity" is, in my view, utterly misguided.

26. Kant, *Foundations of the Metaphysics of Morals*, trans. Lewis Beck (Indianapolis and New York: The Bobbs-Merrill Company, Inc., 1959), 11–13.

27. Karol Wojtyla, *The Acting Person*, 320–23.

28. See John F. Crosby, "Karol Wojtyla on Treating Patients as Persons."

29. Karol Wojtyla, *Sources of Renewal: The Implementation of Vatican II*, trans. P. S. Falla (New York: Harper and Row, Publishers, Inc., 1980), 23.

30. Ibid., 17–18.

31. Buttiglione argues that *DH* stands at the very center of the Council's work and the originality of its vision. See Rocco Buttiglione, *Karol Wojtyla: The Thought of the Man Who Became John Paul II*, trans. Paolo Guietti and Francesca Murphy (Grand Rapids, MI: William B. Eerdmans Publishing Co., 1997), 177–231. My interpretation of Wojtyla in this study owes much to this valuable study.

32. Address to the participants of the Congress on Responsible Parenthood, Rome, September 17, 1983.

33. These audiences have been published as *The Theology of the Body* (Boston: Pauline Books & Media, 1997).

34. St. Thomas Aquinas, *Summa Theologica*, I–II, q. 93, articles 5 and 6.

35. Alasdair MacIntyre, *After Virtue*, 2nd ed. (Notre Dame, IN: University of Notre Dame Press, 1984), 21–35.

36. "The freedom or immunity from coercion in religious matters which is the right of individuals must also be accorded to men when they act in community. Religious communities are a requirement of the nature of man and of religion itself. Therefore, provided the just requirements of public order are not violated, these groups have a right to immunity so that they may organize themselves according to their own principles" (*DH*, 4).

37. Here is an answer to those who think that John Paul, by linking freedom to truth, will in the end favor immunity from coercion primarily for those with a true faith, that is, only for Catholics. What this makes clear is that non-Catholics need the "immunity from coercion" championed by *DH* in order to be in the best possible "position" for considering the claims of Catholicism.

38. Thus, Wojtyla's personalism lends particular support to this *DH* affirmation that "the private and public acts by which men direct themselves to God according to their convictions transcend of their very nature the earthly and temporal order of things. Therefore the civil authority, the purpose of which is the care of the common good in the temporal order, must recognize and look with favor on the religious life of the citizens. But if it presumes to control or to restrict religious activity it must be said to have exceeded the limits of its power" (*DH*, 3).

39. Rico, 169–82. "The focus of John Paul II's proposal in this encyclical [*EV*] is not the patient formation of consciences, progressively changing the predominant values in culture and, through that change, achieving the transformation of the social consensus. His aim right now is the search for a protection and promotion of traditional Catholic morality by civil law, even if against the grain of the positions of the majority" (175–76).

40. Nor is the criminalization of abortion an attempt to impose what *DH* calls "public morality" (*DH*, 7), an important point overlooked by Rico, 212–13.

An Unfinished Argument: *Dignitatis Humanae*, John Courtney Murray, and the Catholic Theory of the State

Kenneth L. Grasso

$\mathcal{M}$y topic here is a subject that *Dignitatis Humanae* (*DH*) addresses but does not attempt to resolve in any type of definitive fashion, namely, the intellectual foundations of the right whose existence it affirms and whose contours it outlines.[1] The Declaration, of course, does offer an argument in support of this right. The Council, as John Courtney Murray points out, felt "it was necessary . . . to present an argument for the principle of religious freedom, lest anyone should mistakenly think that the Church was accepting religious freedom merely on pragmatic grounds or as a concession to contemporary circumstances,"[2] in order to make it clear "that the affirmation of religious freedom is doctrinal."[3] It was also necessary lest the Church's embrace of religious liberty be assumed to involve an embrace of the "skepticism with regard to religious truth, or . . . moral relativism, or . . . religious indifferentism, or . . . secularist conceptions of the functions of government" with which this principle has been so closely associated both "today" and in "other times."[4]

This posed a problem, however, because, as Richard J. Regan observes, the Declaration's supporters were "deeply split on how to articulate a rationale for the principle of religious freedom."[5] As a result, he shows, the argument of the final text was deliberately designed to be a "compromise" combining elements of the various justifications for religious freedom that had emerged in the course of the Conciliar debates so as to secure a consensus in support of the Declaration.[6] As Murray remarks, this compromise argument, which "pleased . . . no one in all respects," was not intended to be "final and decisive," but merely to indicate "certain lines or elements of argument" which the Council thought might be worth pursuing.[7] In doing so, as Regan writes, it "left to professional theologians, philosophers and political scientists the task of critically evaluating specific arguments," of systematically elaborating the intellectual foundations of the right outlined by *DH*.[8]

Toward this end, what I want to examine here are the Declaration's implications for the Catholic understanding of the role of the state in the overall economy of social life. In exploring these implications, I will draw on both the Declaration itself and the work of John Courtney Murray. My reasons for choosing Murray's work in this context are obvious. Not only did it lay the groundwork for *DH*, but the portions of the Declaration addressing the political dimensions of religious liberty are to a significant degree Murray's handiwork. Indeed, his writings during and after the Council represent the most powerful treatment available to us of these dimensions.[9] Specifically, my argument will be essentially threefold. First, I will seek to show that Murray is correct in contending that the intellectual foundations of the right affirmed by *DH* must necessarily include an account of the proper role of government in the overall economy of human social life and thus provide a full-fledged theory of the state. Second, I will seek to show that Murray's own effort to lay the foundations of such a theory is in important respects neither complete nor fully satisfying both in itself and in relation to the affirmations about the nature and role of the state that inform both *DH* and contemporary Catholic social teaching as a whole. Finally, I will offer some brief suggestions about how Catholic thinkers should proceed in attempting to elaborate the theory of the state presupposed by *DH*. Before turning to these subjects, however, it is first necessary to return to *DH* and examine more carefully the nature of the right it proclaims.

THE RIGHT TO RELIGIOUS FREEDOM IN *DH*: A BRIEF OVERVIEW

The construction of a secure foundation for the right outlined by *DH* presupposes clarity about the nature and scope of the right whose existence it affirms. The major points in this regard are as follows:

1. The subject of *DH* is the right to "religious freedom . . . in *civil society*."[10] Thus, as Murray notes, it does not address the questions of "the theological meaning of Christian freedom" or the proper scope of religious freedom "within the Church."[11] Indeed, *DH* makes "a clear distinction between religious freedom as a principle in the civil order and the Christian freedom which obtains . . . inside the Church. These two freedoms are distinct in kind; and it would be perilous to

confuse them."[12] They are distinct in kind, as Avery Dulles suggests, because the Church is a different "kind of society" than a body politic.[13] Likewise, the Declaration touches only lightly on the nature and proper scope of religious liberty in the full range of diverse groups and institutions in which "the social nature of man" (*DH*, 3) finds expression. Its focus is on political society, on the understanding of the nature and scope of religious freedom that should inform "the constitutional law whereby society is governed" (*DH*, 2).

2. While the Declaration proclaims that religious freedom "is to be recognized" as a basic "civil right" (*DH*, 2, 187), the Council makes clear that this right "has its foundation in the very dignity of the human person, as this dignity is known through the revealed Word of God and by reason itself" (*DH*, 6).[14] It has its foundation in man's very ontological dignity as a person, in the dignity, as Pavan writes, "that every human person possesses always and everywhere simply by being a person, and not by behaving rightly in the moral field. It is the dignity that flows from the being of the person and inheres in the being of the person and does not depend on the deeds of the person."[15] Inasmuch as the right to religious freedom "has its foundation, not in the subjective disposition of the person, but in his very nature" (*DH*, 2), this right is, as Pavan concludes, a "natural," rather than a mere "positive" right.[16]

3. As "a natural right, that is, one grounded in the very nature of man," Pavan observes, "it is a right which belongs to *all* human beings: Catholics and non-Catholics, Christians and non-Christians, believers and unbelievers or atheists."[17] Indeed, it belongs even to those who refuse to take seriously their "obligation to seek the truth, especially religious truth" and "to order their whole lives in accord with" its "demands." This right thus "continues to exist even in those who do not live up to their obligation of seeking the truth and adhering to it" (*DH*, 2). "Everyman," as Pavan observes, "has a right to religious freedom because he is a person."[18]

4. The right of religious freedom, as Pavan has written, does not concern "the relation of the person to truth," but rather "the relation between person and person."[19] Man, as Murray points out, lives his life in two orders of reality, namely, the "vertical" order of his relationship to God and truth and "the horizontal order of interpersonal relations among men, between a man and organized society and especially between the people—as individuals and as associated in communities, including religious communities—and the powers of government."[20] It is with this latter order, the juridical order, that the right proclaimed by the

Declaration is concerned. *DH* is clear that, in Murray's words, "no man may plead 'rights' in the face of truth or . . . the moral law."[21] On the contrary, rights can only be affirmed against others; they concern only the order of "intersubjective relations among men."[22]

Thus, the right to religious liberty that *DH* affirms "leaves untouched" both "traditional Catholic doctrine on the moral duty of men and societies toward the true religion and toward the one Church of Christ" (*DH*, 1) and men's "moral obligation to seek the truth" and, "once it is known," to "order their whole lives" in accordance to its demands (*DH*, 2). Rather, it "has to do with immunity from coercion in civil society" (*DH*, 1).

5. As far as its content or object is concerned, the right to religious freedom encompasses a twofold "immunity from coercion" (*DH*, 1). "In matters religious," the Declaration affirms, man "is not to be forced to act in a manner contrary to his conscience. Nor . . . is he to be restrained from acting in accordance with conscience" (*DH*, 3). As an immunity, rather than an empowerment—as a "freedom from," rather than a "freedom for"—the right has an essentially negative character. It does not, as Francis Canavan remarks, assert, "a person's moral right to propagate his belief," but rather "his freedom from being impeded in his propaganda by civil laws and coercive measures."[23]

"It is important," as Pavan remarks, "to be clear about the negative nature of the object [of this right], so as to avoid the idea that the object of the right to religious liberty is connected with the content of religious faith,"[24] so as to avoid the idea that "the object of the right is a faculty, recognized and legally protected, to profess one's own religion." This would involve the claim that individuals have a moral right—an empowerment—to profess their religion, whatever it might be, or even to profess atheism. This claim, however, is untenable. "If a religion is not true or contains false elements," Pavan notes, "anyone who professes it thereby contributes to the spreading of error, and the spreading of error is a bad thing; therefore, it cannot be the object of a right."[25] It cannot be the object of a right because "no one has the right" to commit "evil."[26] "A natural right," in short, "cannot be founded on an objective error."[27] In Murray's terse formulation: "neither error nor evil can be the object of a right, only what is true and good."[28]

6. The right to religious freedom encompasses, in Murray's words, "immunity from coercion in what concerns religious worship, observance, practice and witness—in all cases, both private and familial, and also public and social"[29] within the limits set by "the just requirements of

the public order" (*DH*, 6). Hence, while the right itself is "inalienable" as Pavan remarks, its "exercise" can be suspended in cases of grave "abuse."[30] As the Declaration puts it, because this right "is exercised in human society," it follows that "its exercise is subject to certain regulatory norms" designed to protect society from "possible abuses committed on pretext of freedom of religion." "These norms arise out of the need" for an "effective safeguard of the rights of all citizens and for the peaceful settlement of conflicts of rights," "an adequate care of genuine public peace, which comes about when men live together in good order and justice," and "a proper guardianship of public morality." Taken together, "these matters constitute" that "basic component of the common welfare" which *DH* designates as "public order." The "protection" of society through the enforcement of these norms— through the vindication of the demands of public order—is "the special duty of government" (*DH*, 7).

In determining and safeguarding "the just requirements of public order" (*DH*, 4), *DH* insists, the state must act in "conformity with the objective moral order" and be guided by the principle "that the freedom of man [must] be respected as far as possible, and curtailed only when and in so far as necessary" (*DH*, 7). Nevertheless, in enforcing these requirements, as Canavan observes, "government does not act arbitrarily or violate religious freedom, even if it prevents people from doing things that their religious beliefs authorize or perhaps even command (ritual murder, sacred prostitution and polygamy are extreme, but not fantastic, examples)."[31]

7. Finally, the right to religious liberty affirmed by *DH* entails neither the privatization of religion nor a posture of governmental indifference toward it. On the one hand, *DH* makes clear that "it comes within the meaning of religious freedom that religious bodies should not be prohibited from undertaking to show the special value of their doctrine in what concerns the organization of society and the inspiration of the whole of human activity" (*DH*, 5). On the other hand, it emphatically rejects as incompatible with religious liberty what Murray describes as the view "that secular government may maintain a neutrality of indifference to religion, or that secular society may excise religion from its concept of the common good."[32] If government has the duty to "safeguard" "the religious freedom of all its citizens," it also has the obligation "to help create conditions favorable to the fostering of religious life, in order that the people may be truly enabled to exercise their own religious rights and to fulfill their religious duties, and also in order that society may itself profit by the moral

qualities of justice and peace which have their origin in men's faith-
fulness to God and to His holy will" (*DH*, 6). Indeed, "since the function of government is to make provision for the common welfare," it
is obligated "to take account of the religious life of the people and
show it favor" (*DH*, 3).

RELIGIOUS LIBERTY AND THE CATHOLIC
THEORY OF THE STATE

There was overwhelming agreement at the Second Vatican Council about
the existence of the right to religious liberty whose nature and content were
just outlined. The problem that confronted the Council was, as Murray
notes, "how to construct the argument—whether derived from reason or
from revelation—that . . . [would] give solid foundation to what the Declaration affirms" (*AHR*, 230). The problem that confronted the Council, in
other words, was how to construct an argument grounding these affirmations
that was (a) internally coherent; (b) capable of grounding the full range of
DH's conclusions regarding the nature, scope, and implications of the right
it proclaims; and (c) consistent with the core principles constitutive of the
Catholic tradition.

Among these principles, as Canavan points out,

> are the following: There is a divinely revealed truth about man and his re-
> lation to God, of which the Church is the infallible custodian. Men are not
> free to take or leave this truth as they choose; it is God's will that they ac-
> cept His revealed truth and live by it. Society as well as individuals must
> guide its activities in the light of this truth. Since the same persons are
> members of the Church and citizens of the state, Church and State must
> act in harmony so that men may achieve both their temporal and eternal
> goals.[33]

They also include a commitment to a metaphysical and moral realism; the
idea of a natural moral law discernible by human reason; the naturalness of
social and political life; and the responsibility of the state not merely to suppress violence but affirmatively to foster the human good. Thus, theories of
religious truth that involve commitment to religious indifferentism or subjectivism, or which deny that social and political life should take its bearings
from the truth about man and the human good conveyed through divine revelation and the natural moral law, are unacceptable from the perspective of
Catholicism. The same is true of theories which elevate choice to the status

of the human good and assert that the state should be neutral on all questions of religious and moral truth or which deny that religious truth makes an essential contribution to the good of society.

As we have seen, the right affirmed by the Declaration encompasses a twofold immunity from coercion: in religious matters, as long as "the just requirements of public order are observed" (*DH*, 3), no one was to be forced to act against his conscience, nor was anyone to be restrained from acting in accordance with his conscience. It was not difficult to construct an argument grounded in the Catholic tradition to justify the first immunity. "The Church," as Regan observes, had "long affirmed the right of the individual to freedom from coercion in the profession of the Catholic faith."[34] Indeed, as the Declaration affirms, "one of the major tenets of Catholic doctrine"—a tenet "contained in the Word of God" and "constantly proclaimed by the Fathers of the Church" —was the principle "that man's response to God in faith must be free" because "the act of faith is of its very nature a free act" (*DH*, 9). What proved to be difficult was the construction of an argument for religious liberty rooted in the Catholic tradition to undergird the second immunity, to ground the right of individuals and groups not to be restrained from acting in accordance with their consciences within the limits sets by the exigencies of public order. The recognition of this immunity, as *DH* notes, constitutes a development in Catholic social teaching (*DH*, 1).

As Murray points out, to justify this second immunity it was necessary to consider the whole question of

> the juridical relationship among human beings in civil society. The concept of a juridical relationship properly includes the notion of a correspondence between rights and duties. To one person's right there is a corresponding duty incumbent on others to do or give or omit something. In our case [i.e., in the case of the second immunity], the human person demands by right the omission of all coercive action impeding a community or the person from acting according to its conscience in religious matters. Therefore, the affirmation that every person has a right to such immunity is simultaneously an affirmation that no other person or power in society has a right to use coercion. On the contrary, all others are duty-bound to refrain from coercive action. The second immunity, then, requires a compelling argument that no other person can raise, as a right or duty, a valid claim against that immunity, or, put positively, that all are obliged to respect that immunity.

To place the right affirmed by *DH* on a secure foundation, therefore, it was necessary to formulate a compelling argument rooted in the Catholic tradition justifying this immunity, demonstrating, in Murray's phrase, its "juridical actuality" (*AHR*, 231).

The problem of constructing such an argument was not solved by the Council. In the course of the Council's deliberations, as Regan shows, four arguments designed to ground the right affirmed by *DH* emerged: an argument from the duties and rights of the individual conscience; an argument from the limits placed on the powers of government by man's dignity as a person; an argument from Scripture and "Christian freedom"; and an argument from our obligation to pursue truth in a manner consonant with our dignity and social nature as persons.[35] In the face of this disagreement regarding the foundations of religious liberty, the Council decided to put forward a brief, highly schematic, and, in any case, tentative argument incorporating elements of the lines of argument advocated by each of four schools of thought.

In the compromise argument of the final text, the arguments "from the right and duty to follow conscience" and from the limits of government were invoked but "in a subsidiary rather than a central role."[36] The argument from Scripture and Christian freedom was used but relegated to the second chapter and employed merely to show that religious freedom was, in the words of the Declaration, "consonant" with "revelation" (*DH*, 9). "Primacy" was afforded to "the argument from the duty and right to pursue the truth" and "from the social nature of man," which enjoyed "undisputed first place in both position and the number of lines devoted to it."[37]

As the principal advocate of what is sometimes called the political or constitutional argument for religious liberty, Murray shared in the widespread dissatisfaction with the argument of the final document. His preference for the political argument, however, did not mean he saw no validity in the other lines of argument which emerged in the course of the conciliar debates. He was, it's true, highly critical of the argument from the rights of conscience that played a central role in the early drafts of what became the Declaration. Although an individual has "the duty to act according to his conscience" even if it is "erroneous," Murray insisted, the fact remains that "another's error of conscience can create no duties" in others (*DRF*, 24–25). The fact that "I mistakenly think you owe me five dollars," for example, does not obligate you to pay me.[38]

Nevertheless, he readily admitted that the argument from our obligation to pursue truth conveys important truths. As far as it goes, it is "valid and on target" (*AHR*, 234). Indeed, he advocated its incorporation into the broader political argument he championed (*AHR*, 238–39). Likewise, he acknowledged that situating the "juridical-social" right to religious liberty affirmed by the Council in the context of "a full and complete theology of freedom" would have been "a far more satisfactory method of procedure from a theological point of view" and would have issued in a "doctrine . . . much richer in content" than that ultimately contained in *DH*. Such an approach, however, would have been a far more ambitious undertaking than the narrower argument from Christian freedom and Scripture championed by the proponents of the "theological argument" at the Council, and was, for that reason among others, open to a series of insurmountable practical objections. In any case, whatever merits these lines of arguments may possess, Murray insisted that they were ultimately incomplete because they fail to address the political issues raised by *DH*.[39]

Inasmuch as the state by right possesses a monopoly on the instruments of coercion, Murray argued that, in order properly to ground the immunity from coercion, it was first necessary to address the question of "the criteria which must govern the action of the public powers in limiting the free exercise of religion" (*PRF*, 140). Although "there is no doubt" that "spreading religious errors or practicing false forms of worship is per se evil in the moral order" and may be destructive of "the common good," *DH* denies the state "the right to repress religious opinions, practices and rites [simply] because they are erroneous and dangerous to the common good." The obvious question then is: "on what justifying argument does this denial rest?" Why, in short, "may the limitations placed on the public power in matters of religion" by *DH* "be considered just and legitimate?" To address these questions, it is necessary to engage the whole subject of "the duties and rights of the public power—their nature, their extent, and their limits" (*AHR*, 232). An argument designed to ground the immunity affirmed by the Declaration, in short, must necessarily include a theory of the state.

A quick examination of the central argument of *DH* illustrates Murray's point. This argument begins with "the moral obligation" of "all men" "to seek the truth especially religious truth." Indeed, they have an obligation "to adhere to the truth, once it is known, and to order their whole lives in accord with the demands of truth" (*DH*, 2). Since the duty to pursue truth and adhere to it must proceed freely, it follows that "men cannot discharge these obligations in a manner in keeping with their own nature unless they enjoy immunity from external coercion as well as psychological freedom" (*DH*, 2). We thus have a right to search freely for and, when found, adhere to the truth, a right to religious freedom.

This argument, however, would seem to be open to an obvious objection. "The fact that a person has a right to *search* for truth," says Regan, "would not necessarily of itself give him a right to *communicate* what he thinks is true but which is in fact false."[40] As Murray points out, the "repression" of "false forms of worship or religious errors" is perfectly compatible with man's moral obligation to seek the truth in order to act according to it. For such repression does not in the least prevent the quest for truth, nor does it prevent acting according to the truth. What it does prevent are public activities that proceed from a basis in error and that thus cause harm to the public good" (*AHR*, 235–36). The fact is that after "searching for religious truth or not searching for it," many people "actually cling to more or less false opinions that they wish to put into practice publicly and to disseminate in society" (*AHR*, 234).

Murray asks that we envision the "public powers" answering "those who profess more or less false opinions that they wish to put into practice publicly and disseminate in society" in the following fashion:

> We acknowledge and deeply respect the impulse to seek truth implanted in human nature. We acknowledge, too, your moral obligation to conform your life to truth's demands. But, sorry to say, we judge you to be in error. For in the sphere of religion we possess objective truth. More than that, in this society we represent the common good as well as religious truth—in fact religious truth is an integral part of the common good. In your private and in your family life, therefore, you may lawfully act according to your errors. However, we acknowledge no duty on our part to refrain from coercion in your regard when in the public life of society, which is our concern, you set about introducing your false forms of worship or spreading your errors. Continue then, your search for truth until you find it—we possess it—so that you may be able to act in public in keeping with it.

This proclamation, as Murray notes, is hardly "imaginary." Governments have "time and again" made such claims. Indeed, it closely tracks the argument employed both by the defenders of the "Catholic states" of the modern era and the small minority of bishops at the Council who opposed the promulgation of the Declaration (*AHR*, 235).

This rejoinder by the state admits no convincing answer so long as we remain within the horizon of the argument from the person's duty to seek truth. It admits no such answer because one can concede an obligation to seek the truth while denying that the state is obligated to allow those in error to "act in public according to their consciences" and to freely disseminate their errors. To defeat the line of argument embodied in this proclamation it is necessary to address a subject that the argument from the duty to seek truth ignores: "the duties and rights of the public power—their nature, extent and limits." It is necessary, in short, to move from "the moral" to "the juridical order" (*AHR*, 232).

The proponents of the argument from the obligation to pursue religious truth sought to counter this objection by situating the duty to seek truth in a social context. On the one hand, as Regan reports, they invoked the social nature of the person, maintaining that the "search for truth is necessarily a social enterprise involving communication and exchange."[41] Indeed, they argued, in Murray's words, that there exists a "necessary connection between internal acts of religion and those outward acts by which, in keeping with his social nature, a human being displays his religious convictions in a public way. Given this connection, the argument runs as follows: A purely human power cannot forbid internal acts; it is therefore equally powerless to forbid external acts" (*AHR*, 237).

As Murray points out, however, this argument involves "the fallacy of begging the question" because "it supposes that in society no power exists with authority reaching far enough to warrant its legitimately forbidding [external] acts of religion, even acts that transgress objective truth or divine law or even the common good." The difficulty, however, is that "this is what must be established; it is the very heart of the matter under discussion." That no such power exists is not proven simply by stating that because man possesses a social nature the pursuit of religious truth is a social enterprise which "must proceed in a public and communitarian manner" (*AHR*, 237).

The point is that appeals to our obligation to pursue truth do not suffice to establish the Declaration's conclusions. What Murray calls the political argument—the argument from the principle of limited government—is of "primary importance" because "without it any other argument would not sufficiently settle the question. For the very question [of religious freedom] concerns the limits of public power in religious matters" (*AHR*, 237). When all is said and done, a theory of religious freedom cannot avoid "the crucial issue" of "the competence of the powers with regard to passing judgment on forms of religious expression in society" (*PRF*, 151). A persuasive argument to ground the right affirmed by *DH* simply cannot be constructed without engaging the question of why "the public power" possesses neither "the duty" nor "right to repress opinions, practices, religious rites" that "are erroneous and dangerous to the common good" (*AHR*, 232).

Thus, as Murray points out, in articulating the foundations of the right to religious liberty, it is not sufficient "to attend only to the theological and ethical aspects of the issue. The political aspect becomes decisive. It is necessary to confront the question, whether and under what conditions, government has the right to restrain citizens from public action according to their beliefs" (*DRF*, 31). To construct a persuasive argument for this right, therefore, it is necessary, to provide an account of, and justification for, such a state. Insofar as *DH* fails to provide such a theory, its account of the foundations of the right it affirms is incomplete.

RELIGIOUS LIBERTY AND THE CATHOLIC THEORY OF THE STATE: THE POLITICAL ARGUMENT REVISITED

The obvious question concerns the precise nature of the political theory presupposed by *DH*. Our inquiry into this question must begin with the

Declaration itself, with the claims it makes regarding the nature and limits of the state. Several of these claims have already been elaborated in the context of our analysis of the right itself: the existence of a right to religious liberty as a twofold immunity from coercion; "public order" as the source of the norms limiting the scope of this liberty; the ideas that this order represents "the basic component of the common welfare" and that its "protection" is entrusted in some "special" sense to the state; the insistence that in the organization of social life "the freedom of man [must] be respected as far as possible, and curtailed only when and in so far as possible"; and the affirmation that, properly understood, religious liberty involves neither the privatization of religion nor a posture of governmental indifference to religion.

Over and above these claims, the Declaration makes a number of other assertions that bear on the nature of political life. To begin with, it affirms that "the demand" that "constitutional limits should be set to the powers of government, in order that there may be no encroachment on the rightful freedom of the person and of associations" is "in accord with truth and justice" (*DH*, 1). Second, it connects the legitimacy of this demand with the growing recognition of "the dignity of the human person" by virtue of which "the demand is increasingly made that men should act on their own judgment, enjoying and making use of a responsible freedom, not driven by coercion but motivated by a sense of duty" (*DH*, 1). This dignity, it suggests in turn, is the source of an order of human rights—"the inviolable rights of man" (*DH*, 6)—which the state must respect, an order that includes the right to immunity from coercion in matters religious. (This dignity would also seem to ground *DH*'s insistence that, when the state exercises its powers, "the freedom of man [must] be respected as far as possible, and curtailed only when and in so far as necessary" [*DH*, 7].)

Third, *DH* affirms that "the social nature of man" (*DH*, 4) finds expression in a wide variety of institutions. In addition to the state, these institutions and communities include "the family" (which, *DH* is at pains to stress, "is a society in its own original right" [*DH*, 5]), as well as "educational," "cultural," "charitable," "social" (*DH*, 4), and "religious" organizations (*DH*, 3). Fourth, it affirms that the state's "power" is limited to "the order of terrestrial and temporal affairs" (*DH*, 3). Fifth, it defines the common good of the political community as "the entirety of those conditions of social life under which men enjoy the possibility of achieving their own perfection in a certain fullness of measure and also with some relative ease." Finally, it affirms that the political common good "consists chiefly in the protection of the rights, and in the performance of the duties of the human person" and that "the protection and promotion of the inviolable rights of man ranks among the essential duties of government" (*DH*, 6).

Although *DH* hardly articulates a complete political theory, one can discern in it, as Pavan observes, the broad outlines of a model of the state that differs both from "the Catholic-confessional" model[42] of the state championed by Church social teaching prior to the Council and the secularist—"the laicistic or neutralistic"[43]—model rejected by both pre-Conciliar Church teaching and the Declaration. At the heart of *DH*'s vision of political life is the idea of limited government, the idea that the state is to play what Rausch terms "a limited secular role"[44] in the overall economy of human social life. *DH*, as Coleman notes, thus affirms as "normative" the idea of "the limited constitutional state."[45]

It is this conception of the state that undergirds the Declaration's theory of religious freedom. Government, the Declaration insists, is not authorized to forbid religious acts merely because they are erroneous or subversive of the common good. It possesses neither a generalized authority to pass judgment on the truth of the religious beliefs professed by the individuals and groups that compose society nor an open-ended mandate to advance the common good. The state thus exceeds the legitimate scope of its authority if it prohibits religious acts for either of these reasons. It possesses no right to restrict religious freedom—except insofar as its restriction is demanded by its responsibility to protect that segment of the common good *DH* calls the "public order."

From the perspective of the Declaration's understanding of the role of the state, as Murray notes, "the care of religion, in so far as it is a duty incumbent on the state is limited to a care for the religious freedom of the body politic" (*PRF*, 41). This care, as Pavan notes, places a twofold responsibility on the state. On the one hand, it must simultaneously "recognize, respect [and] safeguard" the right to religious freedom and "limit its exercise in those cases where its abuse may consistently compromise public order." On the other hand, it must act "to insure that the citizens do not lack means to exercise their religious rights and fulfill their religious duties." As the latter responsibility underscores, *DH* is quite emphatic that its conception of the limited constitutional state does not authorize a posture of governmental indifference toward religion. On the contrary, as Pavan remarks, "it is integral" to *DH*'s "model of the constitutional state that it should have a positive policy toward religion," albeit one consistent with its "nature," with its limited role in the economy of social life.[46]

As the Declaration's recognition of religion as a fundamental human good, its grounding of the content of public order in "the objective moral order" (*DH*, 7), and its insistence that the right to religious freedom "has its foundation, not in the subjective disposition of the person, but in his very nature" (*DH*, 2, 168) suggest, the limited constitutional state embraced by *DH* is rooted neither in an agnosticism on the question of the human good nor in the view that freedom as such constitutes that good. As Canavan observes, the Declaration's conception of religious freedom operates within the horizon of "the rational, natural-law" framework that "forms so significant a part" of "the Catholic tradition." It thus takes its bearings from the idea of "a universal human nature, whose natural tendencies and needs are knowable to the human mind" and the idea of "God, who is truth, and the truth about whom answers . . . the deepest of human needs."[47]

DH's conception of the limited constitutional state, furthermore, does not entail a posture of governmental neutrality on the question of the human good or the embrace by the state of the principle that the maximization of individual autonomy is the goal of law and public policy. Nor does *DH* reduce the state's role to the suppression of violence. On the contrary, as the positive responsibilities *DH* imposes on the state regarding religious life and its linkage of the public good with "the objective moral order" (*DH*, 7) suggest, the Declaration embodies a substantive conception of the human good and enlists the state in the service of this good, albeit in a manner consistent with the restricted character of its role in the overall scheme of human social life.

From Human Dignity to Public Order: The Contours of Murray's Argument

Of the many questions suggested by the claims made by *DH* regarding the state, we wish to pursue two here. The first concerns the foundations of its vision of limited government. The second concerns the whole question of the function of the state and of the content of the "public order," that portion of the common good whose protection and promotion is "the special duty of government." These questions can best be explored through an analysis of Murray's work, which, although it doesn't offer us a fully developed theory of the state, nevertheless constitutes the most serious exploration to date of the understanding of government presupposed by *DH*.

DH's embrace of the idea of limited, constitutional government presupposes, Murray argues, what he calls a juridical or constitutional conception of a state. In sharp contrast to paternalist conceptions of the state in which the political community "was conceived on the analogy of the family" and the ruler "was conceived to be *pater patriae*, whose paternal power extended to a care for the total welfare of his subject-children" (*PRF*, 51) and in which society was understood "to be built and rendered virtuous from the top down, as it were," the juridical state embodies the idea of government that is limited in its scope, subject in its operations to the rule of law, and responsible to those it governs. The constitutional state embodies the view that "the primary function of government is juridical, namely, the protection and promotion of the exercise of human and civil rights, and the facilitation of the discharge of human and civil duties by the citizen who is fully a citizen, that is, not merely subject to, but also participant in, government." Likewise, it insists that society is to be constructed and rendered virtuous "from the bottom up, as it were," as free persons voluntarily respond to the responsibilities inherent in their human nature.[48]

From the perspective of Catholic social thought, Murray continues, there is nothing particularly novel in this model of the state. Indeed, it has informed the social teaching of the Church since the pontificate of Pius XII and played a central role in the far-reaching transformation Catholic social teaching has undergone during this period.[49] The Declaration is essentially a statement of the implications of this conception of the political order for the question of religious freedom. This is why it states that "in taking up the matter of religious freedom," its intention is "to develop the doctrine of recent Popes on the inviolable rights of the human person and on the constitutional order of society" (*DH*, 1).

The obvious question here concerns the principles on which this conception of the state rests. In a short book that he wrote during the Council exploring the whole topic of the nature, scope, and foundations of religious freedom, Murray argued that the juridical state was informed by four principles. The first is "the distinction between the sacred and secular orders of human life." Because he "exists for a transcendent end," it follows that "the whole of man's existence is not absorbed in his temporal and terrestrial existence." Government, however, is neither "the judge" nor "the representative" of the "transcendent truth" governing "man's eternal destiny." Thus "the powers of government do not reach into this higher sacred order of human existence" but are instead "limited" to "the temporal and terrestrial order." The second principle, in turn, "is the distinction between society and state." In this view, "the state is only one order within society," namely, "the order of public law and public administration." Accordingly, it is "charged with the performance" only of certain limited functions "to be specified in the society's constitutional law, in accord with the consent of the people." Thus, "the purposes of the state are not coextensive with the purposes of society" (*PRF*, 144–45).

From this distinction follows a third principle, namely, "the distinction between the common good and public order." Whereas "the common good includes all the social goods, spiritual and moral as well as material, which man pursues here on earth in accord with the demands of his personal and social nature," the public order is that "narrower" segment of the common good "whose care devolves upon the state." It encompasses certain responsibilities regarding "the material welfare of the people" as well as a care for public peace, public morality, and the order of interpersonal justice. The fourth and final principle is the idea of "freedom under law." Freedom, in this view, is both "a political end" and "the political method *par excellentiam.*" Thus, there should exist "as much freedom, personal and social, as is possible" and "only as much restraint and constraint, personal and social, as may be necessary for the public order" (*PRF*, 145–46). From these premises, Murray concludes, follow both *DH*'s claims about the state and the right it affirms.

If the juridical state rests on these principles, however, the question necessarily arises about the intellectual underpinnings of these principles. Although in the aforementioned volume he touches only lightly on this question, in his other writings during and after Vatican II, Murray consistently seeks to ground *DH*'s conception of the state in the idea of man's dignity as a person. This dignity, he contends, demands that government's role be restricted to the performance of the limited array of functions that together comprise the public order.

Murray's argument begins

> with the traditional truth that every man has the innate dignity of a moral subject. He is endowed with intelligence, with a capacity for self-awareness. He is therefore called to a consciousness of the sense of his own existence—its meaning and purpose as determined by a transcendent order of truth and moral values, which is not created by himself but is to be discovered by him in the total reality of existence itself. Man is also endowed with freedom, a capacity for love and choice. As a subject *sui juris*, he is called to realize the sense of his own existence through a lifelong process of self-determination, motivated by his own personal judgments.

As a moral subject, man is "responsible" both "for the conformity of his judgments of conscience with the imperatives of the transcendent order of truth" and "for the conformity of his external actions with the inner imperatives of conscience" (*DRF*, 38).

By virtue of his status as a moral subject,

> man exhibits three characteristics. The first is personal autonomy. That is to say, in his necessary search for the sense of human existence, he is subject only to the laws that rule the order of truth—truth is so accepted only on pertinent evidence, the assent is to be pursued in free communion with others. The second characteristic is the irreplaceability of personal judgment and choice in the moral life. Moral worth attaches only to a human act done deliberately and freely. The human subject cannot be endowed with moral worth from the outside, by the action of others that would attempt to substitute itself for the inner dynamisms of intelligence and freedom. The third characteristic is inviolability. Man's native condition as a

moral subject, who confronts the demands of a transcendent order of truth and goodness, requires that he be surrounded by a zone or sphere of freedom within which he may take upon himself his ineluctable burden—that of responsibility for his own existence.

This requirement of a zone of freedom is even "more stringent in what concerns man's relation with God" on account of its immediacy, its "person to person" character, and each individual's "personal responsibility" for "the nature" of his or her individual "response" to God's call (*DRF*, 39). For all these reasons

> it clearly appears that coercion brought to bear upon the human subject, especially in what concerns his relation to God, is not only a useless irrelevance but also a damaging intrusion. It does injury to man's personal autonomy. It stupidly seeks to replace what is irreplaceable. It does violence to the very texture of the human condition, which is a condition of personal responsibility. The conclusion is that an exigence for immunity from coercion is resident in the person as such. It is an exigence of his dignity as a moral subject.

This "exigence for immunity from coercion" extends to all those "areas of human life in which the values of the human spirit are directly at stake" and is validly "asserted against . . . other individuals, others organized in social groups, and especially that impersonal other that is the state." It is thus "the source of the fundamental rights of the person—those political-civil rights concerning the search for truth, artistic creation, scientific discovery, and the development of man's political views, moral convictions, and religious beliefs" (*DRF*, 40).

Inasmuch as this "exigence to act on his own initiative and on his own personal responsibility" is "a thing of the objective order . . . rooted in the given reality of man as man," it follows that it is "permanent and ineradicable and altogether stringent." In essence, "it is identically the basic requirement that man should act in accordance with his nature." Thus, the claim to "immunity from coercion, especially in matters religious" is "man's fundamental claim on others" (*DRF*, 40–41).

The only "authority that might possibly enter a counterclaim" overriding this claim is the "government" in its capacity as the agency "responsible for the establishment and maintenance of the juridical order in society." In fact, however, man's claim to immunity from coercion "is valid not only in its objective foundation . . . but also in the crucial instance" of "the citizen's confrontation with" government. In contrast to "the moral claim or right of the person" who "is the foundation, the end and the subject of the juridical order," government's claims "are only derivative, subordinate to the claims of the human person, and enlisted in the support of these claims." The state thus has

> the burden of proving that it has the right to bring coercion to bear. This, however, it cannot do, except when its own fundamental responsibility becomes controlling—in the case of violation of public order; a contravention of the necessary conditions of social coexistence; a public offense that imperils the pillars of society, which are an order of equal justice for all citizens; the public peace which is the work of justice; and that minimum of realizable public morality whose maintenance is the just requirement of the citizenry.

Only government's obligation to fulfill "its fundamental responsibility" of safeguarding public order—of vindicating the triad of goods this order embodies—trumps the claims of the person to immunity from coercion in religious matters (*DRF*, 41–42).

Murray elsewhere adumbrates a slightly different version of this argument. Here he moves from the dignity of the person to the affirmation "that the human person is the subject, foundation, and end of the entire social life." From these two principles, he draws three conclusions. The first is that "freedom not to be restricted unless and insofar as necessary" to safeguard "public order," insofar, this is to say, as its restriction is necessary "to preserve society's very existence." The second is that all citizens, by virtue of their human dignity must "enjoy juridical equality in society." The third is that, as Pius XII had affirmed, "the paramount duty of every public power" is "to protect the inviolable rights proper to human beings and to ensure that everyone may discharge his duties with greater facility" (*AHR*, 238–39).

These "five principles," he concludes, "cohere with one another in such a way that they form a kind of vision of the human person in society and of society itself, of the juridical ordering of society and of the common good considered in its most fundamental dimensions, and finally of the duties of the public power toward persons and society." Taken together, they undergird the juridical conception of the state that *DH* presupposes, the claims about the political order it explicitly makes, and "the notion of religious freedom" it proclaims (*AHR*, 239).

Murray and the Political Theory of the Juridical State: Four Difficulties

Murray's contention that both *DH* and contemporary Catholic social teaching presuppose what he describes as a juridical or constitutional model of the state is persuasive, as is his contention that a convincing effort to ground the right affirmed by *DH* necessarily involves the articulation of the full-fledged theory of politics, the model of man and society, in which the juridical state is rooted.

At the same time, certain questions arise about Murray's account of this theory. Does it contain all the elements necessary to construct the theory of politics he so persuasively argues is required to ground the conclusions of *DH*? Does it persuasively justify the role it attributes to the state? To what degree is its conception of the state consistent with the role attributed to the state by both the Declaration and, more broadly, contemporary Catholic social teaching? Seen in this light, four difficulties immediately emerge.

The first concerns the capacity of Murray's argument to ground the full range of principles constitutive of the juridical state. Although Murray initially insists that the juridical state is informed by the four principles cited earlier, his effort to articulate their foundations seems to give short shrift to two of these principles. Specifically, while his argument attempts to ground the limitation of government's role to the safeguarding of public order and the method of freedom in the exigencies of human dignity, it appears to pass over in silence the distinctions between the sacred and secular orders and between state and society. How, or even if, these principles can simply be generated from the dignity of the person is not immediately clear.

The second concerns the very content of the public order. Unfortunately, not only does Murray never really explore the idea of public order in a sustained fashion, but it is difficult to reconcile what he says at different points in his work regarding its content. At times, his analysis seems to suggest that it possesses a rather thin content. In the previously quoted passages, he at one point equates public order with "the necessary conditions of social existence" (*DRF*, 41) and at another with "the restraint necessary to preserve society's very existence" (*AHR*, 239). In another passage, he describes it as the conditions "necessary for the sheer coexistence of citizens within conditions of elemental social order" (*DRF*, 35).

When it is defined in this minimalist fashion, it would seem difficult to distinguish the conception of the state's role embodied in the idea of the "public order" from that embodied in the idea of the night watchman state. Indeed, as Regan points out, the seeming resemblance of these two ideas caused uneasiness at the Council because the emphatic rejection of the night watchman state is one of the enduring features of contemporary Catholic social teaching.[50] Interpreted in this type of minimalist fashion, it is difficult to see how the idea of public order can be reconciled with the conception of the state's role that informs Catholic social teaching as a whole. It is also difficult to see how it can be reconciled with the role *DH* itself attributes to the state.

It is thus not surprising that, despite the statements cited earlier, Murray never definitively embraces such a minimalist understanding of public order. On the contrary, at a number of points, his analysis seems to attribute a much richer content to this concept. For example, although not pursuing the point as irrelevant to the immediate question of "the criteria" that should govern "the action of the public powers in limiting the free exercise of religion," he suggests that the public order encompasses "the function of the state with regard to the good of 'prosperity,' the material welfare of the people" (*PRF*, 143–44). Similarly, his analysis suggests that the vindication of public order extends beyond the mere suppression of violence and also includes the protection of the "values"—"juridical, political, moral"[51]—that constitute "the pillars of society" (*DRF*, 29). Over and above the safeguarding of public peace, public order extends to a care for "an order of justice" and a "moral order."[52] It thus includes more than the mere suppression of violence, more than the minimal restraint necessary "to preserve society's very existence." Indeed, even public peace itself would seem to involve more than the suppression of violence insofar as the safeguarding of "genuine public peace"—as opposed to a false and inadequate conception of public peace—involves the maintenance of "good order" and "true justice" (*DH*, 7).

Furthermore, since the Declaration is clear that "government has not done its full duty to society when it has guaranteed this immunity [i.e., the twofold immunity from coercion affirmed by the Declaration] and protected it with the legal armature of law,"[53] the state's care for public order assumes a fuller range of affirmative responsibilities in the area of religion. Understood in this fashion, it is clear that the public does not reduce the state to what Murray once described as an "amoral policeman."[54]

Yet a "thick" interpretation of the public order also brings with it certain dangers. If pushed too far, a "thick" reading issues what might be called a maximalist conception of the content of public order.[55] An expansive reading of the concept of public morality might, to take but one obvious example, authorize the state to assume a type of generalized responsibility for the protection and promotion of religious truth incompatible with the natural human right to religious freedom assumed by *DH*. Such a role, it might be argued, is justified in terms of the close relationship between religious truth and moral truth or by the fact that our moral obligations encompass duties of a religious nature. Indeed, it might even be claimed that the government's responsibility to protect public morality authorizes it to proscribe false modes of religious worship and the public advocacy of religious error.

This maximalist reading, however, is ultimately no more satisfactory than the minimalist reading of the public order. The effect of this reading is to collapse the public order into the common good, make the goals of the state coextensive with the goals of society, and thereby efface the distinction between state and society. Accordingly, the maximalist interpretation is inconsistent with the spirit and substance of contemporary Catholic social teaching, which, as J. Bryan Hehir notes, not only "affirms substantial responsibilities for the state" but simultaneously "sets clear limits to its range of activity."[56] At the same time, it is inconsistent with both the spirit and substance of *DH* and the overall thrust of Murray's thought. The concept of "public order," after all, is clearly intended to be more restricted in its scope than the concept of the "common good."

Clearly, what Murray and contemporary Catholic social teaching (including *DH*) have been attempting to do is to articulate a conception of the proper role of the state that avoids both the Scylla of the minimalist reading of the public order and the Charybdis of the maximalist reading, that avoids, as Murray puts it, either elevating the state to an *episcopus externus* or reducing it to an "amoral policeman."[57] The difficulty is that it is clearer what is being rejected than what is being embraced. In the course of his critique of the Declaration, Murray observes that, although the scope of the immunity affirmed by the Declaration is clear, the same cannot be said about its account of the "root" of government's "duty . . . to favor religion."[58] Something similar might well be said of his own treatment of this subject. If it is not clear, this is because neither Murray nor the Declaration addresses with sufficient depth and precision the question of the exact nature of the state's proper contribution to the common good of society, of the state's proper role in the overall scheme of human social life.

The third problem involves the justification for restricting the state's role to the protection and promotion of the public order rather than conferring upon it a generalized and open-ended mandate for promoting all aspects of the common good. As was noted earlier, Murray's argument for limiting the state's role to the protection and promotion of "public order" begins with the idea of human dignity. The dignity of the human person, he maintains, demands "that man in society must be accorded as much freedom as possible" and thus that "freedom is not to be restricted unless and insofar as is necessary" in order "to preserve society's very existence" (*AHR*, 239). The person's dignity, in other words, creates an exigence for the person to act freely that trumps all other claims save those of societal self-preservation, which Murray equates here with "public order."

Because Murray's argument here assumes an untenably thin conception of public order, it would seem incapable of grounding the more substantive conception of this order implicit in *DH*. If freedom truly trumps all claims other than those of societal self-preservation, it would seem to trump the claims of a sufficiently thick conception of public order to do justice to the understanding of the role of the state that informs *DH* and contemporary Catholic social teaching and that the major thrust of Murray's own thought seems to assume. A persuasive argument for the restriction of the state's role to the care of "public order" in the thicker sense operative in *DH* must necessarily begin with the recognition that goods other than societal self-preservation outweigh those of individual freedom and must encompass both the identification of those goods and an explanation of why they trump the claims of freedom.

The final difficulty concerns the tension between *DH* and the main thrust of Murray's own political theory on the one hand and some of his formulations regarding the relationship of the state to the order of truth—in particular, religious truth—on the other.[59] "Inherent . . . in the notion of religious freedom," he remarks, "is the notion of governmental incompetence in matters religious." This notion, Murray stresses, neither presupposes nor entails "an assertion of indifference to the values of religion to man and to society. Nor is it a reassertion of the outworn laicist creed that 'religion is a purely private matter'" (*DRF*, 36–37). As in the case of public order, however, Murray never really explores the meaning or implications of the religious "incompetence" of the state in anything approaching a systematic fashion.

For the most part, his scattered discussions of the subject would seem broadly consistent in both spirit and substance with both the Declaration and his own theory of the state. In this context, one thinks of his insistence that the right to religious liberty proclaimed by *DH* involves the rejection of the idea that government is "*defensor fidei*," that government's "duty and right . . . extend to what had long been called *cura religionis*, a direct care of religion itself."[60] It involves, this is to say, the rejection of the ideas that the "function of government" encompasses a responsibility for "the protection and promotion . . . of religious truth," that "government is to be the judge of religious truth, the defender of the true faith, or the guardian of religious unity,"[61] and that the state's duties encompass a "share in the *cura animarum* or in the *regimen animorum*" (*PRF*, 144). One also thinks here of his contention that this right implies the recognition that "the function of government is secular,"[62] that "its powers are limited to the affairs of the temporal and terrestrial order of man's existence," and thus that the state is neither "the judge or the representative of transcendent truth with regard to man's eternal destiny" nor "man's guide to heaven" (*PRF*, 144).

Nevertheless, several of the stronger claims Murray makes regarding the "incompetence" of the state "in matters religious" would seem to be problematic when seen against the backdrop of the Declaration and his own theory of the state. He remarks, for example, that truths "of the transcendent order" are not "accessible" to "judgment by secular powers."[63] Similarly, he avers that "the positive values inherent in religious belief, profession, and practice" are "juridically irrelevant, however great their religious, moral, and social significance." They are "irrelevant" because

> it is of the nature of a juridical formula—in this case, religious freedom— simply to set outside limits to a sphere of human activity, and to guarantee this sphere against forcible intrusion from without, *but not to penetrate into the interior of this sphere and to pronounce moral or theological judgments of value on the activity itself.* Such judgments exceed the category of the juridical, which is concerned with interpersonal relationships. They likewise exceed the competence of the forces of juridical order—the forces of law and of political authority.

They exceed the competence of the state, he maintains, because whereas that competence is restricted to the juridical order, "the higher ends of human existence," and "the actual pursuit" of these ends "are of the metajuridical order. They are related to the inner dynamism of the human spirit as such, which is remote from direction or control by any forces of the juridical order" (*DRF*, 28–29; my emphasis).

Admittedly, these statements are hardly unambiguous and to be properly understood must be seen in the context of Murray's broader account of the state and the relationship of political life to the order of truth. Nevertheless, at least at first glance, they would seem to point toward a conception of the state's competence in religious matters that is difficult to reconcile with either the affirmative responsibilities toward the order of religion or the thick conception of the content of public order that informs both *DH* and the major thrust of Murray's own thought. Indeed, on the surface, they could well be interpreted as demanding a posture of intellectual agnosticism on the part of the state that is simply incompatible with the spirit and substance of *DH*.

These statements thus raise a whole series of questions. How can the affirmative duties imposed by *DH* on the state in religious matters be reconciled with Murray's claims that "the positive values inherent in religious belief, profession and practice" are "juridically irrelevant" and that "the higher ends of human existence" lie totally beyond the scope of the government's legitimate concerns? How can the state's obligation to "take account of the religious life of the people and show it favor" be reconciled with the view that with regard to religion "the only matters that are juridically relevant are, first, the limits that may reasonably set to the free exercise of religion and, second, the duty of government and of society not to transgress these limits" (*DRF*, 28–29)? How can a conception of public order rooted in "the objective moral order" and hence in the truth about the nature of man and the human good be embraced by a state committed to a posture of intellectual agnosticism? More broadly, inasmuch as a true understanding of the juridical order—involving as it does the proper ordering of intersubjective relations among men—can take shape only in light of the truth about the human person, how can a state arrive at such an understanding if "the higher ends of human existence" lie beyond its cognizance?

Nor are these difficulties completely resolved by arguing, as Murray sometimes does, ~~that~~ that the affirmative responsibilities imposed on the state in religious matters by *DH* extend only to "the secular values of religion," that if government's competence does not extend to "the care of religion itself" insofar as it involves the affairs and truths of "the transcendental order," it does "extend" to "the secular values of religion—such values as affect the common temporal good."[64] To begin with, it is not readily apparent how judgments about "the common temporal good" can be made without the pronouncement of "moral or theological judgments of value." Likewise, insofar as judgments about the common temporal good are necessarily judgments of moral value, does not empowering the state to make such judgments while denying it access to the "truths" of "the transcendent order" effectively force it to embrace not merely a secular morality but a secularist morality? Similarly, does not the conduct of public life without reference to "the transcendent order" necessarily entail the privatization of religion? Finally, inasmuch as the very notion of "the common *temporal* good," as Murray readily admits, is rooted in a prior distinction between "the sacred and secular orders of human life" and thus in a particular theology and metaphysics, it would seem necessarily to presuppose the very type of affirmations about the order of transcendent truth that Murray's stronger statements about the religious "incompetence" of the state would seem to preclude.

This is not to imply that Murray embraces what is sometimes called the naked public square. Rather it is to suggest that, Murray's intentions and the major thrust of his thought to the contrary notwithstanding, his stronger formulations regarding "governmental incompetence in matters religious" could be interpreted as requiring the very privatization of religion and posture of governmental indifference toward religion that he so steadfastly rejected. This whole subject obviously needs to be explored in a far more systematic, precise, and careful fashion than it is in Murray's work.

Obviously, *DH* limits the role of the state—the competence of the state, in Murray's terminology —in religious matters. The pivotal question concerns the character of these limits. The right proclaimed by *DH*, along with the broader understanding of the juridical order and the theory of the state of which it is a part, is rooted in a whole series of moral, anthropological, metaphysical, and theological affirmations. In determining the content of the public order, the state is obligated to act in conformity with the "objective moral order," in accordance with the order of truth. Insofar as the state is asked to embrace this theory, therefore, it is necessarily asked to embrace these affirmations.

The limits *DH* places on the state in religious matters would thus appear to be not in the order of knowledge but in the order of action; they would appear to be jurisdictional rather than epistemological. The theory of the state underlying *DH* asserts neither that the state is incapable of recognizing religious truth nor that it must eschew all judgments of moral or theological value but rather that government's role relative to the order of religion is limited by virtue of its restricted role in the overall economy of social life. This role encompasses neither the promulgation and defense of religious truth nor the ordering of the entirety of human life in accordance with the demands of that truth nor the care of souls but the care of that limited ensemble of social goods that collectively constitute the public order. One wonders, in this context, if the very language of the religious "incompetence" of the state does not invite needless confusion.

These reservations, it should be stressed, are not meant to diminish what Murray accomplished. Among the twentieth-century Christian ethicists who have wrestled with the problems of church-state relations and religious freedom, as Protestant theologian Keith J. Pavlischek recently remarked, Murray "is in a class by himself" in terms of "lucidity of analysis, historical sensitivity, and theological depth."[65] There can be no question that Murray's work on these subjects guarantees him a permanent place among the giants of modern Catholic social thought. Murray, furthermore, did not claim to offer a fully developed theory of the juridical state; he clearly saw his work as doing no more than beginning the process of laying the foundations for such a theory. Whatever its limits, his work not only demonstrates that this right cannot be grounded without the systematic elaboration of such a theory, it also makes an important contribution to the formulation of that theory. Accordingly, it represents an indispensable starting point for those who wish to complete the unfinished agenda of *DH*.

RECASTING THE POLITICAL ARGUMENT: SOCIAL PLURALISM AND THE LIMITS OF GOVERNMENT

If the quest to elaborate the theory of the state presupposed by *DH* is not to be abandoned, the question that must be addressed is what intellectual resources, over and above those employed by Murray, the Catholic tradition offers us to assist in the construction of this theory. One of the most important of these resources—as Murray's repeated invocation of it as a foundational element of the Catholic tradition in social thought suggests—is the distinction between state and society.[66] Although Murray does not explore it at any length, this distinction has its roots in the rich and highly complex ontology of social life that informs both the Church's contemporary social *magisterium* and the work of the generation of thinkers—one thinks immediately here of Pesch, Maritain, Rommen, and Messner—whose thought (along with Murray's) helped lay the groundwork for the broader development in Catholic social teaching of which *DH* is a part.

As Maritain points out, Catholicism's vision of social life is not only personalist but pluralist as well.[67] At the heart of this ontology is what might be called normative pluralism, the idea that, in John Paul II's words, "the social nature of man is not completely fulfilled in the State, but is realized in various intermediary groups beginning with the family and including economic social and cultural groups." These groups are not creations of the state. Nor are they the purely conventional products of contractual agreements among naturally autonomous individuals, the purely arbitrary products of the private desires of individuals. Rather, they "stem from human nature itself."[68]

The state, in this view, is but one of the social forms to which our nature as intrinsically social beings gives rise and thus must share the stage of social life with a wide variety of other groups and institutions. This means, in turn, that society is not simply a collection of individuals united and structured by the authority of the state. Rather, it is a community of communities, "a unity," in Messner's words, "composed of member communities relatively independent, or autonomous, since they have their own social ends, their own common good, and consequently their own functions."[69] If the state supplies these institutions with their "legal hulk," as Rommen observes, the fact remains that these groups, the ends they serve, and the rights and duties that follow from these ends issue from human nature and from man's dynamic orientation toward the perfection of his nature, not from positive law. It is thus the nature of these institutions and "their ends, that control the legal forms, not vice versa." Although "the state may provide the family with its family law," for example, "the essence and the ends of the family form the critical norm for legal forms."[70]

By virtue of their status as communal subjects, furthermore, these groups possess what John Paul II describes as "certain proper and specific rights."[71] Like the rights of the person, the rights of these communal subjects include the right to a large measure of autonomy and to immunity from coercion in matters concerning the values proper to the human spirit. Likewise, as communities of persons, they must be afforded as much freedom to act on their own initiative as is "possible." This understanding of the structure of social life thus issues in a commitment to what Canavan describes as "the self-organization of society."[72] Society, on this view, must be constructed from the bottom up, not from the top down, as persons freely organize themselves into a wide array of diverse but interconnected social groups in order to secure the goods proper to human flourishing.

At first glance, it might not be entirely clear how an account of society's structure and its implications assists us in constructing an adequate foundation for the theory of the state presupposed by *DH*. Indeed, it would seem simply to repeat Murray's argument, merely substituting what are often called "intermediary groups" for the individual. It would thus seem to be open to the very same objection to which Murray's argument is vulnerable, namely, that it begs the critical question of the proper functions of the state. The immunity from coercion it asserts is not an absolute but is trumped by the right—and indeed responsibility—of the state to employ coercion in the pursuit of its legitimate ends. Similarly, the freedom of these groups must be respected—but only "when and in so far" as its restriction is not "necessary" to the state's pursuit of its legitimate ends. The critical question thus concerns the nature of these ends and the nature of the state's proper role in the overall economy of social life. This line of argument seems to leave this fundamental question untouched.

As Coleman suggests, however, Murray's "argument" is in fact "dependent on a strong corollary case for mediating structures."[73] Indeed, the idea of society as a community of communities is absolutely essential to the successful elaboration of the theory of state presupposed by *DH*. On the one hand, this vision plays a critically important role in laying the foundation for a number of political principles that inform the juridical state. It constitutes, for example, the essential foundation of the state-society distinction that is so central to this theory.

Likewise, it plays a vital role in grounding the principle of limited government. From the perspective of Catholicism's pluralist conception of the proper ordering of human social life, responsibility for the common good does not rest with the state alone but is shared by the whole range of institutions that compose society. As *DH* itself affirms, for example, while religious freedom is an integral element of the common good, the responsibility for the protection and promotion of this right "devolves upon the people as a whole, upon social groups, upon government, and upon the Church and other religious communities, in virtue of the duty of all toward the common welfare, and in the manner proper to each" (*DH* 6, 173).

Similarly, as John Paul II notes in *Centesimus Annus*, although the state plays an essential role in "overseeing and directing the exercise of human rights in the economic sector," nevertheless "the primary responsibility" for the protection and promotion of human rights in this area "belongs not to the State but to individuals and to the various groups and associations which make up society."[74]

The point is that, from the perspective of Catholicism's pluralist ontology of social life, different institutions make different contributions to the common good. The state, therefore, is limited by the fact that only certain limited aspects of the common good have been entrusted to its care. The remainder have been entrusted to the care of other institutions, institutions that are, in Rommen's apt phrase, "original entities and original social organizations"[75] in their own right rather than mere creatures of the state. These institutions have a right not only to exist but to discharge their distinctive functions, to pursue their proper ends, and to make their distinctive contributions to human flourishing. For the state to attempt to absorb the functions of these groups would be a grave injustice. The state is thus limited by the limited character of its functions relative to the overall economy of human social life by the responsibilities and the distinctive functions of the institutions with which it shares the stage of social life.

On the other hand, the Catholic conception of society as a community of communities opens the door to the type of systematic inquiry necessary to arrive at an adequate conception of the content of "public order," necessary to arrive at an adequate understanding of the nature, role, and limits of the state. Since a complete account of the proper role of the state in the total scheme of social life cannot simply be deduced from man's nature or dignity as a person, an analysis that moves on the plane of the state and individual alone cannot arrive at a satisfactory theory of the nature and functions of the state. Neither can one that moves on the plane of the individual, the state, and "society" alone without analyzing further society's ontological structure and its specifically pluralist character.

The question of the nature and functions of the state can be fruitfully pursued only against the backdrop of a pluralist understanding of society because it is only in this context that the distinctive character of the state and its purposes can come into view. Without a comprehensive ontology of social life encompassing an understanding of the full range of institutions charac teristic of a differentiated society in which we provide an account of the role of each in the overall economy of social life, the nature of the state's distinctive subsidiary function—the exact nature of its contribution to the common good in contrast to that of other social actors—cannot be specified with any degree of precision.

CONCLUSION

Ironically, Murray's own pre-Conciliar work embodies this recognition. The idea of social pluralism and its implications for the role of the state figures prominently in this effort to rethink Catholic teaching on the whole problem of Church and state.[76] When, during and after the Council, his focus turned from this broader problematic to the specific problem of religious freedom, however, this whole theme almost entirely disappears from view—remaining visible only in the residual form of the frequently invoked but never systematically explored distinction between state and society—and is replaced by a line of argument that moves directly from the idea of man's dignity as a person to an account of the functions of the state without pausing to situate the state in the context of the entire complex of institutions composing what Murray had earlier called civil society. It is precisely because it neglects the whole subject of social pluralism—the whole subject of the nature and role of the full range of differentiated institutions necessary to human flourishing—that this line of argument is incapable of generating the philosophy of the state underlying the Catholic theory of religious liberty.

This is not to suggest, it should be emphasized, that Murray's explorations of the implications of man's nature and dignity as a person to the organization of social life are irrelevant to the whole subject of the nature and the role of the state. A sound anthropology is an essential precondition of an adequate understanding of both society and the state, and as the Church's social *magisterium* and a whole array of important Catholic thinkers have pointed out, the fact that man is a person has profound implications for our understanding of the nature and proper ordering of both social and political life.[77] What it suggests, however, is that, although the road to the political theory presupposed by *DH* indeed must begin with the idea of man's dignity as a person, it necessarily passes through an account of society's pluralist structure.[78]

NOTES

1. Support for this essay comes in part from the Pew Charitable Trusts and the Earhart Foundation. The opinions it expresses are those of the author and do not necessarily reflect the views of either the Pew Charitable Trusts or the Earhart Foundation. The author wishes to thank these organizations for their generous support of his work. An earlier version of this essay appeared as "John Courtney Murray, the 'Juridical State,' and the Catholic Theory of Religious Freedom," in *The Political Science*

Reviewer XXXIII (2005): 1–61. For purposes of convenience, *Dignitatis Humanae* will generally be abbreviated as *DH* in the text.

2. This observation is contained in the notes Murray attached to the text of his translation of *Dignitatis Humanae*, in *The Documents of Vatican II*, ed. Walter M. Abbott, S.J. (New York: Crossroad, 1989; reprint, New York: The America Press, 1966), 680, n. 7. Further citations of these notes will be given as "Murray, *DH*" followed by the page and note number.

3. Murray, "Arguments for the Human Right to Religious Freedom," in *Religious Liberty: Catholic Struggles with Pluralism/John Courtney Murray*, ed. J. Leon Hooper, S.J. (Louisville: Westminster/John Knox Press), 230. Further citations of this work will be given parenthetically with the title abbreviated as *AHR*.

4. Murray, "The Declaration on Religious Liberty," in *Vatican II: An Interfaith Appraisal*, ed. John H. Miller (Notre Dame, IN: Association Press, 1966), 570.

5. Richard J. Regan, *Conflict and Consensus: Religious Freedom and the Second Vatican Council* (New York: Macmillan, 1967), 170.

6. Ibid., 174.

7. Murray, *DH*, 680, n. 7.

8. Regan, 159.

9. For the drafting of the Declaration, see Regan. For an account of Murray's role in its drafting and the debates which preceded it, see Donald E. Pelotte, S.S., *John Courtney Murray: Theologian in Conflict* (Mahwah, NJ: Paulist Press, 1975).

10. *Dignitatis Humanae*, section 1. Further citations of this document will be given parenthetically.

11. Murray, "Religious Freedom," in *The Documents of Vatican II*, 674.

12. Murray, *DH*, 694–95, n. 58.

13. Dulles, *A Church to Believe In: Discipleship and the Dynamics of Freedom* (New York: Crossroad, 1983), 72.

14. It should be mentioned here that the Declaration affirms that the right to religious freedom enjoyed by the Catholic Church and her members ultimately derives not from the dignity of the human person but, as Murray writes, from "the divine mandate laid on her by Christ Himself . . . . No other church or Community may claim to possess this mandate in its fullness." Murray, *DH*, 682, n. 9. For its treatment of what it, in keeping with the Catholic tradition, designates the freedom of the Church, see *DH* 13–14. Although this freedom, as Murray writes, is an "empowerment," in the juridical order it translates into "an immunity from coercive constraint or restraint" (Murray, "The Issue of Church and State at Vatican Council II," in *Religious Liberty: Catholic Struggles with Pluralism/John Courtney Murray*, 208, 211). Thus, if they differ in their foundations, in the juridical order the right to religious freedom belonging to all men and that proper to the Catholic Church and her members are "the same" in their content. See Murray, *DH*, 682, n. 9. As the Declaration affirms, "a harmony exists between the freedom of the Church and the religious freedom which is to be recognized as the right of all men" (13).

15. Pietro Pavan, "Ecumenism and Vatican II's Declaration on Religious Freedom," in *Religious Freedom: 1965 and 1975*, ed. Walter J. Burghardt (Mahwah, NJ: Paulist Press, 1976), 15.

16. Ibid., 13.

17. Ibid., 13.

18. Pietro Pavan, "Declaration on Religious Freedom," in *Commentary on the Documents of Vatican II*, vol. IV, ed. Herbert Vorgrimler (New York: Herder and Herder, 1969), 64.

19. Ibid., 66–67.

20. Murray, "The Issue of Church and State at Vatican Council II," in *Religious Liberty: Catholic Struggles with Pluralism/John Courtney Murray*, 211.

21. Murray, *DH*, 678, n. 3.

22. Murray, "The Declaration on Religious Freedom: A Moment in Its Legislative History," in *Religious Liberty: An End and a Beginning*, 24. Further citations of this work will be given parenthetically with the title abbreviated as *DRF*.

23. Francis Canavan, "Church, State and Council," in *Ecumenism and Vatican II*, ed. Charles O'Neill, S.J. (Milwaukee: Bruce, 1964), 53.

24. Pavan, "Declaration," 65.

25. Pavan, "Ecumenism," 20.

26. Pavan, "Declaration," 65.

27. Pavan, "Ecumenism," 20.

28. Murray, *DH*, 678, n. 5.

29. Murray, "Religious Freedom," in *Freedom and Man*, ed. John Courtney Murray, S.J. (New York: P. J. Kenedy & Sons, 1965), 135.

30. Pavan, "Ecumenism," 18.

31. Canavan, "The Catholic Concept of Religious Freedom as a Human Right," in *Religious Liberty: An End and a Beginning*, 76.

32. Murray, "Religious Freedom and the Atheist," in *Bridging the Sacred and the Secular: Selected Writings of John Courtney Murray, S.J.*, ed. J. Leon Hooper (Washington, DC: Georgetown University Press, 1994), 263.

33. Canavan, "Church, State and Council," 48.

34. Regan, 2.

35. On the debate at the Council, see Regan, *Conflict and Consensus*.

36. Ibid., 174.

37. Ibid., 159 and 174.

38. Murray, "The Problem of Religious Freedom," in *Religious Liberty: Catholic Struggles with Pluralism/John Courtney Murray*, 179–80. Further citations of this work will be given parenthetically with the title abbreviated as *PRF*.

39. "The Declaration on Religious Freedom," in *Bridging the Sacred and the Secular*, 189–90. For the views of the French theologians who championed a theological approach, see Marilyn Wallace, "The Right of Religious Liberty and Its Basis in the Theological Literature of the French Language (1940–1980)" (Ph.D. dissertation, The Catholic University of America, 1988).

40. Regan, 87.

41. Ibid., 88.

42. Pavan, "Ecumenism," 29.

43. Pavan, "Declaration," 64.

44. James S. Rausch, "*Dignitatis Humanae*: The Unfinished Agenda," in *Religious Freedom: 1965 and 1975*, 41.

45. John Coleman, *An American Strategic Theology* (Mahwah, NJ: Paulist Press, 1982), 224.

46. Pavan, "Ecumenism," 31.

47. Canavan, "The Catholic Concept," 71–72.

48. "The Declaration on Religious Freedom," in *Bridging the Sacred and the Secular*, 196–97.

49. On the movement of Catholic social thought toward this model of the state in the period from the pontificates of Leo XIII through that of John XXIII, see Murray, "The Problem of Religious Freedom," 155–78; and Gerald A. McCool, S.J., "The Evolution of Catholic Social Thought in the Last Two Centuries," in *A Moral Enterprise: Politics, Reason and the Human Good*, ed. Kenneth L. Grasso and Robert P. Hunt (Wilmington, DE: ISI Books, 2002), 83–106.

50. Regan, 124–25.

51. Murray, *DH*, 686, n. 20.

52. Ibid.

53. Murray, "The Declaration on Religious Liberty," in *Vatican II: An Interfaith Appraisal*, 580.

54. John Courtney Murray, "Governmental Repression of Heresy," in *Proceedings of the Third Annual Convention of the Catholic Theological Society of America* (Bronx, NY: Catholic Theological Society of America, 1948), 56.

55. For an example of a maximalist reading of public order, see Brian Harrison, *Religious Liberty and Contraception* (Melbourne, Australia: John XXIII Fellowship Co-Op. Ltd., 1988).

56. J. Bryan Hehir, "*Dignitatis Humanae* in the Pontificate of John Paul II," in *Religious Liberty: Paul VI and* Dignitatis Humanae, ed. John T. Ford, C.S.C. (Brescia, Italy: Instituto Paolo VI, 1995), 174.

57. "Governmental Repression of Heresy," in *Proceedings*, 56.

58. Murray, "The Declaration on Religious Liberty," in *Vatican II: An Interfaith Appraisal*, 580.

59. On this point, see Robert P. Hunt, "Catholicism, Liberalism and Religious Liberty," in *A Moral Enterprise: Politics, Reason and the Human Good*, 143–63; and David L. Schindler, "Reorienting the Church on the Eve of the Millennium," in *Communio* 4 (1997): 774–79, and *Heart of the Heart, Center of the Church:* Communio *Ecclesiology, Liberalism and Liberation* (Grand Rapids, MI: William B. Eerdmans Publishing Co., 1996). My discussion of this aspect of Murray's argument is indebted to both Hunt and Schindler. I should stress, however, that I have serious reservations about Schindler's treatment of Murray's work.

60. "The Declaration on Religious Freedom," in *Bridging the Sacred and the Secular*, 192.

61. "The Issue of Church and State at Vatican Council II," in *Religious Liberty: Catholic Struggles with Pluralism/John Courtney Murray*, 206.

62. "The Declaration on Religious Freedom," in *Bridging the Sacred and the Secular*, 192.

63. "The Issue of Church and State at Vatican Council II," in *Religious Liberty: Catholic Struggles with Pluralism/John Courtney Murray*, 209.

64. "Religious Freedom and the Atheist," in *Bridging the Sacred and the Secular*, 258.

65. Keith J. Pavlischek, *John Courtney Murray and the Dilemma of Religious Freedom* (Kirksville, MO: Thomas Jefferson University Press, 1994), 3.

66. This is not to suggest that it is the only additional resource offered by the Catholic tradition relevant that can assist in the elaboration of the theory of the state presupposed by *DH*. One also thinks in this context of its affirmations of the secularity of the state and the rightful autonomy of temporal affairs.

67. Jacques Maritain, *Man and the State* (Chicago: University of Chicago Press, 1945), 24.

68. John Paul II, *Centesimus Annus*, section 13.

69. Johannes Messner, *Social Ethics* (St. Louis: B. Herder Book Co., 1945), 140.

70. Heinrich Rommen, *The State in Catholic Thought* (St. Louis: B. Herder Book Co., 1949), 143–44.

71. John Paul II, *Letter to Families*, section 17.

72. Canavan, "The Popes and the Economy," *Notre Dame Journal of Law, Ethics & Public Policy* 11, no. 2 (1997): 440.

73. Coleman, 213. One wonders, however, whether the language of "mediating structures" is capable of doing justice to the Catholic understanding of the nature and role of these institutions.

74. *Centesimus Annus*, 48.

75. Rommen, 142.

76. See, for example, Murray, "The Problem of State Religion," *Theological Studies* XII (June 1951): 155–78.

77. Maritain's work is particularly important in this regard. See, for example, *The Person and the Common Good* (New York: Charles Scribner's Sons, 1947).

78. It might be added that, by integrating the idea of society's pluralist structure, John Paul's concept of the "subjectivity of society" provides an ideal starting point for reflection on this whole subject. See *Centesimus Annus*, 13, 21.

· 9 ·

The Architecture of Freedom: John Paul II and John Courtney Murray on Religious Freedom

David S. Crawford

The following passage, authored by a self-proclaimed disciple of John Courtney Murray, offers a critical reflection on John Paul II's interpretation of *Dignitatis Humanae*:

> The basic issue at [the] level of the foundation of the right to religious freedom has to do with the kind of definitive answer [we give] to the following question: Where does human dignity ultimately rest in the person? Is that last layer human freedom, a freedom inherent to every person, which can be used well and fulfilled according to its intrinsic orientation, or not, but which, in either case, cannot be tampered with by any external power? Or is it the person's relationship with transcendent truth—truth to be accessed and embraced through freedom, but to which freedom is only instrumental? John Paul II is clearly more on the side of the latter.[1]

Setting aside for a moment the suggestion that giving a priority to truth implies an instrumentalization of freedom, it seems to me that this statement serves as a stark but revealing introduction to the underlying issue contained in the debate over the meaning of "religious freedom." As the passage acknowledges, both freedom and truth are crucial to the concept of human dignity. The question, then, could be put in terms of deciding which—freedom or truth—is more fundamental or, in the words of the passage, constitutes "that last layer."

The passage clearly reflects the pope's repeated insistence on freedom's close and necessary relationship to truth. We can see this insistence in numerous passages, such as those in *Veritatis Splendor* decrying "currents of thought which end by detaching human freedom from its essential and constitutive relationship to truth"[2] or which lessen or deny "the *dependence of freedom on truth*" (*VS*, 34). We can also see it in his criticism of "[c]ertain currents of modern thought [that] have gone so far as to exalt freedom to such an extent that it becomes an absolute, which would then be the source of values" (*VS*, 32) or in his insistence on "the unbreakable bond between freedom and truth" (*VS*, 87, 109). As these passages and many others like them testify, John Paul believes that the central questions and difficulties of our time revolve around one "crucial issue: human freedom" (*VS*, 31). He has therefore devoted a considerable amount of his teaching to the task of deepening the Church's understanding of freedom in all of its forms.

But what does the pope mean by insisting on this "dependence of freedom on truth," this "unbreakable bond"? The relationship described by these phrases is evidently structurally or ontologically grounded, since he speaks of an "essential and constitutive relationship." These affirmations indicate that the acceptance or rejection of truth are not equivalent actualizations of freedom, to be judged only outwardly for their moral character. The pope does not seem to mean that freedom is simply qualified by its conformity or nonconformity with truths that are exterior to its deepest meaning. Not only are the acceptance and rejection of truth not equivalent from an "exterior" point of view (that is to say, from the point of view of an exterior moral evaluation), they are not equivalent from the point of view of *the structure and meaning of freedom as such.*[3] As the pope reminds us, "freedom is not realized in decisions made against God. For how could it be an exercise of true freedom to refuse to be open to the very reality which enables our self-realization?"[4]

Now it would also seem, as our opening quotation suggests, that this understanding of the relation between freedom and truth translates into a particular conception of the nature and role of religious freedom. Authentic civil freedoms, John Paul tells us in his 1995 address to the United Nations General Assembly, possess a certain "moral structure" or "inner 'logic'" or "order" or—as he puts it in a particularly colorful phrase—"inner architecture."[5] Thus, the characterization of civil freedoms as possessing an interior "order" or "inner architecture" serves to connect the pope's belief in freedom's fundamental and interior relation to truth with his understanding of the nature and role of freedom in society as a juridical reality. As we shall see, the pope moreover gives "religious freedom" a particular priority among these freedoms, as their "source and synthesis" (*CA*, 47).

This understanding appears to be at odds with the dominant interpretation of religious freedom, an interpretation reflected in the quotation with which we began and which has been profoundly influenced by the thought of John Courtney Murray. Of course, the nature of the relationship between freedom and truth in *Dignitatis Humanae* has been a bone of contention from the time of the conciliar debates over its drafting through its reception and interpretation.[6] The tremendous prestige of Murray, due to his crucially important contributions both as a *peritus* in the drafting of the document and more generally as a prominent American theologian, has tended to guarantee the influence of his views.

Murray describes the meaning of "religious freedom" in the following passage:

> In positive terms, the Declaration affirmed the free exercise of religion in society to be a basic human right that, in any society pretending to be well-ordered, should be furnished with a juridical guarantee so as to become a civil or constitutional right. Religious freedom, therefore, was clearly stated to be a juridical notion. Moreover, freedom here has the sense of "freedom from." First, no man is to be forcibly constrained to act against his conscience. Second, no man is to be forcibly restrained from acting according to his conscience.[7]

Or again,

> [I]n its juridical sense as a human right, religious freedom is a functional or instrumental concept. Precisely by reason of its negative content it serves to make possible and easy the practice of religious values in the life of men and of society.[8]

As Murray emphasizes in these passages, "religious freedom" is fundamentally an empty freedom, a "freedom from," possessing only "negative content." Far from possessing a structure or "inner architecture," it would necessarily seem to be, in the final analysis, *structureless*. For Murray, therefore, "religious freedom" should be thought of as a "technical" or constitutional-juridical issue arising in the idea of the secular state and notions of limited government.[9]

Like Murray, the pope speaks of religious freedom in terms of noncoercion or immunity.[10] However, when we examine their writings, we see a difference in starting points. If the question of religious freedom begins for Murray as a constitutional-juridical one, for the pope it begins with the philosophical and theological background against which the nature of the relationship between freedom and truth can be given relief. It is only out of this background that the juridical notion of religious freedom can be adequately drawn. Could it be that these differing starting points represent two ways of arriving at the same conclusion? Or does the difference between them, in the end, make a difference? My basic claim is that it does. Indeed, Murray's interpretation of *Dignitatis Humanae*, it seems to me, cannot consistently deliver what it promises, viz. a pure immunity or truly negative content. This is because it necessarily constitutes a particular interpretation of freedom's relation to truth, an interpretation that poses difficulties for an adequate actualization of the religiously based freedom it claims to protect.

In order to argue this claim, we will begin by discussing Murray's interpretation of "religious freedom" in *Dignitatis Humanae*. Next, we will discuss the pope's understanding of "religious freedom" as grounded in freedom as such and as related intrinsically to truth. In this context we will discuss the sense in which this relationship to truth implies freedom's "architecture," arising as it does within the gift-character of creaturehood. As we will see, the pope's teaching regarding freedom casts light on a crucial ambiguity generated by Murray's juridical starting point. Finally, we will ask whether it is possible to recuperate "immunity" within the pope's anthropologically richer conception of freedom.

MURRAY AND *DIGNITATIS HUMANAE*

How can we understand John Paul II's discussion of freedom's dependence on truth? Does this placement threaten human freedom, "instrumentalizing" it to truth? To see the traction of this question, we should discuss Murray's interpretation of *Dignitatis Humanae* in greater detail.[11]

While the problem of religious freedom is especially a juridical and procedural one for Murray, he nevertheless supports his interpretation by offering an "ontological" context: the concept of "independence." His goal is to show the basic "incompetence" of the state in the "transtemporal" or "vertical order" of salvation history.[12] His argument entails five "principles," which he believes are sufficient to support the teaching of the Declaration. He tells us, in the first principle, that the "human person is endowed with a dignity that surpasses the rest of creation because he is independent" or "in charge of himself." Thus, Murray continues, the "primordial demand of that dignity" is that the human person "acts by his own counsel and purpose, using and enjoying his freedom, moved, not by external coercion, but internally by the risk of his whole existence. In a word, human dignity consists formally in the person's responsibility for himself and, what is more, for his world."[13]

When this ontological foundation is augmented by consideration of man's social character (the second principle)—that the person is the "subject, foundation and end of the entire social life"[14]—Murray feels he has adequately grounded his juridical-constitutional understanding of religious freedom. His argument is further supported by the third, fourth, and fifth principles: viz. that "man in society must be accorded as much freedom as possible, and that that freedom is not to be restricted unless and insofar as is necessary" (the "so-called principle of the free society"); that "all citizens enjoy juridical equality in society";[15] and that the public power's "first and principal concern for the common good [is] the effective protection of the human person and its dignity."[16]

With these five principles in place, Murray is confident that the "whole investigation" has been brought "to a point of decision." "For they are sufficient to constitute that relationship between the human person and the public juridical power. Together they fully characterize the notion of religious freedom."[17]

While Murray focuses on "religious freedom" as a juridical and technical aspect of limited government, the first of these principles nevertheless seeks to offer a prejuridical and personalist starting point for the argument. As he explains, the first principle offers the "the ultimate ontological ground of religious freedom as it is likewise the ground of the other human freedoms" since it offers the "objective truth about the human person," a truth that can "impose upon the public power the duty to refrain from keeping the human person from acting in religious matters according to his dignity."[18] Murray, therefore concludes:

> the dignity and the freedom of the human person should receive primary attention since they pertain to the goods that are proper to the human spirit. As for these goods, the first of which is the good of religion, the most important and urgent demand is for freedom. For human dignity demands that in making this fundamental option and in carrying it out through every type of religious action, whether private or public, in all these aspects a person should act by his own deliberation and purpose, enjoying immunity from all external coercion so that in the presence of God he takes responsibility on himself alone for his religious decisions and acts.[19]

Now, this understanding of the ontological and juridical foundations of religious freedom corresponds to a responsibility for transcendent truth, once it is discovered. Moreover, Murray grants that once this truth has been discovered, it will imply a deeper, theological basis for freedom: "The authorities and faithful of the Church are indeed conscious that their freedom is of divine origin—a participation respectively in the freedom of the Incarnate Word and in the freedom of the Holy Spirit."[20] From a Christian point of view, then, juridical immunity allows the individual to actualize his freedom —freedom as such—in this theologically and humanly richer way. If, as we have seen, Murray defines "religious freedom" as a freedom *from*, it might therefore also be called a freedom *for*, insofar as it entails a responsibility for "the risk of [one's] whole existence." Its purpose is to secure the exercise of "independence," the free space for personal discovery and adherence to truth.

To what extent, then, has Murray made freedom "that last layer" in his understanding of human dignity? As we have seen, Murray begins with a concept of human dignity grounded in "independence."[21] As we have also seen, the "primordial demand" of human dignity is that "man acts by his own counsel and purpose." Or again, human dignity consists in "the person's responsibility for himself."[22] Of course, as Murray's argument presupposes, this independence is linked with a "responsibility" for the truth. Indeed, personal discovery and adherence to truth are the very purpose of this freedom. The human creature is free because he possesses the powers of deliberation and purpose. His dignity constitutes a "demand for responsible freedom."[23] In this sense, then, Murray's interpretation presupposes an orientation of freedom toward truth. In the words of Pietro Pavan (Murray's theological ally during and immediately following the Council), "we should cleave to the truth in proportion to the degree of clarity with which it discloses itself to our minds."[24]

Our question concerns the precise character of this orientation. If freedom is to be used correctly, if it is not to stray from its purpose or fall into immorality, then it must choose its objects in accordance with the truth. Since the very purpose of human freedom is that it is called to embrace what is true and good, then the use of freedom in contradiction to perceived truth would constitute a misuse and, in this sense, an undermining of freedom, since it would deny freedom's very purpose. Nevertheless, Murray's sense of religious freedom presupposes a kind of neutrality with respect to any particular truth content. Freedom, for these purposes, is conceived as simply "negative." Thus, despite the duty to seek out and cleave to truth, this way of connecting freedom to truth is founded on a structural extrinsicism. Only with the discovery of truth is freedom taken up into its richer theological domain, as a chosen participation in the freedom of Christ and the Holy Spirit. But as the initial starting point, and as the precondition for this richer theological appropriation of freedom, human dignity and the general context of juridical freedom must remain free of prior determination by any particular truth claim. In this sense, then, the orientation of freedom toward truth remains formal and abstract.

At this point, it is worthwhile to consider briefly one implication of this way of viewing the relationship. While we may grant that freedom serves the person in his capacity to understand and accept truth, and while this certainly implies that the very purpose and "fulfillment" of freedom are to "cleave" to the truth once it is perceived, still, Murray implies that truth primarily relates to freedom by way of obligation and "responsibility." Once the truth is recognized, freedom must act according to its responsibility by embracing that truth. Freedom remains therefore structurally "neutral" or, in the phrase of

Servais Pinckaers, "indifferent" to truth.[25] The abstraction of freedom from truth—however limited to the technical-juridical problem of religious freedom—implies that the acceptance or rejection of truth, along with its attendant practices, remains structurally (albeit not morally)[26] equivalent as actualizations of freedom. Each is presupposed to be equivalent in terms of what "religious freedom" *is*.

Thus, truth necessarily stands outside freedom, as both its object and finally as its judge. Once identified, it effectively narrows the morally legitimate use of freedom. As a result, the fundamental role of truth in relation to freedom is, properly speaking, one of limitation. The basic sense of religious freedom and the antecedent sense of human dignity therefore tend to presuppose a moral (and ultimately moralistic) rather than ontological relationship between freedom and truth. The deeper theological sense of freedom mentioned by Murray is something that has to be chosen from a starting point of "independence." This interpretation of religious freedom therefore tends to perpetuate a cultural sense of ultimates generally, and religious belief in particular, as matters of choice.

JOHN PAUL II AND FREEDOM'S "INNER ARCHITECTURE"

Henri de Lubac once observed that John Paul II is "a man of *Gaudium et Spes*."[27] As de Lubac's observation testifies, John Paul consistently—and from the beginning of his pontificate—grounded his social teaching in the central truths of the Catholic faith, particularly what we could call the Trinitarian Christocentrism of *Gaudium et Spes*. Effectively corroborating de Lubac's statement, the pope himself stated that the central affirmation of *Gaudium et Spes* (found in section 22), that Christ in revealing the mystery of the Father also reveals the deepest mystery and destiny of man, is "one of the basic principles, perhaps the most important one, of the teaching" of the Second Vatican Council.[28] Indeed, some of John Paul's most significant documents place this teaching at their core.[29]

The theological anthropology indicated by the pope's focus on this passage, moreover, justifies his frequent reiteration of Paul VI's claim that the Church is an "expert in humanity" (e.g., *VS*, 3), which in turn is the basis of the Church's social ethics generally. The Church is an expert in humanity precisely because what is most central to her mandate and source, the eucharistic continuation in history of Christ's mission from the heart of the Trinity, discloses the fullness of human nature and the primitive meaning of all human activity. Likewise, the meaning and significance of human freedom are disclosed in the event of Christ's revelation of the Trinity. As the pope states, "What man is and what he must do becomes clear as soon as God reveals himself" (*VS*, 10).

But what does the pope's "Trinitarian Christocentrism" tell us about freedom? The following passage from *Veritatis Splendor* should set us on our way:

> The Crucified Christ reveals the authentic meaning of freedom; he lives it fully in the total gift of himself and calls his disciples to share in his freedom. Rational reflection and daily experience demonstrate the weakness which marks man's freedom. That freedom is real but limited; its absolute and unconditional origin is not in itself, but in the life within which it is situated and which represents for it, at one and the same time, both a limitation and a possibility. Human freedom belongs to us as creatures; it is a freedom which is given as a gift, one to be received like a seed and to be cultivated responsibly. It is an essential part of that creaturely image which is the basis of the dignity of the person. Within that freedom there is an echo of the primordial vocation whereby the Creator calls man to the true Good, and even more, through Christ's Revelation, to become his and to share his own divine life. It is at once inalienable self-possession and openness to all that exists, in passing beyond self to knowledge and love of the other [citation to *Gaudium et Spes*, 24]. Freedom then is rooted in the truth about man, and it is ultimately directed toward communions. (*VS*, 85–86)

As this passage makes clear, the relationship between freedom and truth, as the pope sees it, is not one in which truth dominates freedom from the outside. Nor is the relationship limited to the fundamental obligation to attend to the truth once it is discovered, although freedom certainly does have such an obligation. Rather, passages such as this one indicate the radically interior relationship between truth and freedom the pope has in mind.

As the passage tells us, freedom is "rooted in" or arises from within truth. Thus the "priority" of truth does not simply indicate that truth serves as a limitation to which freedom must accommodate itself if it is to realize its purpose or if it is to be qualified as morally good. It is true that the passage does speak of the limited nature of human freedom. But in doing so it is not speaking of an external limitation posed by the discovery of truth. Rather, the passage refers to freedom's dependent, finite, created character, as well as the injury inflicted on it by sin, which in itself may be characterized as a nonfreedom. Indeed, the very possibility of freedom is given within truth and more specifically within the "truth about man." As such, then, truth is the precondition for freedom's being and realization. Nor is human dignity, of which the passage also speaks, based most fundamentally in freedom or truth as abstracted from each other. In fact, the foregoing passage grounds human dignity in *both* freedom *and* truth.

The passage makes another observation that may help us to understand more fully what the pope has in mind here. The relationship between freedom and truth arises within communion. The passage discusses freedom as a relationship, not only to the idea of truth but to truth as a relationship to God in the person of Christ. As the pope tells us elsewhere, "objectively speaking, the search for truth and the search for God are one and the same."[30] As we shall see, this primary relation to truth in God is also realized analogously among the persons who make up the family, culture, and friendships of all kinds.[31]

Given this grounding, human freedom is in fact also a sharing in Christ's own freedom and, indeed, in the Trinitarian source of freedom. Christ's own freedom is first of all rooted in his relation with the Father in the Holy Spirit. The freedom of the human creature is a sharing in the freedom of the divine persons, who from all eternity freely give and receive their personhood.[32] Being created in the image of Trinitarian love,[33] creaturely freedom retains its rootedness in Trinitarian gift, expressed in the form of creation *ex nihilo* and the call to fulfillment in God's infinite freedom. Freedom is therefore not indifferent to relations, with respect either to the triune Persons or to the human community. Freedom in an absolute sense, then, does not preexist my individual relationship with God as the possibility for my unencumbered choice for or against God; it is not a "neutral" foundation that may *then* be used to accept truth (or, Truth) once it is perceived. Rather, the very structure of freedom itself already constitutes, at its deepest level, relation to God. In short, the kind of "truth" pertinent to "religious freedom" (the truth to which "religious freedom" is supposed to be a juridical-constitutional openness) is, in the final analysis, the triune God—who is also the source of human freedom.

The foregoing allows us to get a better sense of what the claim that freedom possesses an "inner architecture" might mean. For the pope, freedom would seem to move in two directions. It comes to the human actor in the form of a gift. ("Man is the only creature on earth that God wanted for its own sake"[34] [*GS*, 24]). It simultaneously finds its completeness in a returning "gift of self." ("Man can fully discover his true self only in a sincere giving of himself"[35] [*GS*, 24]).

On the one hand, it is an essential ingredient of the *imago Dei*, and as such it is part of the "vocation" within and for which we were made, in which our very being is "constituted." And as such, it is also the basis of both "self-possession" and "self-determination." On the other hand, it offers (perhaps, paradoxically) the possibility and promise of belonging to another ("to become his and to share in his own divine life"). Hence, "freedom is a gift" in the other direction as well, that is to say, in the sense that self-possession finds its completeness or fullness in self-bestowal. As the pope repeatedly tells us, Christ shows his disciples the meaning of freedom in the "total gift of himself." Or as he says in a famous line from *Veritatis Splendor*, *"[P]erfection demands that maturity in self-giving to which human freedom is called"* (*VS*, 17).

Now the concept of "self-bestowal" is more difficult than we commonly think. For one thing, it appears to risk freedom's self-destruction through voiding the self-possession that seems to be at its root. Moreover, we may wonder how self-bestowal, which is so clearly central to the whole idea of Christian freedom, is possible at all. To "make a gift of oneself" (if this phrase is not to be understood in a merely metaphorical and reductive sense—a sense that could not possibly support its constant use by the pope) must entail the freedom and the ability to do so. And yet, self-possession further implies an ability to take up all of oneself so that this "all" might be handed over to another. This implies an ability to stand "outside" myself, as though I were another person, so as to take up all that constitutes me, in terms of my being and temporal existence, my origin and destiny. In other words, the very idea of "self-gift" implies that freedom in its deepest sense is contained within some point of transcendence that precedes the outward movement of the gift itself. This is true, for the pope, not only in relation to God but also analogously in relations at the human level as well, as his discussions of marriage and society more generally show us.[36]

The paradox, then, is that my freedom to give myself to another is itself a gift. Hence, the presence of another's freedom "in" my freedom is a presupposition of my ability to give myself away, to actualize freedom in its fullness. That freedom is grounded in the relationship with another means in the first instance that it is only "mine" insofar as it is received from another and is, therefore, structured from its very beginning back toward its origin. Hence, freedom is structured *ab initio* within abiding communion. Again, we can see the *Trinitarian* foundation of freedom in this last observation: the Son is "free" precisely in his generation by the Father and in his returning himself to the Father (and the circumincession this implies).

Both of these poles of freedom—freedom as received and freedom as completed in returning gift—must be kept in mind if we are to avoid *either* the extreme of so exalting freedom that it comes to be seen as pure spontaneity and self-initiation that must be constantly immunized from the crushing and dictatorial threat of "the other"/"truth" *or* the opposite extreme of freedom so degrading that it becomes a mere passivity in the face of truth that is finally not freedom at all. Either of these alternatives would simply be an extreme version of abstracted freedom.

This leaves us with the question, however, of how this general understanding of the relation between freedom and truth—the idea of an "inner architecture"—relates to the specific topic of "religious freedom." In *CA* John Paul defines religious freedom as "the right to live in the truth of one's faith and in conformity with one's transcendent dignity as a person" (*CA*, 47). As this definition makes clear, the pope associates religious freedom closely with truth. Indeed, the passage suggests the positive ordination to truth evident in the pope's general theory of freedom.

Moreover, the pope seems to attach a particular importance to religious freedom precisely because it relates so directly to the most fundamental truths concerning human destiny, including the deepest ground and nature of human freedom as such. As he says in his first encyclical:

> The Declaration on Religious Freedom shows us convincingly that, when Christ and, after Him, His apostles proclaimed the truth that comes not from men but from God . . ., they preserved, while acting with their full force of spirit, a deep esteem for man, for his intellect, his will, his conscience and his freedom. . . . Since man's true freedom is not found in everything that the various systems and individuals see and propagate as freedom, the Church, because of her divine mission, becomes all the more the guardian of this freedom, which is the condition and basis for the human person's true dignity. . . . Today also, even after two thousand years, we see Christ as the one who brings man freedom based on truth, frees man from what curtails, diminishes and as it were breaks off his freedom at its root, in man's soul, his heart and his conscience.[37]

More significantly, as we have seen, John Paul consistently claims that religious freedom is the fundamental "form"[38] or "source and synthesis" (*CA*, 47) of these other basic freedoms.[39] But it was precisely with respect to the entire panoply of civil freedoms that he had informed us of freedom's interior order or "inner architecture." As he tells us, religious freedom "is only a translation, in institutional form, of that order within which God had ordained that his creatures should be able to know and accept his eternal offer of a covenant, and be able to correspond to it as free and responsible persons."[40] It is precisely because religious freedom "touches the most intimate sphere of the spirit" that it "sustains and is as it were the raison d'être of other freedoms."[41] What is significant here is not simply the priority the pope has given to religious freedom—a priority that is also suggested by Murray—but the evident reason for doing so. He has given it priority because it represents the institutionalization of the basic ordination of the human person to truth.

Thus, to claim that religious freedom is "fundamental," the "source and synthesis," suggests that it discloses and mediates something of what culture, the human person, and therefore freedom as such are. Only on this basis can it constitute the "source and synthesis" of these other civil freedoms.

"Religious freedom" is not, therefore, an entirely "negative" or "empty" freedom. Rather, like freedom as such and like other civil freedoms, religious freedom "depends" on truth. Like Murray, the pope argues that religious freedom represents the human responsibility and obligation to truth. But for the pope, the fundamental relationship to truth is structural or ontological, rather than simply obligational and external.

The pope's claim is not that "religious freedom" should be based on the state's institution of the theological sense of freedom outlined above. Nevertheless, his Trinitarian Christocentrism offers a rich context in which society can understand freedom, much as revelation has already offered the background for many of the most important and characteristic advances of Western thought generally. The pope argues in *Fides et Ratio* that the relationship between faith and reason or theology and philosophy is "best construed as a circle" (*FR*, 73). Within this "circle," faith and reason reinforce each other in ways that do not deprive either of its proper integrity. The historical result for philosophy, according to the pope, is that philosophy has appropriated "certain truths which might never have been discovered by reason unaided, although they are not of themselves inaccessible to reason." "Among these truths," the pope continues, "is the notion of a free and personal God who is the Creator of the world, a truth which has been so crucial for the development of philosophical thinking, especially the philosophy of being" (*FR*, 76).

The pope also indicates the importance of revelation in developing the philosophical notion of the "problem of evil," "the person," "human dignity, equality, and freedom," and "history as event." In effect, the pope tells us, in disclosing man's vocation, revelation "broadens reason's scope for action." Most importantly, however, "In speculating on these questions, philosophers have not become theologians, since they have not sought to understand and expand the truths of faith on the basis of Revelation" (*FR*, 76).

These statements suggest what the pope means by his claim that the Church is an "expert in humanity" and his notion of "the truth about man." According to the pope, it is possible to affirm both the proper autonomy and secularity of social and civil life, including the constitutional-juridical order, without neutralizing ultimates inherent in human life as a whole, however much our understanding of those ultimates has been shaped by a prior theological or revealed source. Thus, the pope tells us that "different cultures are basically different ways of facing the question of the meaning of personal existence." A given culture may be characterized by the position it takes with respect to "the fundamental events of life, such as birth, love, work and death" (*CA*, 24). This wisdom concerning the fundamental events of life finds expression, according to the pope, in various kinds of "philosophical knowledge," such as those which "inspire national and international legal systems in regulating the life of society" (*FR*, 3).

The question, then, is how to formulate this understanding in the context of a genuine philosophical and juridical inquiry into the nature of freedom and its relation to truth. In order to address this issue, we may distill the foregoing discussion into a number of points. First, at least in its fullest sense, freedom is falsified in its very nature and character if it is abstracted from truth. Freedom and truth possess a constitutive relationship, and the two together, precisely in their interior and irreducible relationship, rather than either one as abstracted from the other, form the final ground for human dignity, that "last layer."

Secondly, the relation between freedom and truth is not most fundamentally one of an external limitation or a narrowing of freedom, although truth does constitute a demand and an invitation. It is true, of course, that we very often experience truth as oppression. It is also true that the law, which according to Catholic tradition is an expression of love and truth (*lex injusta non est lex*), possesses an obligational and finally coercive force. In this sense, truth can serve as a limit to "freedom." However, the foregoing shows that the *fundamental structure* of the relationship between freedom and truth is not one of external limitation or diminution. Rather, the pope suggests that freedom is not in the truest sense of the term possible without truth and that the very nature of truth as grounded in communion implies freedom. Thus, when we experience truth as a limitation of freedom, what we are really experiencing is our own concupiscent tendency to abstract freedom from truth.

And third, the truth claims and ultimates religious freedom means to protect are finally relational, finding their term in participation in Trinitarian relations but also by analogy in human relations, such as that of the family or society in general. This implies that the conception of freedom as structurally an "empty space" voids the central meaning of freedom as such, not only as that meaning is grounded theologically but also as it is mediated philosophically and juridically. For the pope, freedom is inherently ordered not only toward an abstract truth but toward an "other."

THE IMPERIAL NEGATIVE

Now an obvious objection will be that Murray specifically attempted to ground his interpretation of *Dignitatis Humanae* in the juridical order to avoid the issues raised thus far. Murray's basic point, after all, is that "religious freedom" as "negative" or "empty," as a human and civil right, is able to offer the space necessary for the actualization of freedom in the frankly theological sense discussed above. Moreover, it is clear that Murray's starting point has the advantage of being more easily communicated in secular terms in a pluralistic society to nonbelievers. It appears impartial. But is it? Just as atheism does not in fact constitute a "lowest common denominator" to which belief can then be appended on a private basis by individuals and social groups, so too freedom as "independence" may not be a neutral starting point to which we can add the further content of freedom as "participation." Our question, then, is whether it is in principle possible to posit a juridical, "empty" freedom without mediating a sense of the meaning of freedom as such. Does Murray's starting point, however much we may value its advantages of clarity and seeming coherence for pluralistic societies, really offer such a "negative content"? If it does, then presumably the two starting points—that of Murray and that of the pope—could be reconciled.

I have already argued that Murray's interpretation of religious freedom tends to perpetuate a cultural tendency to relate the person to the deeper, theological understanding of freedom implied by religion through individual choice. Perhaps these implications can be drawn out more thoroughly. As we have seen, Murray's interpretation of *Dignitatis Humanae* necessarily entails a subtle abstraction in the relation between freedom and truth. Religious freedom, as he proposes it, is "indifferent" or "neutral" with respect to any number of alternative ultimates, although it is morally bound to accept true ultimates when they are discovered. This abstraction therefore means that individuals are left to connect freedom to truth through an act of choice. Indeed, we might say that the whole point of religious freedom is to allow for this connection as an unimpeded exercise of choice (the "so-called principle of the free society"). But this in turn means that the connection of freedom and truth amounts to a development from within freedom conceived as structurally "indifferent." Moreover, any explicit commitment to ultimates made by the individual leaves the basically "indifferent" structure of his freedom intact, since it is choice that gives rise to the commitment. Freedom and truth, therefore, continue to be related extrinsically, or abstractly, by this act of choice.

Thus, the underlying concept of freedom retains the basic abstraction of Murray's starting point. But our understanding of freedom as such necessarily flows from the way we understand our commitment to ultimates. The act of connecting freedom to truth therefore imports this abstraction into the understanding of freedom as such, whether this latter is anchored theologically or philosophically. It necessarily communicates a purely voluntary sense of the relation between freedom and truth. In effect, then, Murray's juridical sense of "religious freedom," as pure immunity, tends to reconstitute Christian freedom into a version of itself, that is to say, as abstract and even moralistic in the sense we have discussed.

The result? Once the relation between freedom and truth has been abstracted in this way, it becomes nearly impossible to see freedom as anything other than a form of immunity. The implication then is that, if a particular actualization of freedom is something other than a form of immunity, it is a potentially alienating nonfreedom, justifiable only as a particular choice among equivalents and a choice that remains forever provisional. Any "intrinsic orientation" of freedom toward truth therefore will in fact only have the significance of an external demand or duty imposed on freedom, but it cannot indicate an interior or ontological structure of freedom as such. It cannot indicate an "inner architecture." Finally, any exercise of freedom contrary to truth will be structurally equivalent (however morally reprehensible) as an actualization of freedom to an exercise in accordance with truth.

These considerations substantially undermine the legitimacy of Murray's starting point. If immunity is really to be immunity as advertised, it must offer the possibility of realizing, as an exercise of autonomy and independence, a "thicker," religious sense of freedom and truth such as that offered by the pope and characterized by Murray in terms of "participation." After all, the very idea of immunity is that it is able to offer the possibility of realizing such a theologically grounded freedom without predetermining it. But in fact, the "negative" character of this freedom generates a cultural and personal sense of freedom that is unstructured and abstract. Hence, a development of freedom —such as that proposed by the pope—that is radically grounded in relation to truth and is primitively structured within the gift character of creaturehood, will be rendered unintelligible. It will appear to be a lack of freedom rather than its fullness.

Religious freedom as proposed by Murray therefore tends to become a kind of first principle in our understanding of the nature of freedom, reconstituting the deepest sense of freedom as choice, indifference, and immunity, even though it claims to offer no particular theory of freedom as such.

My point, then, is that Murray's "purely" juridical sense of religious freedom does not accomplish what it intends; rather, it mediates a false sense of the relation between freedom and truth and, therefore, of freedom as such. My point is also that *any* interpretation of "religious freedom"—including those claiming to offer a neutral field—must necessarily entail *some* interpretation of the nature of freedom as such insofar as any given understanding of "religious freedom" necessarily entails *some* understanding of the relation between freedom and truth. It is impossible to escape the circle. Laws that touch on the ultimates of human life, such as religious belief or the basics of human life (which necessarily are saturated with religious meaning), necessarily mediate *something* about those ultimates. This is true even when they claim not to do so, if for no other reason than that such a claim *in itself* suggests something about the relation of law and freedom to ultimates.[42]

Law simply cannot avoid speaking to ultimates because the freedom to which it gives shape is fundamental to the identity of the culture and community in which those ultimates are ingredient. As Murray himself put it:

> Freedom is an end or purpose of society, which looks to the liberation of the human person. Freedom is the political method par excellence, whereby the other goals of society are reached. Freedom, finally, is the prevailing social usage, which sets the style of society. This progress in doctrine is sanctioned and made secure by "Dignitatis Humanae Personae."[43]

The criterion by which we should judge any given understanding of "religious freedom," therefore, will be the adequacy for society and for the person of the sense of freedom it does in fact mediate.

The broader implications of an abstract or extrinsic sense of freedom and truth underlie some of the problems both the pope and Murray have objected to in Western liberal societies, such as the reduction of civil freedoms generally to arbitrary "choice," the exclusion of truth claims from public discourse, and the ultimately nihilistic presuppositions of that discourse,[44] as well as a corresponding tendency to see a fundamental tension between personal freedom and Church teaching.[45] Moreover, certain tendencies arise with respect to religious truth, given an abstract view of freedom. As we have seen, this abstraction tends to see truth as a moral limitation or diminution of freedom. While truth guides and obligates freedom, the individual's range of legitimate choices is in fact narrowed by his knowledge of the truth. The individual is "free" only insofar as the course of action he would adopt does not run up against the determination of truth. Once it does, however, the range of freedom has effectively been narrowed. The consequence of this is to put freedom and truth subtly at odds.

This problem becomes all the more severe when we realize that the "truth" we are considering is religious truth. Religious truth makes the most comprehensive and radical claim on society and culture generally and on the individual person in particular. But if this is so, religious truth will also be the most dangerous to freedom, as the historical debate over the existence and meaning of "religious freedom" suggests.

Thus, an abstract sense of freedom tends to leave us on the prongs of a dilemma. The first prong has been discussed. It entails the tendency to continue in our theological understanding of freedom along the line dictated by the logic of immunity and choice. Hence, response to the human vocation becomes a development of immunity. My "response" is to do what God "commands" by "free choice." But to the extent that this "command" is seen to limit my options morally or religiously, it will appear to be a form of oppression. More and more this exterior imposition of a rule is seen as a kind of affront to my dignity. Hence, "self-gift," which according to the pope and the Council fathers lies at the heart of authentic freedom, will appear to be a form of alienation. It will be seen as a loss of self-possession and freedom, unless it remains provisional and therefore void of its deepest characteristics as gift.

On the other hand, the second prong tends toward fundamentalism. According to this possibility, human freedom evaporates under the realization that response according to God's will cannot be simply an alternative and remain Christian. But because this realization occurs within the framework of freedom understood most fundamentally as immunity, the result is a rejection of freedom as potentially or actually sinful[46] (consider the legacy of Luther's *servum arbitrium*). Hence, this second possibility tends to crush freedom in the recognition that above all we must be obedient to God's will. Indeed, once we have articulated this second possibility, we recognize that modern fundamentalism possesses a genetic likeness to the liberal-nominalistic concept of freedom as unimpeded choice. Moreover, an abstract sense of freedom would seem to guarantee an interminable struggle between these alternative responses.

Needless to say, these cultural implications go far beyond what can legitimately be laid at the feet of Murray. My point is only that an abstract sense of religious freedom implies anthropological, sociocultural, and ecclesial ambiguities, which in many ways have become ever more manifest and intractable—as the debate has become ever more shrill—since the time of Murray's death.

THERE IS IMMUNITY AND THERE IS IMMUNITY

So where do we find ourselves? We began this essay by noting that both Murray and John Paul speak of religious freedom in terms of immunity. Do their differing starting points simply bring us in the end to the same conclusion, one by means of juridical and natural reasoning (from the "bottom up," as it were) and the other by means of a theological approach (from the "top down")? I do not believe so. It seems to me that the two starting points represent two fundamentally different senses of immunity, and that each mediates a different concept of freedom.

Are we left, then, with a new and gentler version of the so-called thesis/hypothesis theory of Church and state relations? No. The problem with the thesis/hypothesis theory was that, well, it was based on an abstract view of freedom and truth. It posited that the relation between them was "prudential," that where there was necessarily a plurality of religious beliefs the Church could grant prudential support of religious freedom, but that, where it was possible to arrive at a "Catholic" state, religious freedom should be curbed. The thesis/hypothesis theory traded on an abstraction similar to the "liberal" approach of the dominant interpretation of *Dignitatis Humanae*. It saw freedom and truth as structurally at odds, and therefore, it saw truth as fundamentally coercive. For this reason, it sought either the accommodation of Catholic belief or the careful control of non-Catholic belief, depending on historically contingent circumstances.

Although Murray said that *Dignitatis Humanae*'s teaching only sought to clear up a "doctrinal *équivoque*" and to keep "abreast of the consciousness of civilized mankind,"[47] and while he appears to have read the Declaration's version of religious freedom as possessing essentially the same "content" and "object" as the religion clauses of the First Amendment,[48] he also insisted that his task was to discover whether "American Democracy is compatible with Catholicism," rather than vice versa.[49] Certainly, the point of the Declaration is not to codify a belated if inevitable capitulation on the part of the Church to the dominance of liberal culture, a capitulation perhaps required in order to "move on" to more difficult and important topics. Rather, *Dignitatis Humanae*'s purpose is surely both didactic and propositional. Just as surely, it is significant both for the Church's self-understanding and her activity *ad extra*.

The crucial task, then, is to arrive at an adequate interpretation of *Dignitatis Humanae*'s teaching on "immunity." The foregoing suggests that in order to do so we need to take stock of the dangers of abstraction. The discussion has indicated that the relationship between freedom and truth, at least according to the pope, is not in its fundamental structure "coercive." On the other hand, "immunity" as derived from an abstract sense of freedom does tend toward tacit forms of "coercion" (thus falsifying its claim to being an authentic "immunity"), insofar as it converts freedom as such into a version of itself, claiming all the while to allow for the full flourishing of a richer, private, religiously based sense of freedom.

This suggests that a fuller sense of the relation between freedom and truth must underlie our concept of immunity, and that this fuller sense needs to be made explicit in our cultural and sociojuridical discussion of the meaning of "religious freedom." Otherwise, our concept of immunity will mediate willy-nilly a tacit theory of freedom and ultimates, which it cannot do consistently with its claims to neutrality. The "paradox," then, is that for immunity really to be immunity it must make its underlying attachment to ultimates explicit.

If the foregoing is correct, then our choice is not between neutrality and coercion. Our choice is between two possible understandings of immunity, one secretly rooted in a particular concept of freedom and truth and another openly so.

Of course, the immediate objection to making the relation of freedom to truth explicit is that doing so suggests a slide toward the "monism" so heavily criticized by Murray. Certainly, *Dignitatis Humanae* offers a bulwark against these tendencies, a bulwark that has been reinforced by John Paul II. Thus, the pope warns against the attempt of the state to reach beyond its competence either in an attempt to suppress all religion (in the case of atheistic states) or some particular religion (in the case of certain Islamic states, for example). But he is also wary of the way liberalism tends to reinterpret freedom in its own image, which upon reflection turns out simply to be another form of "monism." Certainly, he is very far from seeing the teaching of *Dignitatis Humanae* as an appropriation into the Church's doctrine of the basic content of the First Amendment's religion clauses (particularly as those clauses have been interpreted by the Supreme Court). Rather, as we have seen, he tells us that religious freedom is a translation of humanity's ordination toward truth into the domain of basic law (which in its turn should affect what American Catholics would take to be a legitimate interpretation of the First Amendment).

Again, my point is not that the pope's explicitly theological understanding of freedom must be the foundation of a just society's concept of "religious freedom." Rather, my point is that the pope's Trinitarian Christocentrism changes the significance and the meaning of the juridical-philosophical discussion itself by offering new material that would not otherwise emerge as part of public discourse about the interior structure of freedom in relation to the "other" and "truth." At the same time, this starting point allows that juridical-philosophical discussion to continue precisely as a properly juridical-philosophical and, indeed, secular discussion. That this is possible is confirmed by the fact that it is historically actual, as the pope observes in *Fides et Ratio*. Concepts such as "person," which are now fundamental to society's juridical-philosophical discussion, are originally Trinitarian and Christological[50] and continue to carry some of the nuance of their native theological setting (although it is true that their original richness needs, in many ways, to be recovered).

In short, the starting point by which the idea of immunity is mediated makes a difference in the context and meaning of immunity. This difference can be identified as the presence of a background concept of freedom as such that is rooted in anthropological "ultimates," including their implied religious significance, such as "birth, love, work, and death."

If we follow out the logic ~~of the~~ of the pope's position, we arrive at a new and positive context for immunity, placing the idea of immunity and noncoercion within the prior idea of freedom as such. The pope's starting point turns on the notion, shared by Murray, that religious truth cannot in principle be coerced. It is certainly true that the state must not, in the words of the pope, "arrogate to itself the right to impose or to impede the profession or public practice of religion by a person or a community."[51] However, the ground for this juridical necessity is the more basic understanding of religious freedom—precisely as a civil liberty—as a "translation in institutional form" of the requirements of the fundamental human ordination, a translation that is open about the ultimates out of which its concept of freedom arises.

The pope's starting point, therefore, puts greater stress on the idea that immunity means a rejection of coercion, not simply because religious truth lies beyond the competence of the state (as the argument of this paper implies, the state is constantly legislating and ruling in religiously significant ways, whether it admits to this or not, and indeed it cannot avoid doing so), but because religious truth cannot be coerced without violating its inner principles. The pope's position leaves the way open for religious freedom to be integrated into a social and juridical system that openly expresses the centrality of the truth content of ultimates.

The foregoing leaves us with several considerations. First, the Church needs to be clear about her own understanding of the foundation and significance of "religious freedom" if she is to present that understanding *ad intra* and *ad extra* in a coherent way. This means that her understanding can never be a simple appropriation of what is offered from without. Rather, the Church's understanding if it is to be legitimate must arise from within her own mission and the content of her faith. Second, social institutions need to come clean about the view of ultimates tacitly mediated by their understanding of "religious freedom." This process might constitute a recovery of traditions concerning the true meaning of culture, which, again, for the pope means the truth-content of its approach to such life events as "birth, love, work and death." And finally, whatever our concept of "religious freedom," it must at the very least allow for the intelligibility of a religiously based understanding of freedom such as the pope's if it is to remain consistent with its claim that it simply offers the "space" necessary for private attachments to religious truth.

By way of conclusion, we should consider an obvious objection, posed in the form of the question "Whose ultimates?" Now this question could mean one of two things. On the one hand, it could be rhetorical. It could mean that we need to abstract "religious freedom" from ultimates in order to avoid an intolerant suppression of opposition beliefs. As the argument of this essay shows, however, this sense of the question in fact begs the question, because the abstraction in itself constitutes a theory of freedom in relation to ultimates. Hence, this rhetorical version of the question obscures the fact that the implied abstraction *does* advance a philosophically and theologically freighted concept of freedom and ultimates.

On the other hand, the question could be genuine. It could mean that society needs to engage in a serious dialogue about ultimates as those are embodied in our basic law. Obviously, this opens very difficult, concrete issues to which we must attend in an honest way. The genuine problems presented by pluralism infinitely compound the complexity of realizing this goal. Murray certainly saw the need to make this effort. He emphasized the necessity for a public conversation and what he called "consensus."[52] He insisted that no society could survive once it was cut off from essential truths. The argument of this essay, then, also calls for discussion and the recovery of essential truths. In doing so, however, we cannot begin with a concept of freedom that effectively, if tacitly, obscures the possibilities for genuine conversation.

NOTES

1. Hermínio Rico, S.J., *John Paul II and the Legacy of* Dignitatis Humanae (Washington, DC: Georgetown University Press, 2002), 142. While fundamentally in agreement with Murray, Rico is somewhat critical of Murray's resistance to drawing out the implications of his constitutional-juridical understanding of "religious freedom" for society as a whole and social ethics generally. Ibid., 36–37, 61; see also *infra*, at n. 45. He nevertheless contrasts the pope's position with Murray's basic concept of "religious freedom" as well as with the direction in which Rico believes Murray was moving following the Council. Ibid., 198 et seq.

2. *Veritatis Splendor*, section 4 (1993). Hereafter cited in the text as *VS*.

3. By the term "freedom as such," I mean to indicate freedom as it is considered by theological or philosophical anthropology in relation to ultimates. As we shall see, the pope considers freedom in this sense in relation to what he calls "the truth about man," which is ultimately grounded in man's image of the triune God in Christ but which has implications for secular considerations of "fundamental events of life, such as birth, love, work and death" (*Centesimus Annus*, section 24 [1991]). Hereafter cited in the text as *CA*. Murray, as we shall also see, speaks of freedom as given in our participation in the freedom of Christ and the Holy Spirit.

4. *Fides et Ratio*, section 13 (1998). Hereafter cited in the text as *FR*. It is certainly true that "decisions made against God" rely on freedom for their possibility. Analogous to the relationship between good and evil, however, "decisions made against God" or decisions made contrary to truth are more parasitic on, than a full realization of, freedom.

5. John Paul II, Address to the United Nations General Assembly: "The Fabric of Relations Among Peoples" (October 5, 1995), in *Origins* 25, no. 18 (October 19, 1995): 293–99, 297.

6. See, e.g., John Courtney Murray, "Arguments for the Human Right to Religious Freedom," in *Religious Liberty: Catholic Struggles with Pluralism/John Courtney Murray*, ed. J. Leon Hooper (Louisville, KY: Westminster/John Knox Press, 1993), 236.

7. "This Matter of Religious Freedom," *America* 112 (January 9, 1965), 40–43, at 40.

8. "The Declaration on Religious Freedom: A Moment in Its Legislative History," in *Religious Liberty: An End and a Beginning*, ed. John Courtney Murray (New York: Macmillan, 1966), 19.

9. Compare to "Arguments for the Human Right to Religious Freedom," 232; and "The Issue of Church and State at Vatican II," in *Religious Liberty: Catholic Struggles with Pluralism/John Courtney Murray*, 211–12.

10. See, for example, John Paul II, 1991 World Day of Peace Message: "Respect for Conscience: Foundation for Peace" (December 8, 1990), in *Origins* 20, no. 29 (December 27, 1990): 472–76, at 474; 1988 World Day of Peace Message: "Religious Freedom: Condition of Peace" (January 1, 1988) in *Origins* 17, no. 28 (December 24, 1987): 493–96, at 494. Of course, these texts constitute an interpretation of the idea of "immunity" contained in *Dignitatis Humanae*.

11. It is worth noting that Murray was not entirely satisfied with the final draft of *Dignitatis Humanae*. On this point, see J. Leon Hooper, "General Introduction," in *Religious Liberty: Catholic Struggles with Pluralism/John Courtney Murray*, 13, 15, 36; Kenneth Craycraft, "Religion as Moral Duty and Civil Right: *Dignitatis Humanae* on Religious Liberty," in *Catholicism, Liberalism, and Communitarianism*, ed. Kenneth L. Grasso, Gerard V. Bradley, and Robert P. Hunt [Lanham, MD: Rowman & Littlefield, 1995], 59–80, at 59–60.) He was dissatisfied because what he believed was the strongest argument for religious freedom, namely, the constitutional-juridical one, had been demoted to a secondary position in the final document, behind the more ontological approach favored by French-speaking theologians. Murray discusses this disagreement in "This Matter of Religious Freedom," 40–43, written in January 1965, after postponement of the Council's decision on the document. Murray reports that the French-speaking theologians considered the constitutional/juridical starting point "superficial." They instead favored an argument grounded in "the order of universal truth. The truth is that each man is called by God to share the divine life. This call is mediated to man by conscience, and man's response to it is the free act of faith. The essential dignity of man is located in his personal freedom of conscience, whereby he is truly a moral agent, acting on his own irreducible responsibility before God. Thus religious freedom was conceived to be formally and in the first instance an ethical and theological notion" (42). Nevertheless, following the Council, Murray attempted to interpret the document in a way that would highlight what he thought was its strongest basis for declaring "religious freedom." Rico rightly argues, it seems to me, that John Paul II's interpretation leans in the "French" direction. My disagreement with Rico, on the other hand, is rooted in the sense he gives to the relation between

freedom and truth, which then culminates in a negative valuation of the pope's insistence on the false character of liberal interpretations of freedom.

12. See Murray, "The Issue of Church and State at Vatican Council II," 211. This separation between the "temporal realm" of state and society, on the one hand, and the "religious realm," on the other, arises from within a more primitive nature and grace dualism. This dualism has been strongly criticized by David L. Schindler in *Heart of the World, Center of the Church: Communio Ecclesiology, Liberalism, and Liberation* (Grand Rapids, MI: William B. Eerdmans Publishing Co., 1996), 43–88. Schindler highlights the problematic character of Murray's claim that the religion clauses of the First Amendment are "articles of peace" rather than "articles of faith." (On this point, see Murray's *We Hold These Truths: Catholic Reflections on the American Proposition* ([Kansas City: Sheed and Ward, 1960], 45–78.) Compare also with Gerard V. Bradley, "Beyond Murray's Articles of Peace and Faith," in *John Courtney Murray and the American Civil Conversation*, ed. Robert P. Hunt and Kenneth L. Grasso (Grand Rapids, MI: William B. Eerdmans Publishing Co., 1992), 181–204, which argues that the religion clauses of the First Amendment, far from being merely neutral "articles of peace," are in fact "articles of faith," insofar as they are deeply shaped by their Protestant background.

13. "Arguments for the Human Right to Religious Freedom," 238.

14. Ibid.

15. Ibid., 239.

16. Ibid.

17. Ibid.

18. Ibid., 240.

19. Ibid., 240.

20. Ibid.

21. Ibid., 238.

22. Ibid.

23. Ibid., 241.

24. "Ecumenism and Vatican II's Declaration on Religious Freedom," in *Religious Freedom, 1965–1975: A Symposium on a Historic Document*, ed. Walter J. Burghardt (Mahwah, NJ: Paulist Press, 1977), 22.

25. See *The Sources of Christian Ethics*, trans. Sr. Mary Thomas Noble (Washington, DC: Catholic University Press, 1995), 242 et seq. Pinckaers argues that William of Ockham inaugurated a paradigmatic shift in the understanding of the nature of freedom. According to Pinckaers, Ockham's conceptualization is at the root of the dominant modern patterns of thought, including those advanced by liberalism (332). As Pinckaers points out, Ockham posited an understanding of freedom that was necessarily and radically "indifferent" to the choices it faced. To the extent that any influence outside the pure act of will would influence a choice, freedom would be diminished. Such influences would therefore include not only external limits such as laws but also internal influences such as virtues, where virtues are understood as constituting a predisposition to choose a certain outcome (i.e., the good) (245–46). This concept of freedom differed from the classical approach, according to which virtue, love, desire, the natural inclinations to goodness and happiness, and so forth

are understood as offering a fundamentally positive augmentation and aid to freedom. The point in common between the "indifference" found in Murray's interpretation of "religious freedom" and that of the nominalism described and criticized by Pinckaers is located in the shared presupposition that freedom possesses no real internal structure. Nominalism supposed that any predisposition, even toward the good, on the part of the moral actor was a limitation of freedom. Thus, the concept of freedom generated by nominalism is radically "empty." It envisions freedom as most fundamentally the ability to choose A or B "indifferently." Likewise, Murray's empty freedom supposes that, while freedom's purpose is to find and cling to truth, freedom itself possesses no interior structure in relation to truth. The question of the content of freedom is taken up philosophically in D. C. Schindler, "Freedom Beyond Our Choosing: Augustine on the Will and Its Objects," *Communio* 29 (Winter 2002): 618–53. D. C. Schindler offers an extremely compelling argument showing the nihilistic implications of "indifferent" freedom or freedom viewed most fundamentally as "choice."

26. As Murray puts it, "spreading religious errors or practicing false forms of worship is per se evil in the moral order. About this there is no doubt. But our inquiry is not about the moral but about the juridical order." "Arguments for the Human Right to Religious Freedom," 232.

27. This statement is recorded in J. Bryan Hehir, "John Paul II: Continuity and Change in the Social Teaching of the Church," in *Co-Creation and Capitalism: John Paul II's* Laborem Exercens, ed. John W. Houck and Oliver F. Williams (Lanham, MD: University Press of America, 1983), 131.

28. *Dives in Misericordia*, section 1 (1980).

29. For example, *Redemptor Hominis*, 8, 10 (1978); *Dives et Misericordia*, 1; *VS*, 2, 28; *FR*, 12, 13, 60 (where he says that this section is crucial for philosophy and that it "serves as one of the constant reference points of his teaching").

30. John Paul II, 1991 World Day of Peace Message (January 1, 1991), 472.

31. "Human beings," John Paul tells us, "are not made to live alone. They are born into a family and in a family they grow, eventually entering society through their activity. From birth, therefore, they are immersed in traditions which give them not only a language and a cultural formation but also a range of truths in which they believe almost instinctively. . . . This means that the human being—the one who lives in truth —is also *the one who lives by belief.* In believing, we entrust ourselves to the knowledge acquired by other people. . . . [W]hat is sought is *the truth of the person*—what the person is and what the person reveals from deep within" (*FR*, 31).

32. Compare with *Theo-Drama: Theological Dramatic Theory II: The Dramatis Personae: Man in God,* trans. Graham Harrison (San Francisco: Ignatius Press, 1990), 312.

33. See also *VS*, 34.

34. The pope references this phrase very often: see, for example, *Redemptor Hominis*, 13; *Mulieris Dignitatem*, 7, 18, 20; *Letter to Families*, 9; General Audience (January 16, 1980), in John Paul II, *The Theology of the Body: Human Love in the Divine Plan* (Boston: Daughters of St. Paul, 1997), 63–66.

35. See, for example, *Centesimus Annus*, 41; *Evangelium Vitae*, 96; *Dominum et Vivificantem*, 59; *Mulieris Dignitatem*, 7, 18; *Letter to Families*, 11, 12; General Audience (January 16, 1980), in *The Theology of the Body*, 63–66.

36. Compare with John Paul II, General Audiences (November 7, 14, and 21, 1979, and January 2, 9, and 16, 1980), in *The Theology of the Body*, 42–51, 57–66.

37. *Redemptor Hominis*, 12.

38. "1991 World Youth Day of Peace Message," 474.

39. See also *Centesimus Annus*, 42, in which the pope tells us that economic freedom has to be qualified by a strong juridical framework that places it "at the service of human freedom in its totality . . . the core of which is ethical and religious." For the proposition that religious freedom is fundamental to or is the "basis" for other senses of freedom, see also John Paul's statements in, for example, Post-Synodal Apostolic Exhortation, *Christifideles Laici* (1988), section 39; 1981 World Day of Peace Message: "To Serve Peace, Respect Freedom" (January 1, 1980) in *Origins* 10, no. 30 (January 8, 1981): 465–70, at 468; Message of Pope John Paul II to the United Nations on the 30th Anniversary of the Universal Declaration of Human Rights: "An Appeal for Religious Freedom" (December 11, 1978), in *Origins* 8, no. 27 (December 21, 1978): 417–20; "1988 World Day of Peace Message," 493; and Address to the Diplomatic Corps Accredited to the Vatican: "Serving the Cause of Human Rights" (January 9, 1989), in *Origins* 18, no. 33 (January 26, 1989): 541–44.

40. 1988 World Day of Peace Message, 494; cf. also *Redemptor Hominis*, 12; "Address to the Diplomatic Corps Accredited to the Vatican," 54; Message for the 1981 World Day of Peace, 465–70.

41. 1988 World Day of Peace Message, 495; and 1981 World Day of Peace Message, 468 (quoting "Religious Freedom and the Final Document of Helsinki," in *L'Osservatore Romano*, November 15, 1980).

42. We may illustrate this point by comparing two leading constitutional law cases concerning marriage. The first is the *Maynard v. Hill* case of the United States Supreme Court (125 U.S. 190), decided in 1888. The second is the recent and controversial case from the Massachusetts Supreme Court on "gay marriage," *Goodridge v. Dept. of Public Health* (798 N.E.2d 941 [Mass. 2003]). The gist of *Maynard* is that marriage is a "relation" rather than a private contract and that as such it is entirely subject to determination by the state's legislative authority (the Assembly's "will was a sufficient reason for its action"). *Goodridge* on the other hand represents the end point of developing constitutional doctrine concerning the so-called "right to marry," which is essentially an individual right in the context of marriage choices. Each case attempts to decide the question before it on a strictly "secular" basis. Each is ostensibly ruling on marriage as a "civil" rather than as a "religious" reality. The effect, however, is that each case is tacitly saying something about what marriage most fundamentally *is*. (*Maynard* treats marriage is a legislatively determined "relation"; *Goodridge* treats it as "a voluntary union of two persons as spouses to the exclusion of all others.") *Maynard* essentially tells us that marriage is defined and determined by the legislative and political authority of the state. *Goodridge*, carving out an exception to *Maynard's* general doctrine, essentially tells us that marriage is to be defined and determined, in an absolutely crucial way, by individual choice. Neither case can be reconciled with Catholic belief not only in terms of the moral evaluation of their outcomes (*Maynard* upholding "legislative divorce"; *Goodridge* requiring marriage laws to allow "gay marriage") but more radically in terms of the presupposition

that the civil aspect of marriage can in principle be separated from and ruled or legislated upon in abstraction from its religious content and, therefore, without making what finally amount to theologically freighted decisions. Thus, each case is intolerable from the perspective of Catholic teaching as represented in, say, Leo XIII, *Arcanum Divinae Sapientiae* (1880), which holds that the civil authority cannot determine the substance of marriage because the whole of marriage is a sacred and (in the case of Christians) sacramental reality instituted by God. However one might feel about the outcome or correctness of either of these decisions or about the value and legitimacy of the Church's doctrine on marriage, the fact is that we have here a fundamental clash that cannot be resolved by recourse only to "purely" secular principles, that is to say, without presupposing either tacit or explicit theological positions. While both of these cases attempt to decide the issues before them along strictly secular lines, the fact of the matter is that each mediates a theologically grounded truth claim (i.e., that "civil marriage" can be separated from any religious meaning it might possess privately; i.e., the sacred/religious aspect is a private value to be added voluntaristically to an already constituted civil foundation).

43. Rico, *John Paul II and the Legacy of* Dignitatis Humanae, 199, quoting commentary on *Dignitatis Humanae*, in *The Documents of Vatican II*, ed. W. M. Abbott (New York: America Press, 1966).

44. See the discussion of this tendency in *We Hold These Truths*, 79–96. In practice, Murray's stark distinction between religious freedom in the juridical and constitutional sense and truth-based freedom in the social/cultural and theological senses is difficult to maintain. This becomes clear in some of Murray's own writing. As Rico points out (*John Paul II and the Legacy of* Dignitatis Humanae, 37), Murray grants in several places that immunity implies noninterference by any "other" in the social order: "The right to immunity from coercion . . . is asserted against all 'the others'—other individuals, others organized in social groups, and especially that impersonal 'other' that is the state, the institutionalized agencies of law and government" ("The Declaration on Religious Freedom: A Moment in Its Legislative History," 40). Or again, as he tells us, the function of religious freedom "is to create and maintain a constitutional situation, and to that extent to favor and foster a social climate, within which the citizen and the religious community may pursue the higher ends of human existence without let or hindrance by other citizens, by social groups, or by government itself" (29). More fundamentally, this difficulty is readily apparent in the previous block quotation, at n. 43, *supra*.

45. Indeed, the thrust of Rico's argument is that John Paul II has undercut the significance of *Dignitatis Humanae*'s teaching on "religious freedom" and "freedom of conscience" in encyclicals such as *CA* (economic freedom), *VS* (moral freedom), and *Evangelium Vitae* (political freedom in relation to the "culture of death") (see *John Paul II and the Legacy of* Dignitatis Humanae, 147 et seq). Another good example of this tendency can be seen, for example, in the discussion of "conscience" in Richard M. Gula, *Reason Informed by Faith: Foundations of Catholic Morality* (Mahwah, NJ: Paulist Press, 1989), 152–61.

46. Compare to D. C. Schindler, "Freedom beyond Our Choosing: Augustine on the Will and Its Objects," 623.

47. "The Declaration on Religious Freedom: Its Deeper Significance," *America* 114 (April 23, 1966), 592.

48. See Schindler, *Heart of the World*, 60, n. 16.

49. Murray, *We Hold These Truths*, ix–x.

50. Compare to Josef Cardinal Ratzinger, "Concerning the Notion of Person in Theology," *Communio* 17 (Fall 1990): 439–54; Hans Urs von Balthasar, "On the Concept of Person," *Communio* 13 (Spring 1986): 18–26; and John D. Zizioulas, *Being as Communion: Studies in Personhood and the Church* (Crestwood, NY: St. Vladimir's Seminary Press, 1985).

51. "Message for the 1988 World Day of Peace," 494.

52. Ibid., 27–43.

About the Contributors

Francis Canavan, S.J., is emeritus professor of Political Science at Fordham University. He has written three books on the political thought of Edmund Burke and several others on the liberal tradition of politics, including the liberal theory of freedom of speech. He has also written extensively on the Catholic social tradition and the development of the Catholic theory of the state.

David S. Crawford is assistant dean and assistant professor of Moral Theology and Law at the Pontifical John Paul II Institute for Studies on Marriage and Family at The Catholic University of America. His articles have appeared in *Communio: International Catholic Review* and other publications.

John F. Crosby is professor of Philosophy at Franciscan University of Steubenville. He is the author of *The Selfhood of the Human Person* and *Personalist Papers.* He has published extensively on various aspects of the thought of John Paul II.

Avery Cardinal Dulles, S.J., Laurence J. McGinley Professor of Religion and Society, Fordham University, is an internationally known theologian and lecturer. He is the author of twenty-two books, including *Models of the Church,* and over 750 articles on theological topics. A former president of both the Catholic Theological Society of America and the American Theological Society, he has served on the International Theological Commission and as a member of the United States Lutheran/Roman Catholic Dialogue.

Robert P. George is the McCormick Professor of Jurisprudence and director of the James Madison Program in American Ideals and Institutions at Princeton

University. His books include *The Clash of Orthodoxies: Law, Religion, and Morality in Crisis, Making Men Moral: Civil Liberties and Public Morality,* and *In Defense of Natural Law.*

Kenneth L. Grasso is professor of Political Science at Texas State University-San Marcos. He has coedited several books, including *Catholicism, Liberalism and Communitarianism: The Catholic Intellectual Tradition and the Moral Foundations of Democracy,* and currently serves as Second Vice-President of the Society of Catholic Social Scientists.

Thomas Heilke is professor of Political Science and associate dean of International Programs at the University of Kansas. He is the author of numerous articles and books on various topics in political philosophy and the history of political thought. His current research is focused on political theology and questions of religion and politics including, but not limited to, studies in progress on the political thought of John Howard Yoder and on Anabaptist political thought in the sixteenth century. His previous books include *Eric Voegelin: In Search of Reality* and *Nietzsche's Tragic Regime: Culture, Aesthetics, and Political Education.*

Robert P. Hunt is professor of Political Science at Kean University. He has coedited several books, including *John Courtney Murray and the American Civil Conversation* and *Catholicism, Liberalism, and Communitarianism: The Catholic Intellectual Tradition and the Moral Foundations of Democracy.* His articles have appeared in journals such as *First Things, The Review of Politics,* and *The Catholic Social Science Review.*

David T. Koyzis is professor of Political Science at Redeemer University College in Ancaster, Ontario, Canada. He is the author of *Political Visions and Illusions: A Survey and Christian Critique of Contemporary Ideologies.*

William L. Saunders Jr. is a graduate of the University of North Carolina and of the Harvard Law School. In 2004, he was profiled in Harvard Law School's inaugural Guide to Conservative Public Interest Law. He is Senior Fellow and Human Rights Counsel at the Family Research Council in Washington, D.C. He is a member of the board of the Fellowship of Catholic Scholars.